# *ideals*
# Desserts, Candy & Cookie
## COOKBOOK

Sweet-lovers will find a world of delights in this volume combining three best-selling cookbooks featuring cookies, candies and desserts.

Book I  Nice & Easy Desserts Cookbook
by Cyndee Kannenberg

Book II  Candy Cookbook
by Mildred Brand

Book III  Cookie Cookbook
by Darlene Kronschnabel

Bonanza Books
New York, N.Y.

# CONTENTS

## Book I Nice & Easy Desserts Cookbook

## Book II Candy Cookbook

## Book III Cookie Cookbook

ISBN: 0-517-332507
NICE & EASY DESSERTS COOKBOOK
Copyright © MCMLXXVIII BY CYNDEE KANNENBERG
CANDY COOKBOOK
Copyright © MCMLXXIX BY MILDRED BRAND
COOKIE COOKBOOK
Copyright © MCMLXXVII BY IDEALS PUBLISHING CORPORATION
ALL RIGHTS RESERVED.

THIS EDITION IS PUBLISHED BY BONANZA BOOKS,
A DIVISION OF CROWN PUBLISHERS, INC.,
BY ARRANGEMENT WITH IDEALS PUBLISHING CORPORATION.
a b c d e f g h
BONANZA 1980 EDITION

MANUFACTURED IN THE UNITED STATES OF AMERICA

Book I

# Nice & Easy Desserts
## COOKBOOK

by Cyndee Kannenberg

# CAKES

## CANDY BAR POUND CAKE

8 1¾-oz. Milky Way candy bars
1 c. butter
2 c. sugar
4 eggs
2½ c. sifted flour
½ t. baking soda
1¼ c. buttermilk
1 t. vanilla
1 c. chopped nuts

Combine candy bars and ½ cup of the butter in a saucepan; melt over low heat. Cream sugar with remaining ½ cup butter. Add eggs, one at a time, beating well after each addition. Stir together flour and baking soda. Add alternately with buttermilk, stirring until smooth. Add melted candy; mix well. Stir in the vanilla and nuts. Pour into a greased and floured bundt pan and bake in a 350° oven for 75 to 80 minutes. Cool and frost with Candy Icing. Serves 16 to 20.

### CANDY ICING

3 fun-size Milky Way candy bars
½ c. butter
2 c. sifted confectioners' sugar
1 t. vanilla
Milk

Melt candy bars in butter. Add sugar and vanilla. Blend in just enough milk to make of spreading consistency.

> Before melting chocolate, brush inside of the pan with melted butter. The chocolate will not stick to the pan.

## CANDY BAR CAKE

8 1⅕-oz. milk chocolate bars
1 c. butter
2 c. sugar
4 eggs
¼ t. baking soda
1 c. buttermilk
1 5½-oz. can chocolate syrup
2 t. vanilla
2½ c. flour
½ t. salt
1 c. chopped nuts

Melt chocolate bars in top of a double boiler. Remove from heat. Cream melted chocolate, butter and sugar. Add eggs, one at a time. Dissolve soda in buttermilk. Add to the chocolate mixture. Mix in syrup and vanilla and then flour, salt and nuts. Pour into a greased tube pan. Bake in a 350° oven 75 minutes. Cool 10 minutes. Turn out of pan. Cake freezes well. Serves 16.

## TREASURE TOFFEE CAKE

¼ c. sugar
1 t. cinnamon
2 c. flour
1 c. sugar
1½ t. baking powder
1 t. baking soda
¼ t. salt
1 t. vanilla
1 c. sour cream
½ c. butter, softened
2 eggs
¼ c. chopped nuts
3 1⅛-oz. chocolate toffee bars, coarsely crushed
¼ c. melted butter
Confectioners' sugar

Combine cinnamon and sugar. In mixer, combine remaining ingredients except nuts, candy bars and melted butter. Blend at low speed until moistened. Beat at medium speed 3 minutes. Spoon half of the batter into greased and floured 10-inch bundt pan. Sprinkle with 2 tablespoons cinnamon-sugar mixture. Spoon remaining mixture into pan. Top with remaining cinnamon-sugar mixture. Top with nuts and chopped candy. Pour melted butter over all. Bake in a 325° oven 45 to 50 minutes. Cool upright 15 minutes. Remove from pan and dust with confectioners' sugar. Serves 16.

# HIDDEN TREASURE CAKE

    1 c. butter
2½ c. sugar
    4 eggs
    2 t. vanilla
    4 c. sifted cake flour
    1 T. baking soda
    1 t. salt
    1 c. milk
    1 8-oz. carton lemon yogurt
    Grated rind of 1 lemon
    Juice of 1 lemon

Cream butter until light. Slowly add sugar, beating until fluffy. Add eggs, one at a time, beating well after each addition; add vanilla. Sift together flour, soda and salt. Add dry ingredients alternately with milk and yogurt, beginning and ending with dry ingredients. Blend in lemon juice and rind. Pour batter into lightly greased and floured 10-inch tube pan. Bake in a 350° oven about 70 minutes or until done. Cool upright on wire rack for 10 minutes. Turn out to cool for about 2 hours. Fill and ice. Serves 12.

### FILLING

    1 3-oz. pkg. raspberry gelatin
    1 c. boiling water
    2 8-oz. cartons plain yogurt

Dissolve gelatin in boiling water. Chill until thickened slightly. Add yogurt and blend until smooth. Refrigerate 10 to 15 minutes. Remove center of cake by cutting ¾ inch from outside edge and ¾ inch in from the center hole, cutting within 1 inch of bottom. Carefully remove inside cake in sections, leaving only a shell. Place shell on serving plate. Spoon Filling into shell. Replace cake sections on top of the raspberry mixture to fill center. Refrigerate 30 minutes.

### ICING

    ⅓ c. butter
    1 1-lb. box confectioners' sugar
    ⅓ c. lemon juice
    2 t. vanilla
    1 t. butter flavoring
    Grated rind of 1 lemon
    Whole raspberries for garnish

Cream butter. Slowly beat in sugar, alternating with lemon juice. Stir in vanilla, butter flavoring and lemon rind. Garnish with whole raspberries.

# WELLESLEY FUDGE CAKE

    3 1-oz. squares unsweetened chocolate, melted
2½ c. flour
    1 t. baking soda
    ½ t. salt
    ½ c. butter
    2 c. brown sugar
    2 eggs
    ½ t. vanilla
    ½ c. milk
    ½ c. water

Melt chocolate over double boiler. Sift together flour, soda and salt; set aside. Cream butter and sugar until fluffy. Beat in eggs and vanilla. Add melted chocolate. Combine milk and water and add to mixture alternately with sifted dry ingredients. Pour into 2 greased and floured 9-inch pans. Bake in a 350° oven 30 to 35 minutes. Serves 12.

### FUDGE ICING

    2 c. brown sugar
    ½ c. milk
    3 1-oz. squares chocolate, melted
    2 T. butter

Combine all ingredients, mixing until of spreading consistency.

# CHOCOLATE CAKE ROLL

    ½ c. sifted cake flour
    ¾ t. baking powder
    ¼ t. salt
    3 eggs, beaten
    ½ c. sugar
    1 t. almond flavoring
    1 T. confectioners' sugar
    ½ pkg. dietetic chocolate pudding
1½ c. skim milk
    2 T. toasted chopped pecans

Lightly butter jelly-roll pan. Line with waxed paper and lightly butter paper. Sift together flour, baking powder and salt; set aside. Beat eggs well. Add granulated sugar, a little at a time, beating until thick. Add flavoring. Fold in flour mixture. Pour in pan. Bake in a 400° oven 8 minutes. Loosen cake edges with a knife. Turn out on waxed paper dusted with confectioners' sugar. Peel off waxed paper. Roll up cake, starting at the shorter end; cool. Prepare pudding as directed on the box, using only 1½ cups milk. Add pecans; chill. Unroll cake. Spread with pudding. Reroll and sprinkle with confectioners' sugar. Serves 10.

## MOCHA CUPCAKES

½ c. sugar
6 T. butter
1 egg
1 egg yolk
1 1-oz. square unsweetened chocolate, melted and cooled
1 c. flour
1 t. baking powder
¼ t. salt
¼ t. baking soda
1 T. instant coffee crystals
½ c. milk

Cream sugar and butter; beat in egg and egg yolk until fluffy. Add chocolate. Sift together flour, baking powder, salt and baking soda. Dissolve coffee crystals in milk. Add dry ingredients to chocolate mixture, alternating with milk mixture. Fill 12 paper-lined muffin pans two-thirds full with batter. Bake in a preheated 275° oven 12 minutes. Spoon 1 tablespoon Meringue on top of each cupcake. Bake an additional 10 to 12 minutes until lightly browned. Makes 12 cupcakes.

### MOCHA MERINGUE

1 egg white
1 t. instant coffee crystals
⅓ c. sugar
½ c. semisweet chocolate chips
½ c. chopped pecans

Beat egg white with coffee crystals until soft peaks form. Gradually add sugar, beating to stiff peaks. Fold in chocolate chips and nuts.

## SOUP CAKE

¾ c. shortening
1½ c. sugar
3 eggs
3 c. sifted flour
1 T. baking powder
1 t. baking soda
1 t. cloves
1 t. cinnamon
1 t. nutmeg
1 10½-oz. can tomato soup
⅓ c. milk
1 c. raisins
1 c. chopped nuts

Cream sugar and shortening until fluffy. Add eggs and blend. Use ¼ cup of the flour and toss with raisins and nuts. Sift together dry ingredients and set aside. Combine tomato soup and milk, blending well. Add dry ingredients to creamed mixture, alternating with soup. Fold in nuts and raisins. Pour into a greased and floured 12-cup bundt pan. Bake in a 350° oven 50 minutes or until done. Cool in pan 15 minutes. Turn onto wire rack to finish cooling. Glaze. Serves 24.

### GLAZE

2 c. sifted confectioners' sugar
1 T. softened butter
½ t. pumpkin pie spice
2 to 4 T. milk

Mix first three ingredients. Slowly add milk and mix to spreading consistency.

## BLACK FOREST CAKE

4 eggs
¾ t. vanilla
⅔ c. sugar
⅓ c. cocoa
⅓ c. sifted flour
6 T. clarified butter
½ c. sugar
¾ c. water
¼ c. kirsch
1 c. pitted dark cherries, drained
2 c. heavy cream, whipped
⅓ c. confectioners' sugar
1 4-oz. bar semisweet chocolate, shaved in curls
Maraschino cherries for garnish

Combine eggs, vanilla and two-thirds cup sugar; beat with electric mixer 10 minutes at high speed. Sift together flour and cocoa; fold into egg mixture. Add melted butter, stirring just until mixed. Do not overmix. Pour into 3 greased and floured 6-inch round pans. Bake in a 350° oven 10 to 15 minutes. Cool 5 minutes. Remove from pans and cool on racks. In a saucepan, combine ½ cup sugar and water; boil 5 minutes. Cool to lukewarm and add kirsch. Sprinkle over cake layers. Fold confectioners' sugar into whipped cream. Spread 1 cake layer with cream, sprinkle on half the cherries. Repeat with second layer then add top layer. Frost top and sides of cake with remaining whipped cream and garnish with maraschino cherries and shaved chocolate. Serves 8.

Pictured opposite: Black Forest Cake

## PUMPKIN CUPCAKES

3 c. flour
1 c. sugar
4 t. baking powder
1 t. salt
1 t. pumpkin pie spice
1 c. milk
1 c. canned pumpkin
½ c. melted butter
2 eggs, beaten

Sift together flour, sugar, baking powder, salt and pumpkin pie spice. Stir in milk, pumpkin, melted butter and eggs. Use a wooden spoon to mix just until the batter is moist. Pour batter into 24 well-greased muffin cups, 2½ inches in diameter. Bake in a preheated 400° oven for 20 minutes. Cool in tins 10 minutes. Loosen muffins and invert pan on a wire rack. Makes 24 cupcakes.

## HOLIDAY CAKE

1 8-oz. pkg. cream cheese, softened
1 c. butter or margarine
1½ c. sugar
1 t. vanilla
4 eggs
2¼ c. sifted cake flour
1½ t. baking powder
1 c. chopped candied fruit
1 c. chopped pecans
Cherries for garnish
Pecans for garnish

Blend cream cheese, butter, sugar and vanilla. Mix well. Add eggs, one at a time, mixing well after each. Sift together 2 cups flour and baking powder. Gradually add to cream cheese mixture. Combine remaining flour with the candied fruit and half the nuts. Fold into the batter. Grease a bundt pan. Sprinkle remaining nuts over the inside of pan. Pour batter in pan and bake in a preheated 325° oven for about 1 hour and 20 minutes. Cool 10 minutes. Remove from pan. Pour Glaze over and garnish with pecans and cherries. Serves 16.

### GLAZE

1½ c. sifted confectioners' sugar
2 T. milk
¼ t. vanilla

Stir milk and vanilla into confectioners' sugar, stirring well.

## CHOCOLATE CHERRY FRUITCAKE

2 c. chopped candied cherries
1 c. raisins
1 c. chopped dates
1 c. chopped walnuts
½ c. flour
½ c. butter
½ c. sugar
2 eggs
¾ c. flour
¼ c. cocoa
½ t. baking powder
½ t. salt
⅓ c. buttermilk
Kirsch

Combine cherries, raisins, dates and nuts with ½ cup flour. Set aside. Cream butter and sugar until fluffy. Add eggs, beating well. Stir together remaining flour, cocoa, baking powder and salt. Add to creamed mixture, alternating with buttermilk. Fold in fruit and nut mixture. Pour into 2 greased 8 x 4 x 2-inch loaf pans. Bake in a 275° oven 1½ to 1¾ hours. Cool in pan 10 minutes. Turn out on wire rack and cool completely. Wrap in a kirsch-soaked cheesecloth and then in foil. Store in a cool place from 1 week to 6 months. Resoak cloth once a week. Chill before serving. Serves 10 to 12.

## MOTHER-IN-LAW'S DATE CAKE

1 c. dates, cut up
1 t. baking soda
1¼ c. boiling water
¾ c. shortening
1 c. sugar
2 beaten eggs
1¼ c. plus 2 T. flour
¾ t. baking powder
1 t. salt
1 6-oz. pkg. chocolate chips
¼ c. sugar
½ c. chopped nuts

Stir soda into boiling water; pour over dates and set aside. Cream shortening and 1 cup sugar until fluffy. Stir in eggs, mixing well. Add dates. Sift together flour, baking powder and salt. Add to date mixture. Pour batter into a greased and floured 9 x 13-inch pan. Combine chocolate chips, remaining sugar and nuts. Sprinkle over top of cake. Bake in a preheated 350° oven 35 to 40 minutes (use 325° for glass pans). Serves 12.

## TANGY FRUITCAKE

½ c. butter
¾ c. sugar
2 eggs
1 T. lemon rind
1 t. lemon extract
1⅔ c. sifted cake flour
1½ t. baking powder
¼ t. salt
⅔ c. milk
    Confectioners' sugar
    Sliced and sweetened strawberries
    Heavy cream, whipped

Cream butter and sugar until light and fluffy. Beat in eggs, one at a time, beating well after each addition. Add lemon rind and extract. Sift together flour, salt and baking powder. Add dry ingredients alternately with milk, beating with mixer at medium speed. Begin and end with dry ingredients. Pour batter into a greased and floured 6½-cup ring mold. Bake in a 325° oven for 30 to 40 minutes. Cool on wire rack for 10 minutes. Loosen edges and invert. Sprinkle with confectioners' sugar. Fill center with strawberries and top with whipped cream. Serves 10 to 12.

## ORANGE RUM CAKE

2⅔ c. sifted cake flour
2½ t. baking powder
½ t. salt
¼ t. baking soda
    Pinch ginger
⅔ c. butter
1⅓ c. sugar
3 egg yolks
1½ t. grated orange rind
¾ c. orange juice
¼ c. rum
½ t. almond extract
½ t. vanilla
3 egg whites, beaten stiff
    Confectioners' sugar

Sift together first 5 ingredients twice. Cream butter until light. Gradually add sugar, creaming until fluffy. Add egg yolks, one at a time, beating well after each. Stir in orange rind. Add dry ingredients alternately with orange juice mixed with rum. Beat well; stir in almond extract and vanilla. Fold in egg whites and pour into a buttered 10-inch tube pan. Bake in a 350° oven 45 to 60 minutes. Serve sprinkled with confectioners' sugar. Serves 12 to 14.

## GREAT-GRANDMA'S RAISIN CAKE

1 t. baking soda
1 c. boiling water
1 c. raisins
2 c. flour
½ t. baking powder
½ c. shortening
1 c. sugar
1 egg
½ c. chopped nuts

Dissolve soda in boiling water and pour over raisins. Set aside to cool. Sift together flour and baking powder. Add to raisin mixture. Cream shortening and sugar. Beat in egg and add to raisin mixture. Stir in nuts. Pour in a greased 9 x 5-inch loaf pan. Bake in a 350° oven 60 minutes. Serves 10 to 12.

## PEANUT CANDY CAKE

1¾ c. boiling water
1 c. quick-cooking rolled oats
½ c. butter
1 c. light brown sugar, packed
1 c. sugar
1 t. vanilla
2 eggs
1½ c. flour
1 t. baking soda
½ t. baking powder
¼ t. cinnamon
¼ t. salt
5 .6-oz. chocolate peanut butter cup candies

Combine water and oats; mix well. Cool to room temperature. Cream butter, brown sugar, sugar and vanilla. Beat in eggs, then oatmeal mixture. Sift together dry ingredients and add; beat 1 minute. Pour batter into a greased and floured 9 x 13-inch pan. Crumble candies and sprinkle on top, having a thicker layer around the edges. Bake in a 350° oven 40 to 45 minutes until done. Frost with Chocolate Icing. Serves 12.

### ICING

½ c. cocoa
2⅔ c. confectioners' sugar
6 T. butter
⅛ t. salt
4 to 5 T. milk
1 t. vanilla

Combine cocoa and sugar. Cream butter and salt with one-third of the cocoa mixture. Gradually add milk, vanilla and remaining cocoa mixture. Beat until smooth.

# APPLE CAKE

1 T. butter
½ c. sugar
2 c. flour
2 t. baking powder
1 egg plus milk to make 1 cup
6 to 8 apples, peeled and sliced

Combine butter, sugar, flour and baking powder; stir well. Add milk and egg, mixing to blend. Spread in 2 greased and floured 8-inch pans. Cover with apple slices. Sprinkle Topping over apples and, if desired, coconut or cinnamon on the top. Bake in a preheated 375° oven for 30 minutes. Makes two 8-inch cakes, or stack layers for one cake.

### TOPPING

2 T. flour
1 c. sugar
2 T. melted butter

Mix all ingredients together with a fork.

# ECONOMICAL CARROT CAKE

3 eggs
2 c. sugar
1 c. vegetable oil
1 t. salt
1 t. baking powder
1 t. baking soda
1 t. cinnamon
1 t. vanilla
½ t. nutmeg
⅛ t. cloves
3 c. flour
2 c. shredded carrot
¼ c. milk

Measure all ingredients except flour, carrot and milk into a large mixing bowl. Beat ½ minute on low speed; beat on medium speed for 1 minute. Gradually stir in flour, carrot and milk. Pour into two greased and floured 10-inch cake pans. Bake in a 350° oven 30 to 35 minutes. Cool in pan 10 to 15 minutes. Remove from pan and cool on rack. Makes 16 servings.

### CREAM CHEESE ICING

2 c. confectioners' sugar
1 3-oz. pkg. cream cheese, softened
1 T. milk
1 t. vanilla

Combine all ingredients in a small bowl. Beat on medium speed until smooth and of spreading consistency, about 3 minutes.

# MERINGUE CAKE

4 egg whites
¼ t. cream of tartar
1 c. sugar
½ c. finely chopped pecans
1 1-oz. square unsweetened chocolate, grated
1 c. sugar
½ c. butter
1½ t. vanilla
4 egg yolks
2 c. sifted cake flour
3 t. baking powder
½ t. salt
¾ c. milk

Grease a 10-inch tube pan. Line the bottom with waxed paper. Beat egg whites and cream of tartar at medium high speed until soft peaks form. Gradually add the first cup of sugar, beating at high speed until stiff peaks form. Gently fold in chocolate and pecans. Spread meringue evenly over the bottom and 3½ inches up the sides and center of the tube. Set aside. Cream remaining sugar, butter and vanilla until fluffy. Add egg yolks, one at a time, beating well after each addition. Sift together flour, baking powder and salt. Add to the creamed mixture alternately with the milk, beating well after each addition. Carefully spoon into the meringue-lined pan. Bake in a 325° oven 55 to 60 minutes. Do not invert pan. Cool in pan on rack 20 minutes. Loosen around sides and center tube; invert on cake rack to cool completely. Serves 16.

# ORANGE RIND CAKE

1 c. raisins
½ c. nuts
Rind of 2 oranges
1 c. sugar
½ c. butter
2 eggs
1 c. buttermilk
1 t. baking soda
2½ c. flour

Put raisins, nuts and rind through a grinder. Set aside. Cream butter with sugar; stir in eggs and buttermilk, mixing well. Add soda, flour and ground mixture. Pour batter into a greased and floured bundt pan. Bake in a 350° oven 45 to 60 minutes. Serves 10 to 12. Frost with Fudgy Chocolate Icing, page 18.

## CHEESE TOPPED PINEAPPLE CAKE

2 8-oz. pkgs. cream cheese, softened
½ c. sugar
1 t. vanilla
1 egg
1 pkg. pineapple or lemon cake mix
2 eggs
1 c. water
1 16-oz. pkg. frozen strawberries, thawed

Cream 1½ packages cream cheese until fluffy. Gradually add sugar, vanilla and 1 egg. Beat well. Spread mixture evenly in a greased and lightly floured 9 x 13-inch pan. Blend cake mix, remaining cream cheese, 2 eggs and water; beat 4 minutes. Spread over cheese mixture. Bake in a 350° oven 40 to 50 minutes until a toothpick inserted in the middle comes out clean. Cool in pan 5 minutes. Remove from pan and cool completely. Cut into 12 pieces and serve topped with strawberries. Serves 12.

## COLA CAKE

1 c. butter, softened
1⅓ c. sugar
2 eggs
2 c. flour
1 t. baking soda
3 T. cocoa
½ c. buttermilk
1 t. vanilla
1 c. cola
1½ c. miniature marshmallows

Cream butter and sugar until fluffy. Add eggs, one at a time, beating after each. Sift together flour, baking soda, cocoa and add, alternating with buttermilk. Stir in vanilla and cola, blending well. Fold in marshmallows. Pour into a 13 x 9-inch well-greased pan. Bake in a 350° oven 40 to 45 minutes. Cool and frost with Cola Icing. Serves 12.

### COLA ICING

4 c. confectioners' sugar
½ c. softened butter
3 T. cocoa
⅓ c. cola
1 c. chopped pecans (optional)

Cream sugar, butter and cocoa. Add cola, beating until smooth. Stir in pecans. Makes 12 servings.

## SPECKLED BANANA CAKE

1 pkg. yellow cake mix
1 c. hot water
½ c. vegetable oil
1 3-oz. pkg. instant banana pudding mix
4 eggs
¼ c. poppy seed

Mix cake mix, water, oil and dry pudding mix. Beat until smooth. Add eggs, one at a time, beating well after each addition. Stir in poppy seed. Pour batter into greased and floured tube pan. Bake in a preheated 350° oven 45 minutes. Serves 16.

---

Mix a tablespoonful of gelatin powder into a thawed package of frozen berries. Stir well. Use as a topping for sherbets or plain cake.

---

## FAVORITE CAKE

3 c. sifted cake flour
4 t. baking powder
¼ t. salt
1 c. butter
2 c. sugar
1 t. vanilla
4 eggs
1 c. milk

Have all ingredients at room temperature. Sift flour three times with baking powder and salt. Cream butter thoroughly, using medium speed of mixer; add sugar gradually. Cream well; add vanilla. Add eggs, one at a time, beating well after each. Using low speed of mixer, add dry ingredients, alternating with milk. Pour into 2 greased and floured 9-inch pans. Bake in a 375° oven 25 minutes. Frost with Fluffy Custard Frosting. Serves 12.

### FLUFFY CUSTARD FROSTING

2 T. flour
¾ c. milk
¾ c. butter
¾ c. sugar
⅛ t. salt
1 t. vanilla

In a saucepan, add a small amount of milk to flour. Stir, making a smooth paste. Add remaining milk. Cook over medium heat, stirring constantly, until mixture boils and thickens. Cool. Cream butter, using medium speed of mixer. Gradually add sugar and salt; beat well. Add cooled milk mixture. Whip until light and fluffy. Add vanilla.

# FEATHER CAKE

2 c. sifted cake flour
3 t. baking powder
½ t. salt
½ c. butter
1 c. sugar
1 t. vanilla
4 egg whites
½ c. milk

Have ingredients at room temperature. Sift flour, baking powder and salt 3 times. Cream butter thoroughly, using medium speed of the mixer. Slowly add sugar and cream well. Add vanilla and egg whites, one at a time, beating well after each. Using low speed of the mixer, add sifted dry ingredients alternately with milk. Pour into 2 greased 8-inch pans. Bake in a preheated 375° oven for 20 minutes. Cool. Put layers together with Nut Filling. Ice with a boiled icing. Serves 10.

## Nut Filling

½ c. sugar
¼ t. salt
2½ T. flour
1 c. milk
1 egg, beaten
½ t. vanilla
⅓ c. chopped nuts

Combine sugar, salt and flour; add milk. Cook over low heat or in top of double boiler until thick. Pour slowly over beaten egg, stirring constantly. Simmer another 2 to 3 minutes. Cool and add vanilla and nuts.

## ANGEL DESSERT

2 T. unflavored gelatin
4 T. cold water
1 c. boiling water
1 c. orange juice
2 T. lemon juice
1 c. sugar
⅛ t. salt
1 pt. heavy cream, whipped
1 angel food cake
Coconut for garnish

Soften gelatin in cold water and set aside. Combine boiling water, juices, sugar and salt. Refrigerate until slightly thickened. Stir gelating mixture into whipped cream. Fold in orange juice mixture. Tear angel food cake in chunks. Layer cake and whipped cream mixture in a 9 x 13-inch pan. Garnish top with coconut. Refrigerate at least 6 hours or until ready to serve. Serves 12.

# CARIOCA CUPS

4 c. miniature marshmallows
½ t. salt
¼ c. milk
1 6-oz. pkg. semisweet chocolate chips
2 t. instant coffee
¼ t. cinnamon
1 c. heavy cream, whipped
8 sponge cake dessert shells
1 c. finely chopped and whole pecans

Combine first three ingredients in the top of a double boiler. Cook and stir over boiling water until marshmallows are melted. Remove from heat and stir in chocolate chips, coffee, and cinnamon. Fold ½ cup of the chocolate mixture into the whipped cream. Cover and chill. Frost tops and sides of cakes with remaining chocolate mixture. Sprinkle nuts over. Spoon cooled filling in the center of the shells. Chill. Garnish with whole pecans. Serves 8.

# VERY SPECIAL CARROT CAKE

2 c. sugar
1¼ c. vegetable oil
4 eggs
2 c. flour
1 t. cinnamon
½ t. nutmeg
1 t. salt
2 t. baking soda
3 c. grated carrot
1 c. pecans
½ c. raisins
1 c. crushed pineapple, drained

Cream sugar and oil. Add eggs, one at a time. Add flour, spices, salt and baking soda, mixing well. Add grated carrot, pecans, raisins and pineapple. Pour into a greased and floured 13 x 9-inch pan and bake in a 375° oven 50 to 60 minutes. Cool and frost with Cheese Icing. Serves 12.

## Cheese Icing

1 8-oz. pkg. cream cheese
½ c. butter
1 1-lb. box confectioners' sugar
1 t. vanilla

Cream cheese and butter. Gradually add sugar, beating until fluffy and of spreading consistency. Stir in vanilla.

## PINK DIVINE CAKE

1 pkg. white cake mix
3 T. flour
1 3-oz. pkg. raspberry gelatin
½ c. water
1 c. vegetable oil
½ 10-oz. pkg. frozen raspberries, thawed
4 eggs

Combine cake mix, flour and gelatin; mix well. Add water, oil, berries with juice and eggs. Beat well. Pour into 3 greased and floured 8-inch cake pans. Bake in a 350° oven 25 minutes. Cool 10 minutes. Remove from pans and ice. Serves 10.

### RASPBERRY ICING

½ c. butter
1 1-lb. box confectioners' sugar
½ 10-oz. pkg. frozen red raspberries, thawed

Mix all ingredients together.

## STRAWBERRY CAKE

1 pkg. yellow cake mix
2 c. fresh strawberries
1¼ c. macaroon crumbs
2 egg whites
   Pinch cream of tartar
⅛ t. salt
1 c. strawberry jelly, slightly whipped

Mix cake according to package directions; bake in two 8-inch cake pans. Cool layers. Split cake layers horizontally to make 4 thin layers. Set aside a few berries for garnish. Mash remaining berries with a fork and let stand 10 minutes. Mix with cookie crumbs. Assemble layers, using strawberry filling between layers. Combine the egg whites, salt and cream of tartar. Beat until soft peaks form. Gradually beat jelly into the whites until stiff. Spread over tops and sides of cake and garnish with reserved berries. Serve immediately or refrigerate until serving time. Serves 10.

## HOW TO SPLIT A CAKE FOR FILLING

Measure the cake with a ruler. Using toothpicks, mark into 3 equal depths. With picks as a guide and using a serrated knife, cut cake with a light sawing motion.

## PEPPERMINT AND ICE CREAM CAKE

¾ c. round hard peppermint candies
¼ c. water
2 c. heavy cream, whipped
¼ c. confectioners' sugar
½ t. vanilla
1 angel food cake
1 pt. vanilla ice cream

In blender container, blend ½ cup candies on high speed until coarsely crushed. Remove to waxed paper. Blend remaining ¼ cup candies but leave in the blender. Add water; blend until syrupy. In small bowl with mixer at medium speed, beat cream, sugar and vanilla until stiff peaks form. Slice cake into 3 layers. Sprinkle bottom layer with 2 tablespoons peppermint syrup. Spread ½ cup whipped cream over the cake; sprinkle with 1 tablespoon crushed candies. Top with second cake layer. Sprinkle with syrup, spread with cream and sprinkle with candies as on the first layer. Invert top layer. Sprinkle cut side with remaining syrup. Place right side up on the cake. Spread remaining cream on top and sides of cake, dusting sides with crushed candies. With a small ice-cream scoop, scoop ice cream into balls. Place ice-cream balls on top of cake. Sprinkle with crushed candies. Freeze until served. Makes 10 servings.

## CHERRY CHIFFON CAKE

1 lemon chiffon cake
1½ 8-oz. pkgs. cream cheese, softened
   Grated rind of 1 lemon
¼ t. salt
1 t. vanilla
4 c. confectioners' sugar
½ c. chopped nuts
1 21-oz. can cherry pie filling

Cut cake into 4 layers. Combine cream cheese, salt, lemon rind and vanilla; beat until smooth. Add sugar, 1 cup at a time, beating well after each addition. Spread one-third of this frosting on the bottom layer of the cake and sprinkle with half the nuts. Top with second cake layer; spread with half the pie filling. Top with third cake layer and spread with one-third of the frosting; sprinkle with remainder of nuts. Add last cake layer, spreading top and sides with remaining icing. (Some of the icing can be set aside and used in a pastry bag to flute around the edge and center hole.) Spread remaining pie filling on top of the cake. Serves 16.

## LEMON SPICE CAKE

1 pkg. yellow cake mix
1 3-oz. pkg. lemon instant pudding
1 t. cinnamon
½ t. ginger
¼ t. cloves
½ t. cardamom
¼ t. allspice
1 c. beer
4 eggs

Mix all ingredients together and beat until smooth. Bake in a 350° oven 45 minutes in a greased and floured tube pan. Remove from pan and pour glaze over cake. Serves 12.

### GLAZE

1½ c. confectioners' sugar
2 T. butter
¼ t. lemon rind
1 t. lemon juice

Mix together all ingredients, stirring until smooth. If necessary, thin with a few drops water.

## SWISS APPLE CAKE

1 pkg. German chocolate cake mix
1 21-oz. can apple pie filling
3 eggs
Whipped cream
Cinnamon

Blend cake mix with pie filling, and eggs. Beat 2 minutes at medium speed of electric mixer. Pour in a greased and floured 9 x 13-inch pan. Bake in a 350° oven 40 to 50 minutes. Serve with whipped cream and a sprinkle of cinnamon. Serves 16.

## CITRUS CAKE

4 eggs
1 pkg. yellow cake mix
1 3-oz. pkg. lemon instant pudding mix
¾ c. water
½ c. buttery flavored oil
2 c. confectioners' sugar
⅓ c. orange juice
2 T. grated orange rind
Orange slices for garnish

Beat eggs. Add cake mix, pudding, water and oil. Beat 10 minutes. Pour into a greased and floured tube pan. Bake in a 350° oven 50 minutes. Cool. Combine sugar and orange juice; heat to boiling. Stir in orange rind and cool. Drizzle over cake. Garnish with orange slices.

## PIÑA COLADA CAKE

1 pkg. white cake mix
1 3-oz. pkg. instant coconut cream pudding mix
4 eggs
½ c. water
⅓ c. dark rum
¼ c. vegetable oil

Blend all ingredients; beat 4 minutes at medium speed of electric mixer. Pour into 2 greased and floured 9-inch round pans. Bake in a 350° oven 25 to 30 minutes. Cool and frost with Pineapple-Rum Frosting. Serves 16.

### PINEAPPLE-RUM FROSTING

1 8-oz. can crushed pineapple
1 3-oz. pkg. coconut cream instant pudding mix
⅓ c. rum
1 9-oz. container frozen whipped topping, thawed

Combine pineapple, pudding mix and rum. Beat until well blended. Fold in thawed whipped topping. Serves 16.

## NUTTY ORANGE CAKE

1 pkg. orange cake mix
2 c. ricotta cheese
2 T. milk
1½ c. confectioners' sugar
¼ c. cut-up candied cherries
¼ c. candied lemon peel
¼ c. finely grated orange peel
¼ c. rum
1 envelope unflavored gelatin
¼ c. cold water
2 c. heavy cream
½ c. sugar
1 c. toasted and coarsely chopped pecans

Mix cake as directed on package and bake in two 8-inch layer cake pans. Cool, split each layer in half, making 4 thin layers. Beat cheese and milk until smooth. Gradually stir in confectioners' sugar. Fold in cherries, lemon and orange peel. Sprinkle each layer of cake with 1 tablespoon rum. Top 1 layer with one-third of the cheese mixture. Continue layering cake and cheese, ending with cake. Sprinkle gelatin over water. Set cup of gelatin in a pan of hot water and stir until dissolved. Cool slightly. Beat cream and sugar until fairly stiff. Slowly add cooled gelatin, beating to stiff peaks. Frost top and sides of cake; sprinkle with nuts. Serves 10.

# EASY MANDARIN CAKE

1 box yellow cake mix
1 11-oz. can mandarin orange slices
4 eggs
½ c. vegetable oil

Combine all ingredients; mix for 2 minutes. Pour into 3 greased and floured 9-inch round layer pans. Bake in a preheated 350° oven 20 to 25 minutes. Remove from pans to wire racks. When cool, frost top and sides with Frosting. Serves 10.

### FROSTING

1 9-oz. carton frozen whipped topping, thawed
1 20-oz. can crushed pineapple
1 3-oz. pkg. instant vanilla pudding

Combine all ingredients, mixing well.

# POPPY SEED CAKE

1 pkg. white cake mix
¼ c. poppy seeds
1⅓ c. water
2 egg whites

Pour one-third cup water over poppy seeds. Let stand 30 minutes. Combine cake mix, egg whites, poppy seed mixture and remaining 1 cup water. Blend all and beat according to package directions. Bake in a greased and floured 9 x 13-inch pan in a 350° oven for about 30 to 35 minutes. Cool, fill and ice. Serves 12.

### FILLING

½ c. sour cream
2 egg yolks
¼ c. milk
1 3-oz. pkg. vanilla instant pudding mix

Mix together the first 3 ingredients. Stir in pudding mix. Spread on cooled cake.

### ICING

2 egg whites, room temperature
¼ t. cream of tartar
¼ t. salt
¼ c. sugar
¾ c. light corn syrup
1¼ t. vanilla

Add cream of tartar and salt to egg whites; beat at high speed of electric mixer until soft peaks form. Gradually beat in sugar until smooth and glossy. Gradually add corn syrup and vanilla, beating until stiff peaks form, about 7 minutes.

# YELLOW MOON CAKE

1 pkg. yellow cake mix
1⅓ c. water
2 eggs
2 t. instant tea
  Grated rind of 1 lemon
2 T. butter
½ t. cinnamon
2 T. brown sugar
1 3-oz. can chow mein noodles
⅓ c. apricot preserves

Combine cake mix, water, eggs, tea and grated lemon rind. Beat with electric mixer on high speed for 2 minutes. Pour into 2 greased and floured 9-inch cake pans. Bake according to package directions. Meanwhile, combine butter, cinnamon and brown sugar in a skillet. Heat until butter is melted. Add noodles and stir over low heat until syrup is absorbed. Cool. Coarsely crumble half of the noodle mixture; stir into apricot preserves. Use as a filling for the cake. Frost with a boiled icing. Garnish with remaining noodles. Serves 12.

---

To produce a fancy marbled cake, remove half of the cake batter and set it aside. Add flavored gelatin powder to remaining batter and pour into the cake pan. Pour the reserved plain batter over flavored batter. Swirl by cutting through batter with a rubber spatula.

---

# ALMOND CREAM MOCHA CAKE

1 pkg. chocolate cake mix
1⅓ c. water
2 eggs
3 T. instant espresso
1 3-oz. pkg. instant vanilla pudding
½ t. almond extract
1¼ c. milk
1 c. heavy cream, whipped
1 can cherry pie filling
  Toasted almonds

Combine cake mix, water, eggs and espresso. Beat on high speed for 3 minutes. Pour batter into two 9-inch round pans and bake as directed on the package. Cool. Combine pudding mix, almond extract and milk. Beat until pudding thickens. Fold in whipped cream. Assemble cake, using pudding between layers and topping cake with cherry pie filling. Garnish with toasted almonds. Serves 16.

## OLD-FASHIONED CHEESECAKE

1 pkg. active dry yeast
¼ c. warm water
1 T. sugar
½ c. butter, softened
2 c. flour
1 egg
½ t. vanilla

Soften yeast in warm water. In large mixer bowl, combine sugar, butter and flour. Mix until crumbly. Mix in softened yeast, egg and vanilla. Mix until a dough forms. Roll two-thirds of the dough to a 16 x 12-inch rectangle. Place dough in a greased 9 x 13-inch pan, pressing dough up the sides of the pan. Spread Pineapple Filling over, then carefully spread Cheese Filling on. Roll out remaining dough to a 9 x 13-inch rectangle, and place on top, sealing edges by pressing dough together. Cover and let rise in a warm place 60 minutes. Bake in a 375° oven 30 to 35 minutes. While warm, spread on Glaze. Cool. Refrigerate until served. Serves 14.

### PINEAPPLE FILLING

3 T. sugar
2 T. flour
⅛ t. salt
1 13¼-oz. can crushed pineapple, undrained

Combine sugar, flour, salt and pineapple in a saucepan. Cook over medium heat, stirring constantly, until thick. Cool.

### CHEESE FILLING

2 eggs
¾ c. sugar
2 T. flour
1 t. vanilla
2 c. creamed small-curd cottage cheese
1 8-oz. pkg. cream cheese, softened
½ c. flaked coconut

Combine eggs, sugar, flour and vanilla. Beat at medium speed until thick. Add cheeses and coconut, blending well.

### GLAZE

1 c. confectioners' sugar
2 T. milk
½ t. white vanilla

Combine all ingredients and blend until smooth.

## CHOCOLATE-FILLED ANGEL FOOD CAKE

1 1-oz. square unsweetened chocolate
1 king-size milk chocolate bar
1 c. butter
1 c. confectioners' sugar, sifted
4 eggs
1 T. creme de cacao
1 angel food cake
Whipped cream

Melt chocolate in a double boiler; cool. Cream butter and confectioners' sugar. Add eggs, one at a time, beating after each addition. Add cooled chocolate and creme de cacao. Cut out inside of cake, leaving a ½-inch shell on sides and bottom. Lift inside out and set aside. Pour chocolate mixture into shell. Press cake which has been removed back into the chocolate center, allowing the chocolate to ooze over the sides. Refrigerate overnight or freeze. Serve with whipped cream. Serves 12 to 16.

## FUDGY CHOCOLATE ICING

¼ c. instant hot cocoa mix
3 T. water
¼ t. salt
⅔ c. shortening
1 egg white
¼ c. cocoa
4 T. chocolate syrup
1 1-lb. box confectioners' sugar
1 t. white vanilla

Combine instant cocoa mix with water and salt. Beat until smooth. Add remaining ingredients, beating with an electric mixer 25 minutes. Add warm water, a teaspoon at a time, until of spreading consistency. Makes enough icing to fill and frost one 8-inch layer cake.

## BOILED ICING

½ c. sugar
2 egg whites
2 T. water
1 7-oz. jar marshmallow creme
½ t. vanilla
Food coloring (optional)

Combine sugar, egg whites and water in top of a double boiler. Beat with electric mixer over boiling water until soft peaks form. Add marshmallow creme and beat to stiff peaks. Remove from heat. Beat in vanilla and a few drops food coloring, if desired. Makes enough to frost a 10-inch cake.

*Pictured opposite:*
*Cranberry Freezer Pie, p. 21*

# PIES

## OIL PASTRY

2 c. flour
1 t. salt
½ c. vegetable oil
3 T. cold water

Toss flour and salt together. Add oil and mix with a fork until mixture looks like fine crumbs. Sprinkle with enough cold water to moisten. Gather into a ball with a fork. Roll out on floured board. Makes 2 single crusts or 1 double 9-inch crust.

## PRETZEL CRUMB CRUST

1½ c. pretzel crumbs (use hard twisted pretzels)
½ c. sugar
¼ c. melted butter

Combine all ingredients, mixing well. Firmly press into the sides and bottom of a 9-inch pie pan. Bake in 400° oven 10 to 12 minutes. Makes one 9-inch pie shell.

## PASTRY FOR ONE-CRUST PIE

1 c. flour
½ t. salt
1 T. sugar
⅓ c. shortening or lard
2 T. cold water

Toss flour, salt and sugar to mix. Cut in shortening with pastry blender or two knives until mixture looks like coarse meal. Sprinkle with water. Gather into a ball with a fork. Roll on a lightly floured board to a circle 1 inch larger than the inverted pie pan. Ease pastry into pie pan; fold edges under even with the pan rim. Flute edges. To bake before filling: prick pie shell with a fork. Bake in a 475° oven 8 to 10 minutes. Cool before filling. Makes one 9-inch pie shell.

## COOKIE DOUGH PIE CRUST

1 c. flour
½ t. salt
2 T. sugar
½ c. butter

Toss flour, salt and sugar to mix. Add butter and work into a dough. Press into bottom and up sides of a 9-inch pie pan. Use for open-faced fruit pies. To use for chiffon and other cooked pudding pies: chill, prick and bake in a 400° oven 15 minutes or until golden brown.

## FROZEN CRUST

1 c. creamed cottage cheese
⅓ c. sugar
1 t. vanilla
1 egg yolk
1½ pts. vanilla ice cream, softened

In blender, mix cheese, sugar, vanilla and egg yolk. Blend smooth. Stir into ice cream, mixing well. Place in freezer 45 minutes. Chill a 9-inch pie plate. Spoon mixture in and freeze 30 minutes. Using back of a spoon, spread evenly on sides and bottom of pan. Freeze solid. To serve, fill with sweetened fresh fruit. Makes one 9-inch pie shell.

## GRAHAM CRACKER CRUST

1¼ c. graham cracker crumbs (19 crackers)
¼ c. sugar
6 T. melted butter

Combine all ingredients, mixing well. Press into a 9-inch pie pan. Chill 45 minutes for a chilled crust or bake in a 375° oven 7 minutes. Cool.

### VARIATIONS

*Peanut Butter Crust:* Follow recipe for graham cracker crust, using only 4 tablespoons butter. Add ¼ cup creamy peanut butter. Mix well.

*Spiced:* To graham cracker crust; add 1 teaspoon cinnamon.

*Orange:* To graham cracker crust, add 1 tablespoon grated orange peel.

*Nutty:* To graham cracker crust, add ½ cup finely chopped nuts.

## WALNUT CRUST

1¼ c. finely chopped walnuts
3 T. sugar
2 T. butter, softened
¼ c. unsifted flour

Combine all ingredients, mixing well. Press onto sides and bottom of a 9-inch pie pan. Bake in a 400° oven 8 to 10 minutes. Cool and fill. Makes one 9-inch pie shell.

## HEALTH CRUST

¾ c. graham cracker crumbs
½ c. wheat germ
2 T. sugar
½ c. butter, softened

Combine all ingredients until well mixed. Press evenly into bottom and sides of a greased 9-inch pie pan. Refrigerate 15 minutes. Firmly press crust against pan. Bake in a 400° oven 8 to 10 minutes. Cool. Spoon in filling. Makes one 9-inch pie shell.

## FESTIVE ICE CREAM PIE

1 c. M and M candies
2 T. butter
2 T. water
1 7-oz. can flaked coconut
1½ qts. peppermint ice cream

In a saucepan, combine M and M candies, water and butter. Cover and heat slowly 10 minutes, stirring smooth. Stir in coconut. Press against sides and bottom of a 9-inch pie pan. Chill. Scoop ice cream into the shell. Freeze. Serve with M and M Sauce. Serves 7.

### M and M Sauce

1 c. M and M peanut candies
½ c. light cream
¼ c. light corn syrup
⅛ t. cream of tartar

Combine candies, cream, corn syrup and cream of tartar in a saucepan. Cover. Place over low heat 10 minutes. Uncover and stir until smooth. Chill. Thin with light cream if necessary. Serves 7.

## NUT CRUST

3 oz. semisweet chocolate
2 T. butter
1¼ c. blanched almonds, toasted and finely chopped

Melt chocolate and butter over low heat. Stir in nuts, coating well. Refrigerate about 35 minutes. Spoon into a greased 9-inch pie pan. Press against bottom and sides. Refrigerate 2 hours before filling. Before serving, dip pan in hot water for 10 seconds, and serve at once. Makes one 9-inch pie shell.

## CRANBERRY FREEZER PIE

1¼ c. cinnamon-graham cracker crumbs
6 T. melted butter
1 8-oz. pkg. cream cheese, softened
½ t. vanilla
1 c. heavy cream
¼ c. sugar
1 16-oz. can whole cranberry sauce

Combine crumbs and butter. Press into the bottom and up the sides of a 9-inch pie pan. Chill. Beat cheese and vanilla until fluffy. Whip cream, sugar, cheese, beating until smooth and creamy. Set aside a few whole cranberries for garnish. Fold remaining sauce into cream mixture. Pour into crust and freeze firm. Remove from freezer 10 minutes before serving. Garnish with reserved cranberries and additional whipped cream. Serves 10 to 12.

## PUFFY PEANUT PIE

1 8-oz. pkg. cream cheese, softened
1 c. crunchy peanut butter
1 14-oz. can sweetened condensed milk
¼ c. lemon juice
1 t. vanilla
1 4½-oz. container whipped topping, thawed
1 graham cracker crust
Chopped peanuts for garnish

Cream cheese until fluffy. Beat in peanut butter and slowly add milk. Stir in lemon juice and vanilla. Fold in topping. Pour into the crust, garnish and chill 2 hours. Serves 7.

## CHERRY PIE

1 9-inch graham cracker crumb crust
1 8-oz. pkg. cream cheese, softened
1 14-oz. can sweetened condensed milk
⅓ c. lemon juice
1 t. vanilla
1 21-oz. can cherry pie filling

Beat cheese until fluffy. Gradually add condensed milk, stirring well. Blend in lemon juice and vanilla. Pour into crust and refrigerate 3 hours. Top with pie filling. Serves 8.

## STRAWBERRY CHEESE TARTS

24 ladyfingers
1 t. almond extract
1 t. vanilla
2 c. confectioners' sugar
2 8-oz. pkgs. cream cheese, room temperature
1 pt. heavy cream, whipped
1 3-oz. pkg. strawberry gelatin
1 c. boiling water
1 16-oz. pkg. frozen strawberries

Line a torte pan or a 9 x 13-inch glass pan with 24 ladyfingers. (Cut in half, lengthwise, to fit sides of pan.) Combine almond extract, vanilla, confectioners' sugar and cream cheese. Fold in whipped cream. Pour into crust. Dissolve gelatin in boiling water. Add strawberries, chill until slightly thickened. Pour over cheese mixture and refrigerate until ready to serve. Serves 12.

## MAI-TAI PIE

2 c. flaked coconut
¼ c. melted butter
1 8-oz. pkg. cream cheese
1 14-oz. can sweetened condensed milk
1 6-oz. can unsweetened orange juice concentrate, thawed
⅓ c. light rum
2 T. orange-flavored liqueur
1 4½-oz. container frozen whipped topping, thawed
Orange slices

Combine coconut and butter, mixing well. Press into the bottom and up the sides of a 9-inch pie pan. Bake in a 300° oven 25 minutes. Cool. Beat cheese until fluffy. Add milk and orange concentrate and beat until smooth. Add rum and liqueur. Fold in whipped topping. Pour into cooled crust and refrigerate 6 hours. Garnish with orange slices. Serves 7.

## PUMPKIN CHEESE PIE

1¼ c. cinnamon-graham cracker crumbs
2 T. sugar
1 t. cinnamon
¼ c. melted butter
1 8-oz. pkg. cream cheese
¾ c. sugar
2 T. flour
1 t. cinnamon
¼ t. nutmeg
¼ t. ginger
1 t. grated lemon peel
1 t. grated orange peel
¼ t. vanilla
1 16-oz. can pumpkin
3 eggs
Salted pecans

Combine graham crumbs, sugar, cinnamon and butter. Mix thoroughly. Press mixture firmly into bottom and up the sides of a 9-inch pie plate. Bake in a 350° oven 10 minutes. Cool. In a large mixing bowl, blend cream cheese, sugar and flour. Add remaining ingredients and beat until smooth. Pour into crust. Cover the edge with a strip of foil to prevent excessive browning. Bake in a 350° oven 50 to 55 minutes or until a knife inserted in the center comes out clean. Remove foil after 35 minutes of baking. Immediately spread on Topping. Refrigerate at least 4 hours. Garnish with salted pecans. Serves 8.

### TOPPING

¾ c. sour cream
1 T. sugar
¼ t. vanilla

Combine all ingredients, mixing well.

## DAIQUIRI PIE

1 9-inch graham cracker crust, baked and cooled
1 8-oz. pkg. cream cheese, softened
1 14-oz. can sweetened condensed milk
1 6-oz. can frozen limeade concentrate, thawed
⅓ c. light rum
Green food coloring
1 4½-oz. container frozen whipped topping, thawed
Lime slices

Beat cream cheese until light and fluffy. Add milk and limeade, beating smooth. Add rum and food coloring; fold in whipped cream. Pour into pie shell and refrigerate 6 to 8 hours. Garnish with slices of lime, if desired. Serves 7.

*Pictured opposite:*
*Daiquiri Pie*

22

## CHOCOLATE BANANA PIE

1 c. vanilla wafer crumbs
½ c. chopped pecans
⅓ c. melted margarine
1 6-oz. pkg. semisweet chocolate chips
½ c. milk
3 c. miniature marshmallows
1 3-oz. pkg. vanilla pudding mix
1½ c. milk
½ c. heavy cream, whipped
2 bananas, thinly sliced

Combine crumbs, nuts and margarine; press into a 9-inch pie pan. Bake in a 375° oven 5 minutes. Combine chocolate chips, milk and 1 cup marshmallows. Stir over low heat until melted; pour into crust. Chill. Prepare pudding as directed on package, using 1½ cups milk. Cover with waxed paper and chill thoroughly. Fold whipped cream and remaining marshmallows into pudding. Arrange bananas over chocolate layer; pour pudding over bananas. Chill several hours. Garnish with additional bananas, whipped cream and chocolate pieces, if desired. Serves 6 to 8.

## MILE-HIGH CHOCOLATE PIE

1 envelope unflavored gelatin
¼ c. cold water
3 1-oz. squares unsweetened chocolate
½ c. water
3 egg yolks
½ c. sugar
1 t. vanilla
¼ t. salt
½ c. sugar
3 egg whites, beaten stiff
1 9-inch baked pie shell
  Whipped cream
  Chocolate curls

Dissolve gelatin in ¼ cup cold water and set aside. In top of double boiler, combine chocolate and ½ cup water. Stir until blended. Remove from heat and add gelatin, stirring until dissolved. Beat egg yolks and gradually add ½ cup sugar, beating until light. Add chocolate mixture, vanilla and salt. Cool to room temperature. Gradually beat ½ cup sugar into beaten egg whites. Fold into chocolate mixture. Pour into pie shell. Chill until firm. Top with whipped cream and garnish with chocolate curls. Serves 7.

## LEMONADE PIE

1 9-inch graham cracker crust
1 14-oz. can sweetened condensed milk
1 3-oz. can frozen lemonade concentrate
1 9-oz. container frozen whipped topping, thawed
  Fresh slices of lemon

Chill milk; beat well. Add frozen lemonade concentrate; beat until thick. Fold in whipped topping and pour into the crust. Chill 1 hour. Will keep a week in the refrigerator. Before serving, top with lemon slices. Serves 7.

## GRASSHOPPER CHEESE PIE

1 8-oz. pkg. cream cheese, softened
1 14-oz. can sweetened condensed milk
⅓ c. lemon juice
½ c. green creme de menthe
1 9-oz. container frozen whipped topping, thawed
1 9-inch graham cracker pie crust
  Chocolate curls for garnish

Beat cheese until fluffy. Slowly add the milk, beating until smooth. Stir in lemon juice and creme de menthe. Fold in topping; pour into crust. Garnish with chocolate curls. Chill 2 hours. Serves 7.

## POLKA DOT PIE

½ c. butter
¼ c. corn syrup
½ c. semisweet chocolate chips
2 c. cornflakes
1½ 8-oz. pkgs. cream cheese, softened
¾ c. sugar
2 T. brandy
½ c. maraschino cherries, drained and quartered
½ c. chopped pecans
2¼ c. whipped topping, thawed
  Chocolate curls for garnish

In a saucepan, combine butter, corn syrup and chocolate chips. Melt over low heat, stirring constantly. Remove from heat and add cornflakes, stirring until well coated. Gently press into a well-buttered 9-inch pie pan. Chill. Beat cheese until smooth. Gradually beat in sugar and brandy. Fold in cherries, nuts and whipped topping. Spread onto crust. Garnish with chocolate curls. Freeze 4 hours. Let stand at room temperature 15 minutes before cutting. Serves 7.

# TORTES

## BUTTERSCOTCH TORTE

6 egg yolks
1½ c. sugar
1 T. baking powder
2 t. vanilla
1 t. almond flavoring
6 egg whites
2 c. graham cracker crumbs
½ pt. heavy cream, whipped
1 c. chopped walnuts

Beat egg yolks well. Combine sugar and baking powder; add to beaten egg yolks with flavorings. Beat egg whites stiff, but not dry. Fold into egg yolk mixture. Fold in cracker crumbs and nuts. Line two 9-inch pans with waxed paper and grease. Pour in mixture and bake in a 325° oven for 25 to 35 minutes. Cover with whipped cream and top with Butterscotch Sauce. Serves 8 to 10.

### BUTTERSCOTCH SAUCE

1 c. brown sugar
1 T. flour
¼ c. butter
½ c. water
1 egg, beaten
½ t. vanilla
¼ c. chopped nuts

In a saucepan, combine first 4 ingredients. Cook over low heat or in top of double boiler until thick. Pour slowly over beaten egg, stirring constantly. Simmer another 2 to 3 minutes. Cool and add vanilla and nuts.

## APPLE TORTE

1¼ c. flour
½ t. salt
1 t. sugar
1 t. baking powder
½ c. butter, softened
1 egg yolk
2 T. milk
3 to 4 apples, peeled and sliced

Sift together dry ingredients and combine with butter. Add egg yolk mixed with milk. Pat into the bottom of a lightly greased and floured 8-inch square pan. Arrange apples over crust. Top with Streusel. Bake in a 375° oven 45 minutes. Serves 6.

### STREUSEL

¾ c. sugar
1½ T. flour
2 T. butter
¼ t. cinnamon

Combine ingredients, mixing thoroughly.

## CHOCOLATE REFRIGERATOR TORTE

½ lb. box chocolate wafers, finely crushed
¼ c. melted butter
½ lb. marshmallows
⅓ c. milk
¼ c. maraschino cherry juice
¾ c. sliced maraschino cherries
½ c. chopped walnuts
½ c. heavy cream, whipped
Whipped cream

Pour melted butter over wafers; blend well. Press ¾ of the crumbs on the bottom of a greased 9 x 9-inch square pan. Melt marshmallows in milk and cherry juice in top of double boiler. Cool. Combine cooled marshmallow mixture, cherries, walnuts and whipped cream. Pour over crumbs. Refrigerate 3 to 4 hours. Cut in squares, top with whipped cream. Serves 8.

## RED, WHITE AND BLUE DESSERT

1 can sweetened condensed milk
⅓ c. lemon juice
2 t. grated lemon peel
2 c. plain yogurt
2 c. miniature marshmallows
½ c. chopped pecans
1 pt. fresh strawberries, sliced
1 c. fresh blueberries

In a large bowl combine the condensed milk, lemon juice and lemon peel; mix well. Stir in yogurt, marshmallows and nuts. Spread half this mixture in a 9 x 13-inch dish. Place half the strawberries and half the blueberries on top. Repeat, using remaining fruit and yogurt mixture. Cover with foil and freeze. Remove from freezer 10 minutes before serving. Makes 15 servings.

## STRAWBERRY TOPPED MERINGUE TORTE

6 egg whites
½ t. cream of tartar
¼ t. salt
1¾ c. sugar
½ t. almond flavoring or vanilla
2 3-oz. pkgs. cream cheese, softened
1 c. sugar
½ t. almond flavoring *or* 1 t. white vanilla
2 c. heavy cream, whipped
2 c. miniature multicolored marshmallows
2 to 3 pkgs. frozen strawberries, thawed

In a large bowl, beat egg whites, cream of tartar and salt until foamy. Gradually beat in 1¾ cup sugar (1 tablespoon at a time). Using high speed of mixer, beat until stiff and glossy. Add flavoring; mix well. Spread in a buttered 9 x 13-inch pan. Bake in a 275° oven for 60 minutes. Turn off oven and let cake set in oven at least 12 hours. *Do not open oven door.* Blend cream cheese, remaining sugar and flavoring until fluffy. Carefully fold in whipped cream and marshmallows. Spread over meringue. Chill 24 hours. Top with strawberries. Serves 12.

## PRIZE-WINNING POTATO TORTE

1 c. butter
2 c. sugar
5 eggs
1 c. sour milk
1 t. baking soda
2 c. flour
1 t. cinnamon
½ t. cloves
¼ t. nutmeg
1 t. allspice
½ t. ginger
1 bar German sweet chocolate, melted
1 c. mashed potato (not instant)
½ c. chopped nuts
1 t. vanilla

Cream butter with sugar; stir in eggs. Combine sour milk and baking soda and add to butter mixture. Combine dry ingredients; beat in chocolate, potato, nuts and vanilla. Add to butter mixture. Pour into a greased and floured 10-inch tube pan. Bake in a 350° oven 60 minutes. Serves 16.

*Pictured opposite:*
*Coconut Strawberry Torte*

## AUNT VIRGINIA'S RASPBERRY TORTE

1 c. flour
½ c. butter
¼ c. brown sugar
¾ c. chopped nuts
36 large marshmallows
1 c. milk
1 c. heavy cream, whipped
2 3-oz. pkgs. raspberry gelatin
2 c. boiling water
2 10-oz. pkgs. frozen raspberries

Combine flour, butter, brown sugar and nuts. Press into a 9 x 13-inch pan. Bake in a 350° oven 15 to 20 minutes. Melt marshmallows in milk; cool. Fold in whipped cream and spread on crumb crust. Combine boiling water and gelatin, stirring to dissolve completely. Chill until slightly thickened; add raspberries. Spread raspberry gelatin over top. Refrigerate overnight and cut in squares to serve. Serves 10 to 12.

## COCONUT-STRAWBERRY TORTE

1 10-oz. pkg. frozen strawberries
2 envelopes unflavored gelatin
1 c. sugar
¼ t. salt
2 eggs, separated
3 8-oz. pkgs. cream cheese, room temperature
Red food coloring
1 c. heavy cream, whipped
1 c. flaked coconut
Fresh strawberries, sliced

Drain syrup from strawberries and set aside. In top of double boiler combine gelatin, ¾ cup sugar and salt. Beat together strawberry syrup and egg yolks and add to gelatin mixture. Heat over simmering water 10 minutes. Cool to room temperature and add thawed strawberries. Stir. Whip cheese until fluffy. Beat in strawberry mixture and food coloring. Chill. Stir occasionally until mixture mounds when dropped from a spoon. Beat egg whites until stiff but not dry. Fold into gelatin. Fold in whipped cream. Pour into a 9-inch round springform pan. Sprinkle with half the coconut. Chill several hours. When ready to serve, run knife dipped in hot water around the edge of pan. Press remaining coconut into sides and top of cake. Garnish with sliced strawberries. Serves 14.

## CRANBERRY CREAM TORTE

1 c. graham cracker crumbs
¼ c. melted butter
2 c. cranberries
1 c. sugar
½ c. water
2 T. orange marmalade
¼ c. chopped nuts
1 8-oz. pkg. cream cheese
⅓ c. sifted confectioners' sugar
1 T. milk
1 t. vanilla
1 c. heavy cream, whipped

Combine crumbs and butter, mixing well. Press into the bottom of an 8-inch square pan. In a saucepan, combine cranberries, sugar and water. Bring to a boil. Simmer 20 minutes. Stir in nuts and marmalade, stirring to melt marmalade. Set aside and chill to be used as a topping. Combine cream cheese, sugar, milk and vanilla. Mix until well blended. Fold whipped cream into the cream cheese mixture. Spread on graham cracker crust and top with cranberry mixture. Chill until serving time. Serves 8.

## BANANA SPLIT DESSERT

2 c. graham cracker crumbs
½ c. melted margarine
2 eggs
2 c. confectioners' sugar
½ c. margarine, softened
1 16-oz. can crushed pineapple
2 bananas
1 9-oz. container frozen whipped
   topping, thawed
   Chopped pecans
   Maraschino cherries

Mix graham crumbs and melted margarine. Pat into a 9 x 13-inch pan. Bake in a 350° oven 3 to 5 minutes. Beat 2 eggs, confectioners' sugar and margarine. Spread over crust. Drain pineapple, reserving juice. Cut bananas into ½-inch slices. Soak in reserved juice for 10 minutes; drain. Arrange drained pineapple and sliced bananas over second layer. Cover the banana layer with whipped topping. Garnish with nuts and cherries. Chill. Serves 12.

## CHOCOLATE CHIP TORTE

10 eggs, separated
¼ t. salt
2 t. cream of tartar
1 c. sugar
1 c. sifted cake flour
1 t. vanilla
1 8-oz. bar German sweet chocolate,
   grated

Beat egg whites with salt and cream of tartar until foamy. Slowly add sugar and beat until stiff peaks form. Fold in flour, vanilla and grated chocolate. Beat egg yolks until lemon colored; fold into mixture. Pour into ungreased 10-inch tube pan. Bake in a 350° oven 60 minutes. Invert pan to cool. Split cake horizontally. Assemble cake, using Filling between layers and frost with Icing. Serves 12.

### FILLING

½ c. butter, softened
1 6-oz. pkg. semisweet chocolate chips,
   melted and cooled
1 egg yolk
½ t. vanilla
2 t. cognac

Cream butter until fluffy. Beat in cooled, melted chocolate, egg yolk, vanilla and cognac. Refrigerate until of spreading consistency.

### ICING

5 oz. milk chocolate
2¾ T. sugar
   Pinch salt
3 T. water
3 egg yolks
½ pt. heavy cream, whipped

Cook chocolate, sugar, salt and water until smooth. Remove from heat and beat in egg yolks, one at a time. Cool completely. Fold in whipped cream.

To make chocolate curls or shavings, slightly soften chocolate candy bar with the heat of your hands. With a vegetable peeler, shave the narrow edge into curls.

## MOCK CHEESE TORTE

2 c. graham cracker crumbs
2 T. melted butter
½ t. cinnamon
½ c. sugar
3 eggs, separated
1 can sweetened condensed milk
Juice and rind of 1 lemon
2 c. applesauce
4 T. sugar
¼ t. salt

Combine cracker crumbs, butter, cinnamon and ½ cup sugar. Mix well. Set aside ¼ cup for garnish. Pat remaining mixture into a greased 10-inch springform. Beat egg yolks; add condensed milk, lemon juice and rind and applesauce. Beat egg whites until stiff; add remaining sugar and salt. Beat until soft peaks form. Fold into applesauce mixture. Pour into springform pan and sprinkle with crumbs. Bake in a 350° oven 50 minutes. Serves 10 to 12.

### STRAWBERRY TORTE FLUFF

½ c. flour
¼ c. brown sugar
¼ c. margarine
⅓ c. chopped pecans
2 T. lemon juice
1 7-oz. jar marshmallow creme
1 16-oz. pkg. frozen strawberries, thawed
2 c. heavy cream, whipped

Combine flour and sugar; cut in margarine. Add nuts. Press into the bottom of a 9-inch springform. Bake in a 350° oven 20 minutes. Cool. Slowly add lemon juice to marshmallow creme. Mix until well blended. Stir in strawberries; fold in whipped cream. Pour over crumb crust. Freeze until serving time. Serves 8 to 10.

### FREEZER MOCHA DESSERT

18 cream-filled chocolate cookies, crushed
⅓ c. melted butter
2 1-oz. squares unsweetened chocolate
½ c. sugar
⅔ c. evaporated milk
1 qt. coffee-flavored ice cream
1 c. heavy cream
¼ c. creme de cacao
Shaved chocolate

Add melted butter to cookie crumbs and mix well. Press on bottom and up sides of an 8-inch springform pan. Bake in a 350° oven 8 to 10 minutes. Chill in freezer. Melt chocolate in top of double boiler; stir in sugar. Slowly add evaporated milk. Cook over low heat until thick, stirring occasionally. Chill. Let ice cream stand until soft. Spread ice cream over crust. Spread cooled chocolate mixture over the ice cream. Whip cream and add creme de cacao. Spread on top of torte and sprinkle with shaved chocolate. Freeze until served. Serves 10 to 12.

### WAFER TORTE

1⅓ c. vanilla wafer crumbs
1 c. confectioners' sugar
½ c. butter
2 eggs
1 c. chopped pecans
1 15¼-oz. can crushed pineapple
½ pt. heavy cream, whipped

Grind wafers. Place half of crumbs into bottom of buttered 9 x 13-inch pan. Cream butter and sugar until fluffy. Stir in eggs, one at a time. Spread butter mixture on top of crust. Top with a layer of chopped nuts. Add a layer of drained crushed pineapple, and a layer of whipped cream. Cover with remaining crumbs. Chill 24 hours. Cut and serve topped with whipped cream. Serves 10.

### LEMON BISQUE

1⅔ c. vanilla wafer crumbs
3 T. confectioners' sugar
1 t. cinnamon
1 T. melted butter
1 3-oz. pkg. lemon gelatin
1 c. boiling water
Rind of 1 lemon
½ c. sugar
3 T. lemon juice
½ t. salt
1 13-oz. can evaporated milk, chilled
1 10-oz. bottle maraschino cherries, drained

Combine crumbs, confectioners' sugar, cinnamon and melted butter; mix well. Press into bottom of a 10-inch springform. Dissolve gelatin in boiling water. Add lemon rind, juice, sugar and salt. Chill until slightly thickened. Beat milk until stiff. Add gelatin mixture and beat an additional 10 minutes. Fold in cherries and spread on crust. Refrigerate 24 hours. Serves 10 to 12.

## PINEAPPLE TORTE
### CRUST

2½ c. flour
1 t. baking powder
Pinch salt
1 c. margarine
3 T. sugar

Combine all ingredients, mixing well. Press into the bottom of a 15½ x 10½-inch pan. Bake in a 350° oven 15 minutes, until light brown.

### FILLING

1 20-oz. can crushed pineapple
½ c. sugar
2 T. cornstarch
1 6-oz. pkg. vanilla pudding
2 c. milk
2 c. heavy cream, whipped
2 t. vanilla

In a saucepan, combine pineapple, sugar and cornstarch; boil until thickened. Cool and pour over crust. Make vanilla pudding according to package directions, using the 2 cups milk. Pour over pineapple filling; chill. Fold vanilla into whipped cream and spread over top of torte. Makes 25 servings.

## PRETZEL TORTE

2⅔ c. crushed pretzels (8-oz.)
¾ c. melted margarine
3 T. sugar
1 envelope whipped topping mix
½ c. milk for topping
1 8-oz. pkg. cream cheese, softened
1 c. sugar
1 6-oz. pkg. strawberry gelatin
3 c. boiling water
1 16-oz. pkg. frozen strawberries

Combine first 3 ingredients and pat in a 9 x 13-inch pan. Bake in a 350° oven 10 minutes. Cool. Prepare whipped topping according to package directions, using the ½ cup milk. Combine cheese, topping and remaining sugar and spread on top of cooled pretzel base. Dissolve gelatin in boiling water. Chill until slightly thickened; fold in frozen strawberries. Pour over cream cheese layer. Sprinkle additional crushed pretzels over the top. Serves 12.

## SHERBET TORTE

1 pt. orange sherbet, softened
1 3-oz. pkg. ladyfingers
1 pt. raspberry sherbet, softened
2 c. frozen whipped topping, thawed
1 c. miniature multicolored marshmallows
Toasted pecan halves

Stir orange sherbet until smooth and pour into a 9 x 5-inch loaf pan. Cover with 12 double ladyfingers placed end to end. Stir raspberry sherbet until smooth and pour over ladyfingers. Freeze until almost solid. Stir marshmallows into the topping and spread over the top. Freeze firm. About 1 hour before serving fill a large bowl with hot water. Quickly lower pan in and out of the water. Loosen loaf with a spatula. Invert on platter. Place pecans on top. Return to freezer until serving time. Makes 10 to 12 servings.

## LINZER TORTE

1 c. unsalted butter
1 c. sugar
2 eggs
2 c. sifted flour
1 t. cinnamon
¼ t. cloves
1 c. finely chopped blanched almonds
1 T. lemon juice
1 t. vanilla
1 10-oz. jar red raspberry jelly
Confectioners' sugar

Cream butter and sugar and beat until fluffy. Add eggs and blend well. Sift together flour, cinnamon and cloves. Add to batter and mix well. Add nuts, lemon juice and vanilla. Mix until smooth. Spread half of the batter in the bottom of a greased 10-inch springform. Spread jelly over the batter. Place remaining batter in a pastry bag that has a half-inch tube. Pipe batter around the sides forming a 1-inch ring. With the remaining batter, pipe a lattice over the top. Bake in a preheated 325° oven for 55 to 60 minutes until pastry is golden brown. Remove from oven. Cool 10 minutes. Remove sides of form and cool completely. Sprinkle torte with confectioners' sugar. Serves 10 to 12.

## VALENTINE'S DAY TORTE

2 c. sifted flour
1 T. baking powder
½ t. salt
1½ t. cinnamon
¼ t. cloves
1½ c. graham cracker crumbs
¾ c. butter, softened
¾ c. sugar
4 eggs, separated
¾ c. milk
Sliced almonds

Sift flour, baking powder, salt, cinnamon and cloves; stir in graham cracker crumbs and set aside. Cream butter with sugar until creamy. Add egg yolks, beating until light and fluffy. Stir in dry ingredients, alternating with milk, beginning and ending with dry ingredients. Beat egg whites until stiff, but not dry. Fold into graham mixture. Grease two 5½-cup heart-shaped pans; line with waxed paper and grease paper. Pour mixture into pans. Bake in a 350° oven 30 to 35 minutes. Cool in pans 10 minutes. Turn out on rack; peel off waxed paper. Cool completely. Split cake into 4 layers. Fill and frost with Chocolate Frosting. Garnish with sliced almonds. Serves 12.

### CHOCOLATE FROSTING

½ c. butter, softened
2 eggs, separated
1½ c. confectioners' sugar
4 1-oz. squares unsweetened chocolate, melted

Cream butter until fluffy. Add egg yolks, beating until blended. Whip egg whites until foamy; gradually beat in sugar, beating until thick. Fold into butter mixture. Gradually stir in chocolate, blending well.

## PUMPKIN CHEESE SPICE TORTE
### CRUST

24 graham crackers, crushed
⅓ c. sugar
½ c. melted butter

Combine all ingredients, mixing well. Press into the bottom of a 9 x 13-inch pan.

### FILLING

2 eggs, beaten
¾ c. sugar
1 8-oz. pkg. cream cheese
2 c. pumpkin
3 egg yolks
½ c. sugar
½ c. milk
½ t. salt
1 T. cinnamon
1 envelope unflavored gelatin
¼ c. cold water
3 egg whites
¼ c. sugar
½ pt. heavy cream, whipped

Combine eggs, ¾ cup sugar and cream cheese, mixing well. Pour over crust. Bake in a 350° oven 20 minutes. In a saucepan, combine pumpkin, egg yolks, ½ cup sugar, milk, salt and cinnamon; cook until mixture thickens. Remove from heat. Dissolve gelatin in cold water and add to pumpkin mixture; cool. Beat egg whites until foamy. Add remaining sugar and beat until soft peaks form. Fold into pumpkin mixture. Pour over cooled layer. Serve topped with whipped cream. Serves 8.

## VIENNESE TORTE

½ c. butter
1 c. confectioners' sugar
1½ 1-oz. squares unsweetened chocolate, melted
3 eggs, separated
2 c. heavy cream, whipped
Shaved chocolate
½ lb. vanilla wafers, crushed
1 c. chopped nuts

Combine butter, sugar, melted chocolate and egg yolks; mix until well blended. Beat egg whites until stiff; fold into chocolate mixture. In a 9-inch square pan, layer half the wafers then half the chocolate mixture. Repeat for two more layers and sprinkle with nuts. Top with whipped cream and garnish with shaved chocolate. Serves 8.

# COOKIES

## CHOCOLATE RAISIN COOKIES

½ c. shortening
½ c. brown sugar
¼ c. sugar
1 egg
½ t. vanilla
1 c. plus 2 T. flour
½ t. salt
½ t. baking soda
1 c. chocolate-covered raisins
½ c. coarsely chopped pecans

In a mixing bowl, with mixer at medium speed, cream shortening and sugars until fluffy. Mix in egg and vanilla. Sift together flour, salt and soda. With mixer at low speed, beat flour mixture into shortening mixture until smooth. Fold in raisins and nuts. Drop by spoonfuls onto greased cookie sheets. Bake in a 350° oven 10 to 12 minutes until lightly browned. Remove to wire rack to cool.

## PEANUT DROPS

1 c. peanut butter
2¾ c. confectioners' sugar
½ c. butter, softened
¼ block paraffin
1 6-oz. pkg. chocolate chips

Cream peanut butter, sugar and butter. Roll into balls and stick with toothpicks. Refrigerate 2 hours. Melt paraffin and chocolate chips in a double boiler. Dip each ball into chocolate; chill. Makes 3 dozen drops.

## GIANT CREAM-FILLED CHOCOLATE COOKIES

⅔ c. shortening
¾ c. sugar
1 egg
1 t. vanilla
2¼ c. sifted flour
1 c. instant chocolate-flavored mix
1 t. salt
½ t. baking soda
1 c. milk

Cream together shortening and sugar. Beat in egg and vanilla. Sift together flour, chocolate-flavored mix, salt and soda. Stir dry ingredients into creamed mixture alternately with milk. Drop by teaspoonfuls onto greased cookie sheets. Bake in a 400° oven 8 minutes. Cool on cookie sheet 2 to 3 minutes before removing. When cool, put 2 cookies together with Marshmallow Filling. Makes about 3 dozen cookies.

### MARSHMALLOW FILLING

¾ c. butter, softened
2 c. sifted confectioners' sugar
2 c. marshmallow creme

Cream butter with sugar until light. Stir in marshmallow creme, blending well.

## MOM'S CHOCOLATE CHIP COOKIES

½ c. butter
½ c. sugar
¼ c. brown sugar, firmly packed
1 egg, well beaten
1 c. sifted flour
½ t. salt
½ t. baking soda
1 6-oz. pkg. chocolate chips
1 c. coconut
1 t. vanilla

Cream butter and sugars until light and fluffy. Add beaten egg and mix thoroughly. Sift flour with salt and soda. Add flour in 2 parts to egg mixture and mix well. Stir in chocolate chips, coconut and vanilla. Mix well. Bake in a 350° oven 10 minutes. Makes 36 to 40 cookies.

## CHERRY COBBLER BARS

1 pkg. yellow cake mix
¼ c. melted butter
2 eggs
1 21-oz. can cherry pie filling
1 pkg. coconut pecan frosting mix
2 T. melted butter

Combine cake mix, ¼ cup butter and eggs, mixing well. Pat into a 9 x 13-inch pan that is greased only on the bottom. Pour pie filling over, smoothing well. Combine frosting mix and remaining butter. Sprinkle over cherries. Bake in a 350° oven 30 minutes. Cool and cut into bars. Makes 24.

## LEMON-CHEESE BARS

1 pkg. lemon cake mix
½ c. melted butter
1 egg, slightly beaten
1 pkg. lemon frosting mix
1 8-oz. pkg. cream cheese, softened
2 eggs

Combine cake mix, butter and 1 egg. Stir with fork until moist. Pat into a 13 x 9-inch pan, which has been greased on the bottom only. Mix cream cheese and frosting mix. Reserve ½ cup of the cream cheese mixture. Add remaining eggs to frosting mixture and beat 3 to 5 minutes. Spread over cake mixture. Bake in a 350° oven 30 to 40 minutes. Cool. Spread with reserved frosting. Makes 40 squares.

## DAINTY COOKIES

2¾ c. sifted flour
1 t. baking soda
½ t. salt
1 c. butter
1 3-oz. pkg. gelatin, any flavor
½ c. sugar
2 eggs
1 t. vanilla
½ t. almond extract
½ c. milk

Sift flour, baking soda and salt. Set aside. Cream butter, sugar and gelatin until light and fluffy. Add eggs, one at a time, beating after each addition. Stir in flavorings. Add flour mixture, alternating with milk, and beating well after each addition. Drop by teaspoonfuls onto ungreased cookie sheets. Bake in a 375° oven 10 minutes, or until edges are lightly browned. Makes 5 dozen.

## ORANGE BALLS

4 c. vanilla wafer crumbs
1 c. confectioners' sugar
1 c. finely chopped nuts
¼ c. melted margarine
1 6-oz. can frozen orange juice, thawed
Confectioners' sugar

Combine crumbs, sugar and nuts. Add margarine and mix well. Stir in orange juice. Mix well. Form 1-inch balls; roll in confectioners' sugar; refrigerate. Makes 4 dozen.

## CLOUD PUFFS

5 egg whites
1 c. sugar
1 c. semisweet chocolate chips

Beat egg whites to soft peaks. Gradually add ¼ cup of the sugar; beat 3 minutes. Sprinkle remaining sugar over and fold in as gently as possible with a rubber spatula. Carefully fold in chocolate. Drop batter by spoonfuls onto a greased cookie sheet lined with waxed paper. Bake in a 275° oven 50 to 60 minutes. Puffs should be very dry and crisp. Makes 24 large puffs.

## EGGNOG BARS

½ c. margarine, softened
1 c. sugar
1 t. rum flavoring
2¼ c. flour
1 t. baking soda
¼ t. nutmeg
¼ t. salt
1 c. eggnog
1 c. chopped maraschino cherries
½ c. chopped toasted almonds

Cream margarine and sugar until fluffy. Blend in rum flavoring. Combine flour, soda, nutmeg and salt. Add alternately with eggnog. Stir in cherries and nuts. Spread in a greased 15 x 10-inch jelly-roll pan. Bake in a 350° oven 18 to 20 minutes. Drizzle Icing over warm cake. Cool and cut into 48 bars.

### ICING

¾ c. sifted confectioners' sugar
½ t. rum flavoring
3 to 4 t. milk
Green food coloring

Mix all ingredients until smooth.

*Pictured opposite:*
*Cherry Cobbler Bars*
*Eggnog Bars*

34

## DREAMY CHOCOLATE BROWNIES

1¼ c. flour
½ t. salt
1 c. shortening
4 1-oz. squares unsweetened chocolate
2 c. sugar
4 eggs, well beaten
1 t. vanilla
1 c. chopped nuts

Sift together flour and salt. Set aside. In top of double boiler, melt shortening and chocolate. Add sugar, mixing well. Stir in eggs and vanilla. Gradually add flour and salt, stirring well. Remove from heat and add nuts. Spread batter in a well-greased 8 x 12-inch baking dish. Bake in a 400° oven for 18 minutes. Cool and frost with Chocolate Icing. Makes 32 servings.

### CHOCOLATE ICING

2 1-oz. squares unsweetened chocolate
3 T. hot water
1 T. butter
2 c. sifted confectioners' sugar
½ t. vanilla
1 egg, beaten

Combine chocolate and hot water in top of double boiler. Heat, stirring, until chocolate is melted. Blend in butter; cool slightly and stir in confectioners' sugar and vanilla. Beat in egg. Spread on cooled cake.

## PRETZELS A LA BROWNIE

⅔ c. shortening
4 1-oz. squares unsweetened chocolate
2 c. sugar
4 eggs
1 c. pretzel crumbs
1 c. sifted flour
1 t. baking powder
½ t. salt (use only with unsalted pretzels)
2 c. coarsely chopped pecans

In a large saucepan, melt shortening and chocolate. Add sugar and eggs; beat until smooth. Add pretzel crumbs, flour, baking powder and salt, if needed, and nuts. Pour into a greased and floured 9 x 13-inch pan. Bake in a 350° oven 30 to 35 minutes until center is firm to the touch. Cool in pan and cut into squares. Makes 30 squares.

## LEMON BROWNIES

½ c. butter, softened
1⅓ c. flour
¼ c. sugar
2 eggs
¾ c. sugar
2 T. flour
¼ t. baking powder
3 T. lemon juice
Confectioners' sugar

Combine first 3 ingredients. Mix on low speed of mixer about 1 minute. Press into an ungreased 8-inch square pan. Bake in a 350° oven 15 to 20 minutes; edges will be slightly brown. Combine remaining ingredients except confectioners' sugar. Blend well. Pour over partially baked crust and return to oven for an additional 18 to 20 minutes or until filling is set. Sprinkle with confectioners' sugar. Cool and cut into squares. Makes 20 servings.

## MALT COOKIE BARS

1 1-oz. square unsweetened chocolate
½ c. shortening
¾ c. sugar
½ t. vanilla
2 eggs
1 c. sifted flour
½ c. chocolate malted milk powder
½ t. baking powder
¼ t. salt
½ c. chopped walnuts

Melt chocolate; cool. Cream shortening, sugar and vanilla until fluffy. Beat in eggs. Blend in melted chocolate and set aside. Sift together flour, malt powder, baking powder and salt. Stir into creamed mixture; fold in nuts. Spread in greased and floured 8-inch square pan. Bake in a 350° oven 20 to 25 minutes. Frost with Malt Frosting. Makes 32 bars.

### MALT FROSTING

2 T. butter, softened
¼ c. chocolate malted milk powder
Dash salt
1 c. sifted confectioners' sugar
Light cream

Cream butter, malt powder and salt. Slowly beat in sugar. Add cream until of spreading consistency.

## FUDGE SCOTCH SQUARES

1 6-oz. pkg. semisweet chocolate chips
1 6-oz. pkg. butterscotch chips
½ c. peanut butter
1 box coconut pecan or coconut almond frosting mix
1 can sweetened condensed milk

In a large saucepan, combine chips and peanut butter. Melt over low heat, stirring constantly, until smooth. Remove from heat and add remaining ingredients, stirring well. Spread into an ungreased 9-inch square pan. Chill 2 hours. Cut into 1-inch pieces. Makes 6 dozen. Store in refrigerator.

## CHOCOLATE NUT LOGS

1 1-lb. box confectioners' sugar
1 3½-oz. can flaked coconut
1 c. chopped peanuts
1 t. vanilla
1½ c. graham cracker crumbs
½ c. crunchy peanut butter
1 c. peanut oil
4 T. shortening
3 8-oz. pkgs. chocolate chips

Combine all ingredients except shortening and chocolate chips. Mix well, kneading until smooth. Pinch off 1½-inch pieces and roll into a log shape. Melt chips and shortening in the top of a double boiler. Place logs, one at a time, into the chocolate. Turn to cover completely with chocolate. Lift out with a fork. Place on waxed paper. Refrigerate to harden chocolate; store in a cool place. Makes 65 logs.

## SWEDISH ROSETTES

1 large egg
1 c. milk
1 c. flour
1 t. vanilla
Melted shortening for deep frying

Mix egg, milk, flour and vanilla until smooth. Heat shortening to 350°. Dip rosette iron into hot shortening, then into batter and again in fat. Fry about 45 to 60 seconds on each side. Remove from oil and drain on paper towels. Cool and sprinkle with confectioners' sugar. Makes 4 to 5 dozen.

## DATE MALT BARS

6 T. melted butter
¾ c. brown sugar
2 eggs, slightly beaten
½ t. vanilla
¾ c. sifted flour
½ c. chocolate malted milk powder
½ t. baking powder
1 c. snipped dates
½ c. chopped walnuts
½ c. flaked coconut

Blend brown sugar and butter. Beat in eggs, one at a time, and vanilla. Stir in flour, malt powder and baking powder. Mix well. Fold in dates, nuts and coconut. Pour into a greased and floured 9-inch square pan. Bake in a 350° oven 25 to 30 minutes. When cool, ice; cut into bars. Makes 16.

### ICING

1 T. butter, softened
1 c. sifted confectioners' sugar
2 T. chocolate malted milk powder
¼ t. vanilla
1 t. milk

Combine all ingredients and beat until smooth.

## CARROT SPICE NIBBLES

1 c. butter
1 c. firmly packed brown sugar
2 eggs
1 t. vanilla
1 c. flour
1 t. baking powder
1 t. cinnamon
½ t. salt
¼ t. nutmeg
¼ t. cloves
2½ c. quick oats, uncooked
2 c. shredded carrots
¾ c. raisins
¾ c. chopped nuts

Cream butter and sugar until light and fluffy. Add eggs and vanilla. Combine flour, baking powder, cinnamon, salt, nutmeg and cloves. Add to sugar mixture, mixing well. Stir in remaining ingredients. Drop by rounded teaspoonfuls onto ungreased cookie sheet. Bake in a 350° oven 12 to 15 minutes. Makes 5 dozen.

# COCONUT COOKIES

⅓ c. shortening
1 c. sugar
1 egg
1 egg yolk
1½ c. flour
1 t. baking powder
½ t. salt
2 T. milk
½ t. vanilla
½ t. lemon juice

Blend shortening, sugar, egg and egg yolk. Sift together flour, baking powder and salt. Add alternately with milk, blending well. Add vanilla and lemon juice. Spread ¼ inch thick on a greased cookie sheet. Cover with Coconut Meringue. Bake in a 325° oven 30 minutes. Cut in squares. Makes 4 dozen cookies.

### COCONUT MERINGUE

2 egg whites
1 c. light brown sugar
½ t. vanilla
⅔ c. shredded coconut

Beat egg whites stiff. Beat in sugar, ½ cup at a time. Add vanilla and fold in coconut.

## MARSHMALLOW NUT GOODIES

1 12-oz. pkg. chocolate chips
1 12-oz. pkg. butterscotch chips
1 c. peanut butter
1 10½-oz. pkg. miniature marshmallows
3 c. Spanish peanuts

Melt chips and peanut butter over low heat, stirring to blend. Set aside to cool. Add marshmallows and peanuts, mixing well. Pour into a 12 x 9-inch pan or cookie sheet. Cool and cut into squares. Makes 24.

## CHOCOLATE CREAM DROPS

½ c. heavy cream
2 c. confectioners' sugar
8 oz. sweet cooking chocolate, melted

Mix sugar with cream. Bring to a boil. Boil 5 minutes, stirring constantly. Set pan in a dish of ice water. Stir to a soft dough that can be handled. Roll into balls and place on waxed paper. When firm, dip balls, one at a time and quickly, into the chocolate. Return to waxed paper. Chill until served. Makes 3 dozen.

## SOUR CREAM DROPS

3¼ c. sifted flour
1 t. salt
½ t. baking powder
½ t. baking soda
1 c. butter
1½ c. sugar
2 eggs
1 t. vanilla
½ t. almond extract
1 c. sour cream

Sift together flour, salt, baking powder and soda. Set aside. Cream butter with sugar until fluffy. Beat in eggs, vanilla and almond extract. Add dry ingredients alternately with sour cream, blending well. Chill about 2 hours. Drop by level tablespoonfuls onto greased cookie sheets. Bake in a 375° oven 10 to 12 minutes. Cool and frost. Makes 6 dozen.

### ALMOND FROSTING

¼ c. butter
2½ c. sifted confectioners' sugar
1 t. vanilla
½ t. almond extract
2 T. light cream
Toasted almonds

Cream butter and sugar until light and fluffy. Add remaining ingredients except almonds. Cream until smooth. Spread on cookies, topping each with a nut.

## CRISPY FLAKY COOKIES

1¼ c. flour
½ t. baking soda
¼ t. salt
½ c. butter, softened
1 c. sugar
1 egg
1 t. vanilla
2 c. crisp rice cereal
1 6-oz. pkg. semisweet chocolate chips

Sift together flour, salt and baking soda. Set aside. Cream butter with sugar until fluffy. Add egg and vanilla, beating well. Stir in dry ingredients, cereal and chocolate. Drop by spoonfuls onto greased cookie sheets. Bake in a 350° oven 12 minutes. Cool on wire racks. Makes 3½ dozen.

*Pictured opposite:*
*Coconut Cookies*

## PINEAPPLE COOKIES

½ c. shortening
½ c. brown sugar
½ c. sugar
1 t. vanilla
½ c. crushed pineapple, drained
1¾ c. flour
1 t. baking powder
½ t. salt

Cream shortening, sugars and vanilla. Add pineapple. Sift dry ingredients and add. Form into small balls and press onto a greased baking sheet. Bake in a 350° oven 8 to 10 minutes.

---

Cookies can be decorated with a bit of flavored gelatin before baking.

---

## GRAHAM COOKIES

1 1-lb. box graham crackers
1 c. margarine
1 c. sugar
1 egg
½ c. milk
1 c. graham crackers, crushed
1 c. chopped nuts
1 c. coconut

Cover a 10 x 15-inch cookie sheet with whole graham crackers. In a saucepan, combine margarine, sugar, egg and milk. Bring to a full boil, stirring occasionally. Remove from heat and add cracker crumbs, chopped nuts and coconut. Mix well and pour over graham crackers. Frost with Icing and cut in bars. Makes about 45 bars.

### ICING

2 c. confectioners' sugar
½ c. margarine
1 t. vanilla

Cream sugar and margarine until light and fluffy. Add vanilla. If necessary, add milk, 1 teaspoon at a time, until of spreading consistency.

## PUDDING DROPS

1 3-oz. pkg. chocolate pudding
1 c. sugar
½ c. evaporated milk
1 T. butter
1 c. unsalted peanuts

Combine all ingredients except peanuts in a saucepan. Bring to a rolling boil. Lower heat and boil for 3 minutes, stirring constantly. Remove from heat and add peanuts. Beat candy with a wooden spoon until it starts to thicken. Drop by tablespoons onto waxed paper. Makes 34.

## DAD'S FAVORITE SUGAR COOKIES

¾ c. shortening
1 c. sugar
2 eggs
1 t. vanilla or lemon extract
2½ c. flour
1 t. baking powder
1 t. salt

Mix together shortening, sugar, eggs and flavoring. Stir in flour, baking powder and salt. Chill 1 hour. Roll dough ⅛ inch thick on a floured board. Cut out, using a 3-inch cookie cutter. Place on an ungreased cookie sheet and bake in a 400° oven 6 to 8 minutes. Makes about 3 dozen.

## CHEESY EASY SQUARES

1 pkg. lemon cake mix
½ c. melted butter
1 egg, slightly beaten
1 pkg. lemon frosting mix
1 8-oz. pkg. cream cheese, softened
2 eggs

Combine cake mix, butter and 1 egg. Mix with a fork until moist. Pat into the bottom of a 9 x 13-inch pan, greased only on the bottom. Blend frosting mix into cream cheese. Set aside ½ cup of this mixture, and add 2 eggs to the remaining cheese batter. Beat 3 to 5 minutes. Spread over cake mixture in the pan. Bake in a 350° oven 30 to 40 minutes. When cool, spread with reserved frosting. Cut into squares. Serves 24.

# CREPES

## BASIC CREPES

1½ c. flour
1 T. sugar
½ t. baking powder
½ t. salt
2 c. milk
2 eggs
½ t. vanilla
2 T. melted butter

Measure flour, sugar, baking powder and salt into a bowl. Stir in remaining ingredients; beat until smooth. Lightly butter a 6-inch skillet. Heat until butter is bubbly. Pour a scant ¼ cup batter into the pan. Quickly rotate the pan until the batter is evenly distributed on the bottom of the pan. Cook over medium-high heat 30 seconds, until the underside is slightly browned. Turn over and brown the other side, about 15 seconds. While warm, spread with applesauce, jelly, jam or sweetened strawberries. Roll up and sprinkle with confectioners' sugar. Makes 16.

## THREE-EGG CREPE

3 eggs, slightly beaten
6 T. flour
¼ t. salt
1 c. milk
Butter

Beat eggs, flour, salt and milk until smooth. Cover and chill 1 hour. Stir well before using. For each crepe, heat about ½ teaspoon butter in a 7-inch crepe pan over medium-high heat. Pour in a scant ¼ cup batter. Quickly tilt pan to distribute batter evenly over bottom of pan. When light brown on the bottom, turn and lightly brown other side. Makes 12 crepes.

## CHEESE CREPES

1 8-oz. pkg. cream cheese, softened
1 T. butter, softened
⅓ c. sugar
½ t. vanilla
⅛ t. salt
1 t. grated lemon peel
¼ c. plumped golden raisins
12 Three-Egg Crepes
¾ c. heavy cream
Confectioners' sugar

Cream butter, cheese, sugar, vanilla and salt until fluffy. Fold in lemon peel and plumped raisins. Divide evenly among crepes; spread. Fold crepes on 2 sides and roll up. Place side by side in a greased 9 x 13-inch dish. Pour cream over. Bake in a 350° oven 10 to 15 minutes. Serve with warm cream and sprinkle with confectioners' sugar. Makes 12 crepes.

*Note:* To plump raisins, cover with hot water. Let stand 5 minutes and squeeze dry.

## CREPES SUZETTE

⅔ c. butter
¾ t. grated orange rind
⅔ c. orange juice
¼ c. sugar
⅓ c. brandy
⅓ c. orange liqueur
12 Basic Crepes

In a 10-inch skillet, heat butter, orange rind, juice and sugar to boiling, stirring occasionally. Boil and stir 1 minute. Reduce heat and simmer. In a small saucepan, heat brandy and orange liqueur. Do not boil. Fold crepes into quarters. Place in hot orange sauce, turning once. Arrange crepes around edge of skillet. Pour warm brandy mixture in center of skillet. Ignite with match. Spoon flaming sauce over crepes. Place 2 crepes on each plate. Spoon sauce over crepes. Enough for 12 crepes.

# SWEET CHERRY BLINTZES

2 17-oz. cans sweet cherries
2 T. flour
1 T. sugar
1 t. grated lemon peel
¼ t. cinnamon
18 Blintzes
4 T. butter
  Sour cream
  Cherry Sauce

Drain cherries, reserving 1 cup syrup for sauce. Carefully mix cherries with flour, sugar, lemon peel and cinnamon. Prepare blintzes. Place 1 heaping tablespoon cherry mixture on browned side of each blintze. Roll up, tucking in sides. Melt 2 tablespoons of the butter in a shallow 12 x 8-inch dish. Place blintzes side by side. Dot with the remaining 2 tablespoons butter. Bake in a 400° oven 10 minutes. Serve with sour cream and Cherry Sauce. Makes 18.

## BLINTZES

2 eggs
1 c. milk
½ t. salt
¾ c. flour
2 T. vegetable oil
  Butter

Beat eggs and milk. Add salt and flour; beat until smooth. Stir in oil. Chill 30 minutes. Lightly butter a 6-inch skillet. Pour in about 1 tablespoon batter, rotating skillet to coat bottom. Cook until pancake is lightly browned. Turn out, browned side up.

### CHERRY SAUCE

1 T. lemon juice
1 c. reserved cherry syrup
1 T. cornstarch
1 t. water

Add lemon juice to cherry syrup. Dissolve cornstarch in small amount of water. Add to cherry syrup. Cook over medium heat until thick. Makes 1 cup sauce.

## TROPICAL DELIGHT CREPES

3 eggs, beaten
⅔ c. flour
½ t. salt
1 c. milk

Combine all ingredients and beat until smooth. Let stand 30 minutes. For each crepe, pour ¼ cup batter into a lightly greased and hot 8-inch skillet. Rotate skillet to spread batter evenly. Cook until underside is lightly browned. Remove from skillet. Makes 8 crepes.

### TROPICAL FILLING

1 7-oz. jar marshmallow creme
2 T. orange juice
¼ t. grated orange rind
1 c. heavy cream, whipped
2 bananas, sliced
2 8½-oz. cans crushed pineapple, drained
  Toasted pecans

Combine marshmallow creme, orange juice and rind. Mix well. Fold in whipped cream. Spread ¼ cup of this on each crepe. Top with a few slices of bananas, and 2 tablespoons crushed pineapple. Roll up crepe. Serve with remaining marshmallow mixture. Top with pecans.

## CHOCOLATE AND APRICOT CREPES

1 1-oz. square unsweetened chocolate
2 eggs
¼ c. sugar
1 t. salt
¼ t. cinnamon
1 c. water
½ c. light cream
¾ c. flour
  Apricot jam
  Confectioners' sugar
1 c. heavy cream, whipped

Melt chocolate. Beat eggs until thick and light. Gradually add sugar and salt, beating well. Blend in melted chocolate and cinnamon. Combine water with cream and alternately add to chocolate mixture with flour. Pour 2 tablespoons at a time into a hot, well-buttered 8-inch skillet; cook, turning once, until lightly browned. Set crepes aside. Repeat until batter is used up. Spread each warm crepe with 1 tablespoon apricot jam. Roll up and sprinkle with confectioners' sugar. Top with whipped cream. Makes 12 to 14 crepes.

*Pictured opposite:*
*Tropical Delight Crepes*

# HUNGARIAN CHOCOLATE CREAM CREPES

2 eggs
½ c. milk
½ t. vanilla
½ c. flour
1 T. sugar
⅛ t. salt
2 T. melted butter
Vegetable oil

In blender, blend eggs, milk and vanilla. Combine flour, sugar and salt; add to egg mixture. Beat until smooth. Blend in butter. Chill about 1 hour. Heat a 7 to 8-inch omelet or crepe pan over medium heat. Brush lightly with oil. Pour 2 tablespoons batter into pan, tilting pan to spread batter evenly. Cook until brown, about 1 minute. Loosen and turn; cook until lightly brown. Makes about 10 crepes. Place 3 tablespoons Cocoa Filling on each crepe and roll up as for a jelly roll. Top with Apricot Sauce. Refrigerate until served.

## Cocoa Filling

⅓ c. cocoa
¼ t. salt
1 14-oz. can condensed milk
¼ c. hot water
2 T. butter
½ t. vanilla
1 c. heavy cream, whipped

Combine cocoa and salt in top of double boiler. Gradually stir in condensed milk. Place over boiling water. Stir constantly, until thick. Slowly stir in hot water. Cook 5 minutes, stirring frequently until thick. Remove from heat. Add butter and vanilla. Cool to room temperature. Fold whipped cream into chocolate mixture. Chill.

## Apricot Sauce

1 17-oz. can apricot halves, drained (Reserve ½ cup syrup)
¼ c. sugar
4 t. cornstarch
¼ c. water
½ t. lemon juice
1 T. orange-flavored liqueur

Slice apricots and set aside. In a 2-quart saucepan, mix sugar and cornstarch. Gradually stir in reserved syrup and water. Cook, stirring constantly over low heat, until mixture thickens and boils. Add apricots and lemon juice. Heat until fruit is warmed through. Remove from heat and stir in orange liqueur. Serve warm. Makes 1½ cups.

## HOT APPLE CREPE A LA MODE

8 crepes
1 20-oz. can apple pie filling with spice flavorings
¼ c. raisins
4 scoops ice cream
Chopped pecans

Combine pie filling and raisins. Mix well. Fill each crepe with 3 tablespoons of the mixture. Place in a 9 x 13-inch dish. Bake in a preheated 350° oven for 10 minutes. For each serving, top 2 crepes with a scoop of ice cream. Sprinkle with chopped nuts. Makes 4 servings.

## CHOCO-CHERRY CREPES

8 crepes
1 4½-oz. pkg. chocolate instant pudding mix
1¾ c. milk
¼ c. cherry liqueur
⅓ c. chopped maraschino cherries
1 c. heavy cream, whipped
Whipped cream
Cherries

Combine pudding mix, milk and cherry liqueur. Whip until thickened. Stir in cherries; fold in whipped cream. Fill each crepe with about ½ cup of the mixture. Garnish with additional whipped cream and cherries, if desired. Serves 8.

# ORANGE CREPES

⅔ c. flour
2 T. sugar
2 t. finely shredded orange peel
2 eggs
2 egg yolks
1½ c. milk
2 T. melted butter

Mix together flour, sugar and orange peel. Set aside. Combine eggs, egg yolks, milk and melted butter. Stir into dry ingredients, beating smooth. Lightly grease a 6-inch skillet. Heat skillet moderately hot. Remove from heat and spoon in 2 tablespoons batter. Rotate pan, spreading batter evenly over the bottom. Return to heat and brown one side only. Fill crepes with Orange Filling.

## ORANGE FILLING

2 c. vanilla pudding
1 t. finely shredded orange peel
1 T. orange juice
2 egg whites
¼ c. sugar
2 T. orange juice
2 T. brandy

Combine orange peel and orange juice. Beat egg whites to soft peaks. Gradually add sugar, beating to form stiff peaks. Fold into 1 cup of the pudding. Spread 2 tablespoons Filling on each crepe and fold crepe in quarters. Place in ungreased 7 x 12-inch dish. Bake in a 400° oven 10 to 12 minutes. In a saucepan, stir remaining pudding, orange juice and brandy. Heat and pour over warm crepes. Serves 8 to 10.

# AMBROSIA CREPES

4 crepes
1 16-oz. can fruit cocktail
1 c. frozen dessert topping, thawed
1 small ripe banana, sliced
½ c. miniature marshmallows
⅓ c. shredded coconut

Drain fruit, reserving 3 tablespoons of the juice. Reserve ½ cup fruit cocktail for garnish. Combine remaining fruit, dessert topping, banana, marshmallows, coconut and reserved juice. Mix lightly. Fill each crepe with ½ cup of the fruit mixture. Garnish with additional topping and reserved fruit. Sprinkle with additional coconut if desired. Makes 4 servings.

# CHOCOLATE CREPES

3 eggs
1 c. flour
2 T. sugar
2 T. cocoa
1¼ c. buttermilk
2 T. melted butter

Beat eggs in a medium-size bowl. Combine flour, sugar and cocoa; add alternately with buttermilk. Beat until smooth. Beat in butter; refrigerate 1 hour. Drop 2 tablespoons batter on a lightly greased 6-inch skillet that is moderately hot. Rotate pan, spreading batter evenly over the bottom. Brown one side only. Fill with Almond Cream Filling. Makes 20.

## ALMOND CREAM FILLING

1 c. sugar
¼ c. flour
1 c. milk
2 eggs
2 egg yolks
3 T. butter
2 t. vanilla
½ t. almond extract
½ c. ground, toasted blanched almonds
Melted butter
Grated unsweetened chocolate
Confectioners' sugar
Heavy cream, whipped

Mix sugar, flour and milk in saucepan. Cook and stir until thick, then cook and stir 1 to 2 minutes longer. Beat eggs and egg yolks slightly. Stir some of the hot mixture into the eggs, then return to hot mixture. Bring just to a boil, stirring constantly, and remove from heat. Stir in butter, vanilla, almond extract and almonds. Cool to room temperature or refrigerate if not using immediately. Fill crepes; roll up. Place, folded side down, in a buttered 9 x 12-inch dish. Brush crepes with melted butter. Heat in a 350° oven 20 to 25 minutes. Sprinkle with grated unsweetened chocolate. Sift confectioners' sugar over and top with whipped cream. Makes 20.

To freeze crepes, stack with waxed paper between. Wrap in heavy foil or freezer paper, sealing tightly. Will keep 3 months frozen. Thaw at room temperature. Heat in a 350° oven 10 to 15 minutes.

# PASTRIES

## COCOA CREAM PUFFS

1 T. cocoa
1 c. water
1 T. sugar
⅛ t. salt
7 T. butter
1 c. sifted flour
4 eggs
Whipped cream
Shaved chocolate

In a saucepan, combine cocoa, sugar, water, salt and butter. Bring to a gentle boil, melting butter. Add flour, all at once. Stir quickly with a wooden spoon until batter leaves the sides of the pan. Remove from heat and cool slightly. Add eggs, one at a time, beating after each addition. Dough will be smooth and glossy. If it is too soft, refrigerate 30 minutes. Butter cookie sheet and drop dough in 12 mounds. Bake in a 450° oven 10 minutes. Turn heat to 425° and bake 10 minutes, then turn heat to 400° for 10 minutes. Remove from oven and cool 5 minutes. Turn off oven. Cut tops of puffs with a serrated knife and remove them. Return to oven 15 minutes, leaving door ajar. Remove and cool thoroughly. Fill with Cocoa Cream Puff Filling. Garnish with whipped cream and shaved chocolate. Makes 12 puffs.

### COCOA CREAM PUFF FILLING

1 c. semisweet chocolate chips
1 c. butterscotch chips
¼ c. milk
¼ c. sugar
⅛ t. salt
4 eggs, separated
1 t. vanilla

Combine chips, milk, sugar and salt in the top of a double boiler. Cook over hot water until mixture is smooth. Cool slightly. Add egg yolks, one at a time, beating well after each addition. Stir in vanilla. Beat egg whites stiff. Fold into chocolate mixture.

*Pictured opposite:*
*Elephant Ears, p. 48*

## CANNOLI

3 c. sifted flour
¼ c. sugar
1 t. cinnamon
1 t. cocoa
¼ t. salt
3 T. shortening
2 eggs
4 T. red Italian wine
1 egg white, beaten
Fat for deep frying
Confectioners' sugar
Pistachio nuts, finely chopped

Sift together dry ingredients. Cut in shortening, mixing well. Add eggs and wine. Knead by hand. Roll out to ⅛ inch thick. Cut in a circle. Wrap around metal cannoli forms; seal ends by brushing with beaten egg white. Heat fat to 350° and fry until slightly crisp (about 1 to 2 minutes). Cool on a paper towel. When cool, fill with Filling, sprinkle tops with confectioners' sugar and dip ends in finely chopped pistachio nuts. Makes about 3 dozen.

### FILLING

3 lbs. ricotta
2¼ c. confectioners' sugar
1 t. vanilla

Beat ricotta smooth; add sugar and vanilla.

## ALMOND KRANZ

3 c. flour
1 c. butter
1 t. salt
2 T. sugar
1 cake yeast
1¼ c. lukewarm milk
1 T. sugar
3 egg yolks
3 egg whites
1 c. sugar
1 c. chopped nuts
1 t. vanilla

Mix together 2 tablespoons sugar, flour, butter and salt. Set aside. Crumble yeast into a 1-cup measure; add ¼ cup lukewarm milk and 1 tablespoon sugar. Let rise to a cup. Beat egg yolks and remaining 1 cup milk. Add egg yolk mixture with yeast to flour mixture, beating well. Refrigerate overnight. Next day, on a floured board, roll dough out to about ¼ inch thick. Beat egg whites until stiff. Gradually add 1 cup sugar, beating to soft peaks. Fold in chopped nuts and vanilla. Roll up as for a jelly roll. Place in a greased 10-inch tube pan and pinch edges together. Spread egg white mixture over top and let rise until doubled in bulk. Bake in a 350° oven 60 minutes. Makes 16 servings.

## YULETIDE BUNS

1 pkg. hot roll mix
¾ c. warm water
1 egg
¼ c. sugar
½ c. brown sugar
3 T. melted butter
¾ c. chopped nuts
1 c. chocolate chips
½ c. confectioners' sugar
1 T. milk
Red diced cherries

In a large mixing bowl, soften yeast from the mix in warm water. Stir to dissolve. Blend in egg and sugar. Add dry hot roll mix, stirring until blended. Cover and let rise in a warm spot about 1 hour or until doubled in bulk. Combine brown sugar, butter and nuts in a small bowl; blend well. On a well-floured surface, knead dough lightly until no longer sticky. Divide dough in half. Roll each half into a 14 x 7-inch rectangle. Spread one-third of the filling on the dough. Sprinkle with half of the chocolate chips. Starting at longer side, roll up, pressing to seal edge. Cut roll into 1½-inch slices. Arrange rolls, cut side down, on a greased baking sheet. Cover and let rise in a warm spot 1 hour. Bake in a 350° oven 15 to 18 minutes. Combine confectioners' sugar and milk to make a thick glaze. Drizzle glaze over rolls. Garnish with cherries. Makes about 18 rolls.

## TOFFEE SCHNECKEN

2 pkgs. active dry yeast
½ c. lukewarm water
1 c. lukewarm milk
½ c. butter, softened
⅓ c. sugar
2½ t. salt
1 egg, beaten
4¾ to 5¼ c. flour
½ c. butter, softened
⅓ c. sugar
1¼ c. chocolate-toffee candy chunks
½ c. chopped pecans
Corn syrup

Dissolve yeast in warm water. Add milk, butter, sugar, salt, egg and 2 cups of the flour. Beat until smooth. Stir in enough flour to make a stiff dough. Turn onto floured board and knead until smooth and elastic. Cover with plastic wrap and a towel. Let dough rest 20 minutes. Punch down dough. Cut into 2 equal parts. Roll each to a 12 x 9-inch rectangle. Cream butter and sugar. Stir in toffee and pecans. Spread half on each rectangle. Roll up tightly, beginning at wide side. Cut each roll into 12 even slices. Grease muffin tins and place 1 teaspoon corn syrup in each cup. Place slices in cups; cover with plastic wrap. Refrigerate 2 to 24 hours. Remove from refrigerator, uncover and let stand at room temperature while oven is preheating to 350°. Bake 20 to 25 minutes. Turn rolls out of pan to a rack to cool. Serves 24.

## ELEPHANT EARS

1 pkg. dry yeast
¼ c. lukewarm water
2 c. sifted flour
1½ T. sugar
½ t. salt
½ c. butter, softened
1 egg yolk
½ c. milk, scalded and cooled
2 T. butter
1½ c. sugar
3½ t. cinnamon
1 c. chopped pecans
⅓ c. melted butter

Dissolve yeast in lukewarm water and set aside. Mix together flour, 1½ tablespoons sugar and salt. Cut in ½ cup butter. Combine egg yolk, milk and softened yeast. Add to dough, mixing well. Cover and chill at least 2 hours. Turn dough onto lightly floured board. Punch down. Cover with a towel and let rest 10 minutes. Roll to a 10 x 18-inch rectangle. Spread with 2 tablespoons butter. Combine cinnamon and sugar. Sprinkle ½ cup cinnamon-sugar mixture over dough. Roll up as for a jelly roll. Seal edges and cut into 1-inch slices. Dip slices, one at a time, in remaining cinnamon-sugar mixture. Roll out into 18 5-inch rounds. Sprinkle with a few nuts, pressing nuts in gently. Place on ungreased cookie sheets, brush with melted butter and sprinkle each with 1 teaspoon of the cinnamon-sugar mixture. Bake in a 400° oven 12 minutes. Cool on wire racks. Makes 18.

## EVERYONE'S FAVORITE LONG JOHNS

1 c. milk
¼ c. butter
¼ c. sugar
1 t. salt
1 pkg. yeast
½ c. warm water
1 egg, beaten
3½ to 4 c. sifted flour
Fat for deep frying

Scald milk; add butter and stir until melted. Add sugar and salt. Pour into a bowl and cool to lukewarm. Soften yeast in warm water and add to cooled milk mixture. Add egg and mix well. Gradually add flour, beating well after each addition, to form a dough. Knead on a floured surface until smooth and satiny—3 to 5 minutes. Place in a greased bowl and cover. Let rise in a warm place about an hour until doubled in bulk. Punch down dough. Cover and let rise again until light, about 30 to 60 minutes. Roll out dough on a floured board to a 12-inch square. Cut into 4-inch by 1½-inch rectangles. Place on a lightly floured surface and let rise, uncovered, 30 to 60 minutes until doubled in size. Heat fat to 375° and fry 1 to 2 minutes on each side. Dip tops in Maple Icing. Makes about 32.

### MAPLE ICING

2 c. confectioners' sugar
2 T. butter
½ t. vanilla
¼ t. salt
¼ c. maple syrup

Combine all ingredients and mix until smooth. Add syrup until icing is of spreading consistency.

## PUMP MUFFS

1 spice cake mix
1 c. pumpkin
⅔ c. water
2 eggs
1 6-oz. pkg. semisweet chocolate chips
Whipped cream
Pecan halves

Combine cake mix, pumpkin, water and eggs. Beat well. Stir in chocolate chips. Grease and flour 2½-inch muffin tins. Fill two-thirds full with batter. Bake in a 350° oven 15 to 20 minutes. Cool 5 minutes. Remove from pans. When ready to serve, top with whipped cream and a whole pecan half. Makes 24 to 30.

## HOLIDAY PINEAPPLE CLUSTER BUNS

1 8½-oz. can crushed pineapple
1 pkg. active dry yeast
¼ c. warm water
2 large eggs
¼ c. syrup from pineapple
½ c. sugar
¼ c. melted butter
2¼ c. sifted flour
¾ t. salt
¼ t. nutmeg
¼ c. wheat germ

Drain pineapple, reserving syrup. Dissolve yeast in warm water; set aside. Beat eggs. Reserve 1 tablespoon beaten egg for glaze. Stir remaining eggs into the yeast mixture. Add ¼ cup syrup from the pineapple, ¼ cup sugar, melted butter and 1 cup flour. Mix well. Add salt, nutmeg and wheat germ. Gradually blend in remaining 1¼ cups flour, making a stiff dough. Cover bowl and set in a warm place for 1 hour. Place drained pineapple and any remaining syrup into a saucepan, add remaining ¼ cup sugar. Cook, stirring constantly, until thick. Cool. Punch down dough after 1 hour. Roll out on a floured board to a 9 x 12-inch shape. Cut into 3-inch squares. Set aside 1 tablespoon filling for the glaze. Divide remainder among the squares of dough. Fold the corners together to cover the filling. Pinch to seal and round up. Place seam side down in a well-greased 9-inch layer pan. Cover and let rise in a warm place about 45 minutes. Brush with reserved beaten egg. Bake in a 350° oven 30 to 35 minutes. Cool 15 minutes. Spoon Pineapple Glaze over. Serve warm. Makes 12 buns.

### PINEAPPLE GLAZE

1 T. reserved pineapple filling
¾ c. confectioners' sugar
Warm water

Combine filling, sugar and a few drops water. Stir until of spreading consistency. If necessary, add more warm water.

---

To keep muffins from burning around the edges, fill one of the muffin cups with water instead of batter. Bake as directed.

# DIET DESSERTS

## DIET CRANBERRY DELIGHT

1 envelope unflavored gelatin
¼ c. cold water
1 pt. cranberry juice cocktail
1 t. liquid sweetener

Soften gelatin in cold water for 5 minutes. Heat cranberry cocktail. Add gelatin and stir to dissolve. Add sweetener. Pour into 5 individual molds. Chill. Each serving contains 65 calories. Makes 6 servings.

## PUMPKIN SPICE TORTE

2½ c. sifted cake flour
3 t. baking powder
2 t. pumpkin pie spice
½ t. cinnamon
½ t. butter-flavored salt
6 egg yolks
⅔ c. diet margarine
1 c. canned pumpkin
¾ c. brown sugar, firmly packed
Sugar substitute to equal 2/3 cup sugar
6 egg whites
½ t. cream of tartar

Sift together first 5 ingredients. Set aside. Combine yolks, diet margarine, pumpkin, brown sugar, and sugar substitute; beat smooth. Gradually add dry mixture to pumpkin mixture, mixing well. Beat egg whites and cream of tartar until stiff. Gently fold pumpkin mixture into egg whites. Pour into a greased 10-inch non-stick tube pan. Bake in a 325° oven 60 minutes. Invert pan on rack to cool. Serves 16. Each serving contains 160 calories.

## DIET APPLESAUCE CAKE

2 c. raisins
2 c. water
1 c. unsweetened applesauce
2 eggs
¾ c. vegetable oil
2 T. liquid artificial sweetener
2 c. flour
1 t. baking soda
1¼ t. cinnamon
½ t. nutmeg

Cook raisins in water until soft; drain. Add applesauce, eggs, oil and sweetener to raisins. Mix well. Add remaining ingredients. Mix well. Pour into a glass 9 x 13-inch pan greased with diet margarine. Bake in a 325° oven 45 minutes. Serves 16.

## DIET STRAWBERRY PIE

½ c. water
½ c. instant non-fat dry milk powder
4 eggs
¼ t. salt
½ c. sugar
¼ c. flour
1 T. lemon juice
1 t. vanilla
1 1-lb. container small curd cottage cheese
1 qt. whole strawberries
1 9-inch graham cracker crust

Combine first 9 ingredients; blend in blender until smooth. Pour into graham crust. Bake in a 250° oven 60 minutes. Turn off heat and leave pie in oven 60 minutes. Remove and cool. Arrange whole berries on top and brush warm Glaze over. Serves 10. Each serving contains 177 calories.

### GLAZE

1 T. cornstarch
1 c. water
Liquid artificial sweetener
Red food coloring

In a saucepan, combine constarch and water. Cook over low heat, stirring constantly, until thickened and clear. Add liquid sweetener to taste. Stir in a few drops red food coloring. Cool slightly.

*Pictured opposite:*
*Diet Strawberry Pie*

## DIETER'S DELIGHT

1 pt. dry-curd cottage cheese
1 3-oz. pkg. orange gelatin
1 11-oz. can mandarin oranges, drained
1 small can unsweetened crushed
   pineapple, drained
1 4-oz. container frozen whipped
   topping, thawed
   Cherries for garnish

Place cottage cheese in a large bowl. Pour gelatin over and mix gently. Add pineapple and oranges. Mix gently. Fold in whipped topping. For dessert, put a scoop in a dish and top with a cherry. Cover and store in refrigerator. Whip gently before serving. Serves 8 to 10.

## DIET MOLASSES COOKIES

1 egg
½ c. molasses
¼ c. sugar
1 t. lemon extract
1 t. baking soda
½ t. cream of tartar
1 t. liquid artificial sweetener
1 t. ginger
1⅔ to 2 c. flour

Mix all ingredients together. Roll out ⅛ inch thick and cut with 2 or 3-inch cookie cutters. Bake in a 350° oven until lightly browned. Makes about 3 dozen cookies.

*Note:* One teaspoon orange rind can be substituted for ginger.

## DIET SPICE COOKIES

1¼ c. water
⅓ c. shortening
½ t. salt
2½ t. artificial liquid sweetener
½ c. quick rolled oats
2 t. cinnamon
2 c. raisins
½ t. nutmeg
2 eggs
2 c. flour
1 t. baking powder

In a saucepan, combine first 8 ingredients. Boil for 3 minutes. Cool. Add remaining ingredients, mixing well. Drop by teaspoonfuls on a greased cookie sheet. Bake in a 350° oven 15 to 20 minutes. Makes 5 dozen.

## PECAN SURPRISE DESSERT

3 egg whites
¼ c. nonfat dry milk
¼ c. ice water
¾ c. granulated sugar substitute
1 t. baking powder
½ t. baking soda
1 t. vanilla
¾ c. finely chopped pecans
20 snack crackers, crumbled

Whip egg whites, dry milk and ice water until stiff peaks form. Add sugar substitute, baking powder, soda and vanilla. Fold in pecans and cracker crumbs. Spread in a lightly buttered pie pan. Bake in a 350° oven 15 to 20 minutes. Serves 12 at 95 calories each serving.

## DIET SHERBET

1 14-oz. can evaporated milk, well chilled
2 T. liquid artificial sweetener
1 6-oz. can unsweetened frozen orange
   juice concentrate, thawed

Beat evaporated milk, slightly. Gradually add sweetener and orange juice. Blend well. Pour into 3 pint containers. Freeze. One cup equals 140 calories. Yields 3 pints.

## DIET DOTTED COOKIES

¾ c. sugar
½ c. margarine
1 t. coconut flavoring
3 T. skim milk
1½ c. sifted flour
½ t. baking powder
½ t. salt
¾ c. coarsely chopped cranberries, drained
½ c. shredded coconut

Cream sugar, margarine and coconut flavoring until fluffy. Add milk, mixing well. Sift together flour, baking powder and salt. Add to sugar mixture. Fold berries into batter. Divide dough in half. Roll each half into a roll about 1½ inches in diameter. Roll each roll in shredded coconut. Wrap each roll in waxed paper and chill 8 hours. Slice thin. Place on ungreased cookie sheet. Bake in a 375° oven 12 to 15 minutes. Makes 60 cookies. Each serving contains 39 calories.

# CANDY

## ALMOND BARK

2 lbs. chocolate
1 c. sliced almonds

Melt chocolate over boiling water. Line cookie sheet with aluminum foil. Sprinkle nuts in a single layer on foil. Slowly pour chocolate over, spreading gently. Chill. Break into pieces. Makes 2 pounds candy.

## PEANUTTY FUDGE

¼ c. white corn syrup
¼ c. honey
¾ c. chunky peanut butter
½ c. butter, softened
½ t. salt
1 t. vanilla
4 c. sifted confectioners' sugar
¾ c. chopped peanuts

Beat first 6 ingredients together until blended. Add sugar to make a stiff dough. Knead with hands to blend well. Knead in nuts. Press into a well-buttered 8-inch square pan and cool. Cut into squares. Makes 2 pounds.

## FRENCH MINTS

1 c. butter
2 c. confectioners' sugar
4 1-oz. squares unsweetened chocolate, melted
4 eggs
1½ c. crushed vanilla wafer crumbs

Cream butter and sugar, beating until fluffy. Add melted chocolate and beat well. Add eggs, one at a time, beating well after each addition. Put a teaspoon of crumbs into the bottom of paper 2½-inch muffin containers. Fill muffin paper to the top, using about 3 tablespoons of the chocolate mixture. Put remaining crumbs on top of the chocolate mixture. Freeze. Makes 22 to 24 mints.

## PENUCHE

4 c. brown sugar
1 c. milk
2 T. butter
1 c. coarsely chopped pecans

Combine brown sugar, milk and butter. Heat, stirring constantly, until sugar is dissolved. Allow to boil until mixture forms a soft ball (232°) when dropped into cold water. Remove from heat and cool. Add nuts, stirring until mixture is creamy and begins to thicken. Spread into a buttered 12 x 8-inch glass dish. Chill until firm. Cut into squares. Makes 6 dozen.

## MARSHMALLOW PENUCHE

1 c. brown sugar
1 c. sugar
⅔ c. evaporated milk
2 T. butter
1 t. vanilla
½ of a 1-lb. bag miniature marshmallows
1 c. chopped nuts

Butter sides of a 4-quart pot. Combine sugars, milk and butter. Cook, stirring frequently, until mixture comes to a boil. Cook to the soft-ball stage (238° on a candy thermometer). Remove from heat and add nuts, vanilla and marshmallows. Stir until marshmallows melt. Pour into a buttered 9-inch square pan. Cool and cut into 36 pieces.

## SPECKLED CANDY ROLLS

1 8-oz. bar milk chocolate
1 12-oz. pkg. chocolate chips
½ c. butter
1 c. chopped nuts
1 pkg. multicolored miniature marshmallows
1 16-oz. pkg. flaked coconut

Combine chocolate, chocolate chips and butter in top of a double boiler. Stir until chocolate melts. Cool slightly. Stir in nuts and marshmallows. Using 2 pieces of aluminum foil, place half of candy mixture on each piece. Roll candy into 15-inch logs; roll each log in half the coconut. Seal and chill. Candy will keep in the refrigerator indefinitely. To serve, slice into ½-inch slices. Makes 2 rolls.

## WHITE CHOCOLATE CREAM FUDGE

3 c. sugar
1 c. evaporated milk
¾ stick butter
1 pt. jar marshmallow creme
12 oz. white chocolate, cut in small pieces
1 c. chopped pecans
1 4-oz. jar candied cherries (optional)

Bring sugar, milk and butter to a boil over low heat, stirring constantly. Cook to 237°. Remove from heat, add marshmallow creme, white chocolate, nuts and cherries. Stir until marshmallow creme and chocolate are melted. Pour into a 13 x 9-inch buttered pan. Cool before cutting. Makes 6 dozen.

## CRACKER CANDY

2 c. sugar
½ c. milk
¼ lb. soda crackers, finely crushed
1 T. peanut butter
1 t. vanilla

Combine sugar and milk and bring to a boil. Add remaining ingredients and let stand for 5 minutes. Beat and pour into a buttered 8-inch square dish. Cool in refrigerator. Makes 16 squares.

## CARAMEL CORN

Popped corn
½ c. margarine
½ c. brown sugar
½ c. corn syrup
½ t. vanilla
½ t. salt
½ t. baking soda

Butter a 9 x 13-inch baking pan and fill with popped corn. In a saucepan, combine margarine, brown sugar and corn syrup. Bring to a boil and boil 5 minutes. Remove from heat; stir in vanilla, salt and soda. Pour over corn and mix from the bottom. Place in a 250° oven for 50 to 60 minutes. Stir every 15 minutes. Pour onto waxed paper; spread out to cool. Makes 4 quarts.

## NUTTY FUDGE

2 c. chocolate chips
1 14-oz. can sweetened condensed milk
1½ c. chopped nuts
1 t. vanilla

Melt chocolate chips in a double boiler. Add milk. Remove from heat. Stir in nuts and vanilla. Mix well. Pour into a well-buttered 12 x 8-inch glass dish. Let set overnight or until it is dry on top. Cut into squares. Makes 72 pieces.

## HEALTHY CANDY

1¼ c. wheat germ
½ c. creamy peanut butter
2 T. cocoa
2 T. honey
1 t. vanilla
⅛ t. salt

In a large bowl combine 1 cup wheat germ with remaining ingredients, mixing with back of spoon. Sprinkle remaining wheat germ onto waxed paper. Form into about 70 balls, using ½-teaspoonful mix for each ball. Roll balls in wheat germ. Cover and refrigerate. Makes 70.

## SEAFOAM

3 c. sugar
½ c. light corn syrup
⅔ c. water
½ t. salt
2 egg whites
1 t. vanilla
1 c. chopped nuts

Combine sugar, corn syrup and water and boil until thermometer registers to 240° or until mixture spins a thread when dropped from a spoon. Add salt to egg whites and beat until stiff. Slowly pour syrup into beaten egg whites, beating constantly. When mixture thickens, add vanilla and nuts. Drop from a spoon onto waxed paper. Makes 4 dozen.

*Pictured opposite:*
*White Chocolate Cream Fudge*

# DESSERTS

## PARTY ICE-CREAM DESSERT

1½ c. crushed cornflakes
1 c. light brown sugar
½ c. chopped nuts
½ c. flaked coconut
1 c. melted butter
½ gal. Neapolitan ice cream, softened

Mix together all ingredients except ice cream. Pat half of the crumb mixture into a 9-inch square pan. Press ice cream on crust and top with remainder of the crumb mixture. Freeze. Serves 10 to 12.

## PINK CLOUD RICE PUDDING

2 egg yolks, beaten
3 c. milk
3 c. cooked rice
⅓ c. sugar
¼ t. salt
2 T. butter
1 t. vanilla
½ c. chopped maraschino cherries

Beat egg yolks with ½ cup of the milk; refrigerate until needed. Combine rice, remaining milk, sugar, salt and butter. Cook over medium heat until thick and creamy, about 15 minutes. Pour egg yolk mixture over. Cook 2 minutes longer, stirring constantly. Add vanilla. Spoon into serving dishes and chill. Top with Icing and garnish with cherries. Serves 6 to 8.

### ICING

2 egg whites
¾ c. sugar
½ t. cream of tartar
Dash salt
¼ c. maraschino cherry juice
¼ t. almond extract

Beat egg whites until stiff but not dry. In a saucepan, combine sugar, cream of tartar, salt and cherry juice. Bring to a boil. Gradually pour hot syrup over egg whites, beating constantly. Stir in almond extract.

## NUTTY GREEN SALAD DESSERT

1 16-oz. can crushed pineapple
1 3-oz. pkg. instant pistachio pudding
1 c. miniature marshmallows
1 4½ oz. container frozen whipped topping
½ c. chopped pecans
½ c. chopped maraschino cherries

Combine pineapple and pudding; mix until thickened. Add remaining ingredients and chill. Serves 8.

## LEMON FRUIT FREEZE

⅔ c. butter
⅓ c. sugar
3 c. crushed Corn Chex cereal
1 can sweetened condensed milk
½ c. lemon juice
1 can lemon pie filling
1 20-oz. can fruit cocktail, drained
2 c. whipped topping

In a saucepan, melt butter; stir in sugar. Reserve one-third cup crumbs for garnish; stir remainder into butter and sugar. Pat firmly into the bottom of a 9 x 13-inch pan. Bake in a 300° oven 12 minutes; cool. Combine condensed milk and lemon juice. Stir in pie filling and fruit cocktail. Pour over crust. Top with whipped topping and reserved crumbs. Freeze 4 hours. Remove 20 minutes before cutting. Makes 16 servings.

## CRANBERRY CREAM

4 c. fresh cranberries
1 c. cold water
¾ c. sugar
1 3-oz. pkg. pineapple gelatin
¾ c. boiling water
1 c. heavy cream
¼ t. salt
1 c. chopped walnuts

Reserve 12 cranberries; place remaining berries in a saucepan. Stir in sugar and cold water. Bring to a boil over medium heat and cook until berries pop. Force cooked berries through a strainer. Place gelatin in a bowl and add boiling water; stir well. Add cranberry puree and chill in refrigerator until thickened. Whip cream with salt until soft peaks form; fold in nuts. Swirl cream mixture into thickened cranberry mixture, creating a marbled effect. Pour into a 1½-quart mold. Chill. Unmold when firm. Garnish with reserved whole berries. Serves 8 to 10.

## NOEL TORTONI

1 qt. vanilla ice cream
¼ c. chopped toasted pecans
2 T. chopped red maraschino cherries
2 T. chopped green maraschino cherries
1 t. rum extract
1 t. vanilla
½ c. M and M candies
   Jimmies and whole cherries
   Whipped cream

Scoop ice cream into a cold bowl. Stir until smooth but not melted. Stir in pecans, cherries and flavorings. Fold in candies. Spoon into 2½-inch foil baking cups. Freeze. Garnish each with whipped cream, jimmies and a whole cherry. Serves 8.

## ICE CREAM-PUMPKIN SQUARES

2 c. canned pumpkin
1 c. sugar
1 t. salt
1 t. ginger
1 t. cinnamon
½ t. nutmeg
1 c. chopped pecans, toasted
½ gal. vanilla ice cream, softened
36 gingersnaps
   Whipped cream
   Pecan halves

Combine all ingredients except gingersnaps. Mix well. Line the bottom of a 13 x 9-inch pan with half the gingersnaps; top with half of the ice-cream mixture. Repeat for a second layer. Freeze 5 hours. Cut into squares and garnish with pecan halves. Serve with whipped cream. Serves 18.

## CHOCOLATE ANGEL FREEZE

1 6 to 8-oz. angel food cake
1 12-oz. pkg. semisweet chocolate chips
4 eggs, separated
¼ c. sugar
2 c. heavy cream, whipped

Line an 8-inch square pan with waxed paper. Cut cake into 1-inch cubes. Melt chocolate chips in top of double boiler. Remove from heat and cool to lukewarm. Add beaten egg yolks to chocolate mixture. Mix well and cool. Beat egg whites until soft peaks form. Gradually add sugar and beat to stiff peaks. Fold into chocolate with whipped cream. Layer chocolate mixture and cake cubes, beginning and ending with chocolate mixture. Cover and freeze. To serve, garnish with pecans and cut into squares with a serrated knife. Serves 12.

## CHOCO-FREEZE

1¼ c. vanilla wafer crumbs
4 T. melted butter
1 qt. peppermint ice cream, softened
2 1-oz. squares unsweetened chocolate
1 t. butter
3 egg yolks, beaten
1½ c. sifted confectioners' sugar
½ c. chopped pecans
1 t. vanilla
3 egg whites

Mix wafer crumbs with melted butter. Reserve ¼ cup crumb mixture. Press remaining mixture into a 9-inch square pan. Spread with ice cream and freeze. Combine butter and chocolate and cook over low heat until melted. Gradually stir in egg yolks, sugar, nuts and vanilla. Cool. Beat egg whites until stiff. Beat chocolate mixture until smooth; fold in egg whites. Spread over ice cream. Top with reserved crumbs. Freeze. Serves 8.

## A LA FRUITCAKE PUDDING

1 3-oz. pkg. instant lemon pudding mix
2 c. milk
4 slices fruitcake
   Whipped cream

Prepare pudding mix as directed on package, using 2 cups milk. Break fruitcake into small pieces; fold into pudding. Serve in sherbet dishes. Garnish each with dollop of whipped cream. Serves 6 to 8.

## PEANUT BUTTER TORTONI

⅓ c. creamy peanut butter
¼ c. sugar
1 t. instant coffee
1 t. vanilla
1 egg white
1 T. sugar
½ c. macaroon crumbs
⅓ c. chopped peanuts
1 c. heavy cream, whipped

Blend together peanut butter, ¼ cup sugar, coffee and vanilla. Beat egg white to soft peaks. Gradually beat in 1 tablespoon sugar until stiff peaks form. Fold into peanut butter mixture. Combine cookie crumbs and peanuts. Fold half of the crumb mixture into peanut butter mixture, then fold in whipped cream. Spoon into 6 small serving dishes. Garnish with remaining peanut and crumb mixture. Makes 8 servings.

# FRUITY SHERBET

5 ripe bananas
Grated peel of 2 oranges
1 c. orange juice
½ c. lemon juice
2 c. sugar
3 c. cranberry-apple juice
3 egg whites

Mash bananas. Stir in remaining ingredients except egg whites. Pour into a 15½ x 10½-inch pan and freeze until mushy. Mix fruit mixture in mixer at low speed. Beat egg whites stiff. Gently fold into fruit mixture. Return to pan and freeze until mushy. Pour into a bowl and beat; return to pan, cover with foil and freeze. Set out 15 minutes before serving. Spoon into sherbet dishes. Serves 14.

## CHOCOLATE ALMOND VELVET

⅔ c. chocolate syrup
⅔ c. sweetened condensed milk
2 c. heavy cream
½ t. vanilla
⅓ c. chopped and toasted almonds
Almonds for garnish

Combine syrup, milk, cream and vanilla. Chill well. Whip to soft peaks. Fold in nuts. Pour into a freezer ice-cube tray and freeze. Spoon into sherbet dishes. Garnish with almonds. Serves 8 to 10.

## CHERRY CHEESECAKE PARFAIT

1 3-oz. pkg. instant vanilla pudding
2 c. sour cream
1 8-oz. pkg. cream cheese, softened
¼ c. sugar
2 t. almond flavoring
1 t. vanilla
1 can cherry pie filling
1 3½-oz. can flaked coconut

Combine pudding mix, sour cream and cream cheese; whip until smooth. Slowly stir in sugar and flavorings. Spoon into 8 parfait glasses, filling each half full. Add 1 tablespoon pie filling to each glass. Spoon remaining pudding over and top with another spoonful of pie filling. Garnish with coconut. Serves 8.

## TROPICAL SLUSH PARFAIT

Pour tropical-flavored fruit punch into freezer trays. Freeze until mushy, stirring once. Pile in parfait glasses. Serves 8 to 10.

*Pictured opposite:*
*Cherry Cheesecake Parfait*
*Tropical Slush Parfait*
*Frozen Fruitcake Salad, p. 60*

# PEACHY CREAM PARFAIT

1 16-oz. can sliced peaches
1 3-oz. pkg. peach gelatin
2 c. vanilla ice cream

Drain peaches, reserving syrup. Add enough water to syrup to make 1 cup liquid and bring to a boil. Set aside 6 peach slices for garnish. Dice remaining peaches. Dissolve peach gelatin in liquid. Add vanilla ice cream; stir until melted. Add diced peaches and pour into 6 parfait glasses. Chill about 30 minutes. Garnish with reserved peaches. Makes about 3½ cups.

## LAYERED PEPPERMINT CHILL

12 marshmallows
½ c. chopped nuts
½ c. crushed peppermint canes
2 c. heavy cream, whipped
1 c. graham cracker crumbs

Cut each marshmallow into 6 or 8 pieces. Fold nuts, crushed canes and marshmallows into the whipped cream. Butter an 8-inch square pan. Line bottom and sides with half of the graham cracker crumbs. Spoon cream mixture into pan; sprinkle remaining crumbs on top. Chill 24 hours. Serves 9.

## RASPBERRY PARFAIT

2 pkgs. frozen raspberries
2 3-oz. pkgs. vanilla pudding
⅛ t. salt
2 c. water
2 T. butter
1 c. heavy cream, whipped

Force raspberries through sieve to remove seeds. Reserve juice. Combine pudding mix and salt in a large saucepan. Add water and raspberry juice; mix well. Cook and stir over medium heat until mixture comes to a full boil. Remove from heat and stir in butter. Chill. Serve in parfait glasses. Garnish with whipped cream. Serves 8.

## PEACH MOUSSE

1 c. mashed peaches, drained
½ c. sugar
½ pt. heavy cream, whipped
2 egg whites, beaten stiff
¼ t. almond flavoring

Add peaches and sugar to whipped cream. Fold in egg whites and flavoring. Freeze. To serve, spoon into sherbet glasses. Serves 6 to 8.

## PINEAPPLE FLUFF

1 8½-oz. can crushed pineapple, drained
1 10-oz. bag miniature marshmallows
1 T. confectioners' sugar
1 t. vanilla
½ pt. heavy cream, whipped
2 medium-size bananas

Pour pineapple over marshmallows. Place bowl in a larger bowl filled with ice. Set aside for 3 hours. Add sugar and vanilla to whipped cream. Before serving, slice bananas and fold into whipped cream. Serve in sherbet dishes. Serves 6 to 8.

## FLUFFY MARSHMALLOW WHIP

1 3-oz. pkg. strawberry gelatin
1 c. boiling water
1 c. cold water
2 c. frozen whipped topping, thawed
1 c. miniature marshmallows
1 8-oz. can crushed pineapple, drained
Fresh strawberries for garnish

Dissolve gelatin in boiling water. Add cold water and chill until slightly thickened. Set bowl of gelatin in a larger bowl of crushed ice. Whip until light and fluffy on medium speed of mixer. Add 1½ cups whipped topping, beating well. Fold in marshmallows and pineapple. Chill until partially set. Mound in serving dish and garnish with the reserved whipped topping and fresh strawberries. Serves 6 to 8.

## BLACK CHERRY WHIP

1 16-oz. can pitted dark sweet cherries
Cool water
1 3-oz. pkg. black cherry gelatin
1 c. boiling water
1 2-oz. pkg. whipped topping mix
Milk
¼ c. mayonnaise
2 medium bananas, peeled and diced
Whipped cream and toasted pecans for garnish

Drain syrup from cherries and reserve. Add enough cool water to make a cup. Dissolve gelatin in boiling water. Stir in cherry juice. Chill 20 minutes. Prepare topping with milk as directed on package; beat in mayonnaise. Add this to thickened gelatin, mixing well. Fold in cherries and bananas. Spoon into a 1½-quart mold. Chill overnight. Unmold and garnish with whipped cream and pecans. Serves 8.

## FROZEN YULE LOG

1 20-oz. can sliced pineapple
1 c. quartered maraschino cherries
⅔ c. slivered almonds, toasted
¼ c. honey
1 c. mayonnaise
2 c. heavy cream, whipped
Almonds
Mint leaves

Drain pineapple, reserving ¼ cup syrup. Combine reserved syrup with cherries, almonds, honey and mayonnaise. Fold in whipped cream. In a 2-pound coffee can, layer pineapple and whipped cream mixture. Cover with plastic wrap and freeze. To unmold, run spatula around the inside of can, cut around bottom of can and push log out. Sprinkle with additional almonds and garnish with mint leaves. Makes 12 to 14 servings.

## WALKING SALADS

¼ c. honey
1 8-oz. pkg. cream cheese
1 c. sliced banana
1 10-oz. pkg. frozen raspberries, partially thawed
2 c. heavy cream, whipped
2 c. miniature marshmallows

Blend honey and cream cheese. Stir in fruit. Fold in whipped cream and marshmallows. Pour into eight 6-ounce paper cups. Insert a wooden stick in the center of each cup. Freeze until firm. Tear away paper cups and eat. Serves 8.

## FROZEN FRUITCAKE SALAD

1 c. sour cream
½ of a 4½-oz. container frozen whipped topping, thawed
½ c. sugar
2 T. lemon juice
1 t. vanilla
1 13-oz. can crushed pineapple, drained
2 bananas, sliced or diced
½ c. sliced red candied cherries
½ c. sliced green candied cherries
½ c. chopped walnuts
Lettuce
Candied cherries

Blend sour cream, whipped topping, sugar, lemon juice and vanilla. Fold in fruit and nuts. Turn into a 4½-cup ring mold. Freeze overnight. Unmold onto a lettuce-lined plate. Garnish with additional candied cherries. Let sit 10 minutes before serving. Makes 8 servings.

## NAPOLEON CAKE SLICES

½ recipe puff pastry
1 recipe Creme Plombieres
   Confectioners' Sugar Icing
⅛ to ¼ c. chocolate syrup

Roll out puff pastry to a 16-inch square about ⅛ inch thick. Trim with a sharp knife and cut into three 5 x 15-inch strips. Place strips on a greased cookie sheet. Prick all over with a fork and freeze 60 minutes. Bake in a 350° oven 35 minutes until golden. Fill layers with Creme Plombieres, and ice top with Confectioners' Sugar Icing. Fill a pastry bag with chocolate syrup. With a #2 writing tube and working quickly, pipe lines, 1 inch apart, across the cake. Pass blade of knife the length of the cake through the chocolate lines, giving a marbled look. Serves 10.

### CREME PLOMBIERES

3 T. flour
⅛ t. salt
⅜ c. sugar
1 c. light cream
4 egg yolks, slightly beaten
1 t. vanilla
1 envelope gelatin
¼ c. cold water
1 c. heavy cream, whipped
1 T. cognac
1 T. Kahlua
1 1-oz. square unsweetened chocolate, melted

Mix flour, salt and sugar in a heavy saucepan. Blend in a little of the light cream and place on medium heat, stirring constantly. Add remaining light cream and stir until thickened. Stir a little into the egg yolks, then pour yolks into flour mixture. Heat until thick, but do not boil. Remove from heat and stir in vanilla. Set aside. To prevent a skin from forming, brush top with melted butter. Stir before using.

Add gelatin to cold water. Heat in the top of a double boiler until clear. Stir into cream mixture. Fold whipped cream into the entire mixture. Divide mixture in half. Stir cognac into 1 half. Stir Kahlua and chocolate into the other half.

### CONFECTIONERS' SUGAR ICING

1 c. confectioners' sugar
1 t. white vanilla
   Water

Mix vanilla and water into sugar, adding water by the teaspoonfuls until of spreading consistency. Beat until smooth.

## APPLE STRUDEL

½ recipe Puff Pastry
1 c. fine dry bread crumbs
¾ c. melted butter
3 large McIntosh apples, peeled, cored and sliced ¼ inch thick
½ c. sugar mixed with 1 t. cinnamon
⅓ c. raisins
⅓ c. sliced, blanched toasted almonds
   Melted butter
   Confectioners' sugar

Roll dough out on a floured board to ⅛ inch thick. Sauté bread crumbs in ½ cup melted butter. Brush pastry with a thin layer of remaining butter. Spread bread crumbs on two-thirds of the dough nearest you. Spread apples over crumbs. Sprinkle apples with a mixture of cinnamon and sugar. Dot with raisins and nuts. Roll up strudel, beginning with edge nearest apples and pulling it up over apples. Continue to roll to the end. Seal ends. Place on a greased cookie sheet, open edge down, and form into a horseshoe shape. Brush top with melted butter. Bake in a 425° oven 45 minutes until golden brown. When cool, sprinkle with confectioners' sugar. To reheat, bake in a 425° oven 10 minutes. Serves 12.

## QUICK AND EASY PUFF PASTRY

1½ c. unsifted flour
1 c. butter
½ c. sour cream

Cut butter into flour until it resembles crumbs. Stir in sour cream. Turn onto a floured board and knead only until it holds together. Form into a ball. Flatten slightly. Place on waxed paper. Wrap airtight. Refrigerate at least 2 hours or overnight. Work with half of the dough at a time and keep the other half in the refrigerator until ready to use. On a board, with a heavy rolling pin, pound the dough to make it pliable.

*Note:* Use for recipes calling for puff pastry, such as Strudel and Napoleons.

Pictured here clockwise from the top:
Peppermint Ice Cream Cake, p. 15, Cherry
Cobbler Bars, p. 34, Eggnog Bars, p. 34,
Daiquiri Pie, p. 22, White Chocolate
Cream Fudge, p. 54, Cherry Cheese-
cake Parfait, p. 59, Tropical Slush
Parfait, p. 59.

## APPLE CRISP

5 or 6 McIntosh apples, peeled and
   sliced
1 c. sifted flour
1 c. sugar
1 t. baking powder
¾ t. salt
1 egg
⅓ c. melted butter
   Cinnamon
   Ice cream

Butter a 10 x 6-inch baking dish. Fill ¾ full
with apple slices. Mix together flour, sugar,
baking powder, salt and egg. Spread over
apples. Pour melted butter over and sprinkle
cinnamon over top. Bake in a 350° oven 30
to 40 minutes. Serve warm with ice cream.
Serves 6 to 8.

## APPLE BROWN BETTY

4 c. soft bread cubes
½ c. melted butter
¾ t. cinnamon
⅛ t. salt
¾ c. brown sugar
4 c. peeled and chopped tart apples
   Ice cream

Mix the first 5 ingredients together.
Arrange alternate layers of apples and bread
mixture in a greased shallow 1-quart cas-
serole. Cover with foil and bake in a 375°
oven 1 hour. Remove foil for last 15 minutes of baking time. Serve with ice cream.
Serves 4.

## CHERRY COBBLER

2 T. shortening
1 c. sugar
1 c. milk
2 c. flour
2 T. baking powder
2 20-oz. cans sour red cherries
   Additional sweetening to taste
   Ice cream

Cream shortening with sugar. Add milk.
Stir in flour and baking powder. Pour into a
buttered 9 x 13-inch dish. Sweeten cherries
to taste and pour over batter. Bake in a 350°
oven 20 minutes. Serve with ice cream.
Serves 8.

## FRUIT COCKTAIL COBBLER

½ c. butter
1 c. flour
1 c. sugar
2 t. baking powder
¾ c. milk
1 17-oz. can fruit cocktail, drained
   Ice Cream

Melt butter in a 9 x 13-inch pan. In a bowl
mix flour, sugar and baking powder. Stir in
milk until smooth. Stir into pan. Spoon fruit
evenly over the batter. Bake in a 350° oven
45 minutes. Serve topped with ice cream.
Serves 8.

## MINCEMEAT SNACKIN' COBBLER

1 18-oz. jar mincemeat with rum and
   brandy
1 14½-oz. pkg. coconut-pecan snack cake
   mix
1 egg
2 T. butter, softened
   Whipped cream for topping

Heat oven to 325°. Spread mincemeat in an
8-inch square pan. Mix together dry cake
mix, egg and butter until crumbly. Sprinkle
over mincemeat. Bake 45 to 50 minutes or
until light brown. Serve warm. Garnish
with whipped cream. Serves 9.

## PEACH COBBLER

1 c. buttermilk baking mix
4 T. brown sugar
⅓ c. milk
1 29-oz. can sliced peaches, undrained
3 T. cornstarch
2 T. butter
½ t. ginger
   Dash salt
   Whipped cream

Mix baking mix, 1 tablespoon brown sugar
and milk. Set aside. In a 10-inch skillet,
combine remaining brown sugar, peaches,
cornstarch, butter, ginger and salt. Cook
over low heat, stirring constantly, until
thick and bubbly. Drop batter mixture by
tablespoonfuls into hot peach mixture.
Cook, uncovered, over low heat 10 minutes.
Cover and cook an additional 10 to 15
minutes until dumplings are fluffy. To
serve, spoon syrup over dumplings and top
with whipped cream. Serves 6 to 8.

# Book I Index

# Book II
# *Candy*
# COOKBOOK
by Mildred Brand

# CONTENTS

## Book I Nice & Easy Desserts Cookbook

## Book II Candy Cookbook

## Book III Cookie Cookbook

*Pictured opposite: Mint Sandwich, p. 32; Mints Made From Icecap Colored Coatings, p. 31.*

# INTRODUCTION

Candy making is a lot of fun when it is done as a family or group project. Like anything else, there are a lot of things that can help make your candy consistently the way you want it. Here are a few ideas that we have found helpful.

## Thermometer

A good candy thermometer is very important. Even with the best thermometer, readings may vary from day to day, so test your thermometer each day you use it. To test thermometer, place it in enough water to cover the ball of mercury at the base of the thermometer. Bring water to a boil. Let water boil for several minutes or until mercury rises no higher. Read the temperature. If it reads 212°, cook candy to the exact degrees as the recipe instructs. If the reading is higher, cook candy as many degrees higher as the thermometer reads over 212°. For example, if thermometer reads 214° instead of 212° (2 degrees too high), and your recipe calls for 236°, cook candy to 238° (2 degrees higher than 236°). If your thermometer reads low when tested, adjust accordingly. For example, if your thermometer reads 208° instead of 212° in boiling water (4 degrees too low), and your recipe calls for 236°, cook candy to 232° (4 degrees lower than 236°).

Many recipes, especially older ones, will state that candy is to be cooked to the hard ball, soft ball, crack, or thread stage. These terms describe the consistency of a small amount of cooking syrup when it is dropped into cold water. Crack is usually about 290° to 300°, hard ball is about 245° to 250°, soft ball is about 240°, and thread is about 230°. Consistent results are obtained by using a thermometer. An incorrect temperature reading could result in extremely hard candy or candy so soft it cannot be handled.

## Undercooked Candy

If candy is not cooked long enough, several things can be done. In some candy, dry fondant can be mixed with soft candy to make it firm; or melted chocolate (milk, semisweet, white, etc.) can be mixed with candy before it cools. When the chocolate hardens, the candy becomes firm. Often you can cool candy to thicken it and dip it in chocolate. If candy is so soft that it cannot be handled, line molds with chocolate, spoon candy into a mold and cover with chocolate.

## Overcooked Candy

When candy is overcooked by a few degrees, it can easily be saved, as long as the candy is not scorched. Leave candy on the stove cooking; carefully add (¼ to ½ cup) water (or milk or whatever liquid used) to the boiling candy. The candy's temperature should drop a few degrees below the desired temperature. Continue cooking until the proper temperature is reached and you will have the same results had the candy been properly cooked.

## Ingredients

In many recipes, butter and margarine can be used interchangeably; however, always use butter in toffee. As a rule of thumb, use butter when the flavor of the butter contributes to the taste of the candy; and margarine where the taste is predominately another flavor, such as peanut butter, chocolate, etc.

Candy made with milk products will cook with a residue on the bottom of the saucepan; so candy must be stirred while cooking to prevent residue from sticking and scorching. There is an exception; heavy cream or frozen liquid non-dairy coffee cream can be used in most recipes to replace milk. They will not cause sticking, do not need to be stirred, and the candy will taste richer. In addition, with the non-dairy products or heavy cream, there will be very little chance of the candy becoming granular; and you will have a better quality candy.

Candies with a sugar, corn syrup, and water base should be stirred well to mix sugar completely with liquid, then covered and brought to a rolling boil. The lid is removed, thermometer added, and candy cooked to desired temperature without stirring. Covering candy the first few minutes of cooking prevents sugar crystals from forming on the sides of the pan and eliminates the possibility of grainy candy. Use of a lid eliminates the need of washing down the sides of the saucepan with a damp cloth as some recipes call for. Never use a lid, however, with candies calling for milk or

Basic ingredients used in candy making.

Basic equipment used in candy making.

cream, or with mixtures that might boil over.

### About Pans

Candy can be cooked with good to excellent results in a variety of pans. Heavier pans, such as heavy aluminum will give an even heat and help prevent scorching. When making candy with milk, cream, or any milk product, a heavy pan must be used.

When making candy with milk products, use a large pan because the milk will make the candy cook up high. Do not bother stirring candy that does not need it, it may make candy grainy. This is especially true for fudges.

Most recipes can be doubled or tripled with no trouble as long as you have large pans. When doubling a recipe, you may need to increase the size of your pan by three or four times in order to keep the candy from boiling over, especially candies using milk or cream.

If candy does boil over, carefully remove pan from heat and use a different burner to finish cooking candy, or clean off the burner. Candy will be less likely to boil over again if you pour it into a larger pan or wipe down the sides of the pan with a damp cloth.

### To Prevent Boil Overs

Watch candy as it cooks and reduce heat in small steps if the candy threatens to boil over. This is especially important in recipes using cream or milk. Such recipes should be started on high heat, but continually turned down (in small steps only) to prevent boil overs as well as scorching.

## CHOCOLATE

To many people, candy and chocolate are synonymous. To others, candy making with chocolate has been restricted to simple fudges, leaving hand-dipped chocolates to the professional candymaker. Today, however, with the use of summer coatings or chocolate-flavored compounds, even the novice can produce delicious chocolate candy. There are, however, a few simple precautions to follow when using chocolate.

### About Chocolate

In this book, the word chocolate refers to real chocolate, chocolate-flavored coatings or summer coatings; *real* milk chocolate will be specified as such. Either will make exceptionally good candy or candy of a waxy, poor quality, depending on the ingredients used by the manufacturer when producing the chocolate.

The main difference between real and artificial chocolate is the oil base used. Real milk chocolate is made from the cocoa bean by separating the cocoa butter from the powder, processing them separately, and then recombining them. Better quality chocolate-flavored coatings substitute coconut oil for the cocoa butter.

Real milk chocolate, as might be expected, is of a better quality, more expensive, and more difficult to handle. As chocolate coatings are easy to use, beginners will want to use them until they are more secure with candy making methods; but chocolate lovers will eventually want to try the real chocolate.

### Amount of Chocolate to Melt for Dipping

The amount of chocolate needed to dip centers will vary. As a general rule, melt one pound chocolate to coat one pound centers (50 pieces). If the centers are smaller than one-half inch diameter, or the chocolate cooler than specified, more chocolate should be used. Conversely, if the centers are larger than average or the chocolate is warmer than specified, less chocolate per pound will be needed.

## Melting Chocolate

Chocolate must be heated gently, always melting it over hot, not boiling, water rather than over direct heat. Heat water in the bottom of a double boiler. Remove from heat, place chocolate in top of double boiler, and stir to melt. It is important not to allow any water, steam, or milk to drip in chocolate. If you lift the top of the double boiler from the water, dry the base of the pan; should a drop of water fall in the chocolate, dip it out with a spoon. Never stir water into the chocolate.

When chocolate will not melt properly, chances are it is either old or has been exposed to moisture. In this case, stir a tablespoon or two of coconut oil or paramount crystals into chocolate. Vegetable oil can be substituted for coconut oil but the results are not as good.

## Real Milk Chocolate

When dipping in real chocolate, tempering is necessary. Real chocolate that is not tempered properly will take a very long time to set up, and when it is firm will have white streaks and spots in it. If you think you have the chocolate properly tempered, dip one center into the chocolate and wait a few minutes. If the chocolate was tempered properly, it will be set within a few minutes. If it is not set within ten minutes, or if it dries with white streaks in it, you probably need to go through the tempering process again. Although the process of using real milk chocolate is somewhat involved, most real chocolate lovers will agree that the results are worth the extra effort.

## Tempering Chocolate

Tempering chocolate is simply melting, cooling, then bringing chocolate back to the proper dipping temperature. Tempering chocolate before dipping results in a shinier surface to dipped chocolates. Real chocolate *must* be tempered, although chocolate coatings can be tempered for shinier results. To temper chocolate properly, follow the steps below.
1. Bring water in the bottom of a double boiler to a boil; remove from heat.
2. Place chocolate in top of double boiler over hot water. (The temperature of chocolate should not rise over 110°.) Stir frequently until the chocolate is almost melted.
3. Replace hot water in double boiler with warm water (about 120°). Continue stir-

ring until chocolate is melted.
4. Replace warm water with cool water (about 60°). Stir until chocolate becomes very thick, like a thick frosting, and does not run from the spoon (78° for milk chocolate, 80° for dark chocolate, 86° for pastel coatings). Do not allow chocolate to cool enough to solidify.
5. Replace cool water with tepid water (86° to 90°). Stir to loosen chocolate. The chocolate requires time and constant stirring at this point to bring it back up to the proper temperature and consistency.
6. Milk chocolate must be quite thick when used (much thicker than the coatings).

Melted chocolate.

Thickened tempered chocolate ready to reheat.

## Melting Coatings for Dipping

To prepare chocolate coatings for dipping candy centers, follow these easy steps:
1. Heat water to a boil in the bottom of a double boiler (without chocolate near stove).
2. Remove water from heat; place top of double boiler with chopped block chocolate or wafers in it over hot water.
3. Stir occasionally, until chocolate is melted (about 3 to 5 minutes).
4. Remove chocolate from hot water and allow coating to cool for 10 to 20 minutes; or place chocolate over cold water and stir until it thickens slightly.

*Pictured opposite: No-cook Divinity and Seafoam. p. 36; Coconut Kisses, p. 44; Coconut Bonbons, p. 18; Colored Coatings.*

6

5. Replace hot water with warm water in bottom of double boiler.
6. When chocolate has thickened slightly, place it over warm water and it will be ready to dip. If chocolate is too thick to dip centers, warm water slightly. If chocolate is too thin, replace water with cooler water. Lukewarm water should keep chocolate the right temperature for dipping.
7. Keep chocolate stirred while dipping.

### Temperature for Dipping
Real Chocolate:

| | |
|---|---|
| Milk Chocolate | 86° |
| Dark Chocolate | 90° |
| Chocolate-Flavored Coatings | 98° |

### Dipping Chocolate
Successful chocolate dipping is largely dependent upon three factors: using a chocolate especially made for coating or dipping, having the correct temperature and consistency, and stirring thoroughly.

The temperature of the room is as important as that of chocolate. The room should be between 60° and 70°, and results are best for beginners on a clear, cool day in a room free of steam. When dipping, keep chocolate over tepid water and close to the temperature under the heading "Temperature for Dipping."

While dipping centers, continue stirring chocolate rapidly with a circular motion, not allowing chocolate to set up around the rim of double boiler. This stirring results in proper blending of cocoa butter and insures a rich, glossy coating.

### A Short-Cut When Dipping Centers
1. Melt chocolate in 2 double boilers.
2. Temper chocolate in 1 double boiler; cool other chocolate only slightly.
3. Dip a few centers in tempered chocolate. Add 1 tablespoon of untempered chocolate to the tempered; stir well and dip a few more centers. Continue adding a tablespoon of untempered chocolate after dipping a few centers, keeping the level of the tempered chocolate constant, and not adding too much untempered chocolate at a time or you will lose the temper.

### Leftover Chocolate
If you have chocolate left after dipping centers or filling molds, stir in nuts, raisins, crunchy cereal, crushed graham crackers, or any number of other foods. Drop spoonfuls onto waxed paper. You can also dip cookies, crackers, or marshmallows in melted chocolate. For reuse, scrape chocolate out on waxed paper, let it harden, wrap well and use another time.

Rolling fondant balls for dipping.

Dipping fondant.

Chocolate-dipped fondants.

### Molding Chocolate
With the use of chocolate-flavored coatings, chocolate molding has become easy and excellent results can be realized with minimum effort. An endless number of molds are available: chicks and rabbits for Easter, Santas and suckers for Christmas, witches for Halloween, molds for every occasion.

Chocolate-flavored coatings are easiest to mold. To prepare coatings, melt chocolate in double boiler over hot (never boiling) water, or place chocolate in a wide-mouth glass jar and set in a hot water bath. Stir occasionally until melted. The coating is then ready to be molded. Cooling is unnecessary. If you wish to mold real milk chocolate, you *must* temper it before molding. To add flavor to molded candy, melt chocolate and stir in a few drops of *concentrated* flavoring oils.

Although many types of molds will work in molding chocolate, clear plastic molds are best and will be the only ones discussed. There are two main categories of clear plastic molds: the flat-back mold and three-dimensional mold. The flat-back mold will make candy shaped on one side and flat on the other. Some of these molds have grooves at the base to accommodate a sucker stick. Three-dimensional molds are two-piece molds that clip together with paper clips or other fasteners which allow you to make stand-up or fully shaped candy figures. Usually there are indentations in the molds to insure proper alignment. These molds come in two distinct styles: molds with an open base and molds which are closed when clipped together.

The clear plastic molds need to be clean and dry before filling with chocolate. Greasing, spraying, or dusting is not necessary and would ruin the appearance of the finished candy. If molds are used for something else other than chocolate, however, such as marshmallow, jellies, or cooked candies, they must be greased or sprayed with an oiling spray. If a mold is to be filled several times, it does not need to be cleaned between use, as the chocolate will come out cleanly and leave the mold ready for filling. When finished with the mold, wash it in hot water. Detergent will eventually dry out the mold and may crack it.

### Flat-Backed Molds

If you want a solid piece of candy, spoon (or use a candy funnel) the melted chocolate into the mold. Underfill rather than overfill mold as overfilling will cause a "foot" to form at the base of candy. Tap mold on the table to release air bubbles, or lift mold and work bubbles out with a toothpick. Fill all cavities in mold, then chill in freezer for a few minutes. Leave in freezer only long enough for chocolate to harden slightly. Remove from freezer, turn upside down and candy should fall out. If candy does not fall out, flex mold slightly or return to freezer.

For molds with a soft center, use a paint-brush or small spoon to line mold cavity with chocolate, using just enough for a strong layer. Chill mold in freezer long enough for chocolate to harden slightly. Remove from freezer and spoon soft center into the cavity, leaving a small rim of chocolate around top. Spoon a small amount of chocolate over top to seal, chill for a few minutes and unmold.

**Molded Chocolate Covered Cherries, p. 40**

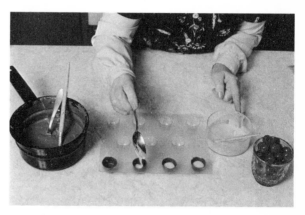

*Pouring liquid fondant into chocolate painted mold.*

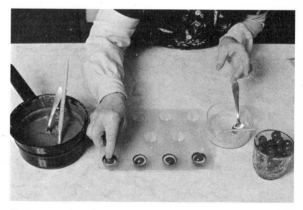

*Placing a maraschino cherry in liquid fondant.*

*Covering cherry and fondant with chocolate.*

9

## Chocolate Painting

Very attractive multicolored chocolate pieces can be molded using clear plastic molds. Melt the colors you wish to use in at least one-pound quantities in separate double boilers, or put small amounts of different colored chocolate in small glass jars and place jars in a hot water bath. Different colors of chocolate can also be placed in the separate cavities of a cupcake pan which is then placed in a hot water bath. In either case, be careful not to get water in chocolate.

When chocolate melts, color it with paste food coloring to produce a darker color or a color not available in chocolate coatings. Too much color will make the chocolate thick and difficult to use, and may prevent it from setting up shiny. Use paste food colors only; if chocolate becomes thick, add a few paramount crystals or liquid vegetable oil. Use chocolate that is nearest the color you desire. If you want red, start with pink coating; if you want black, start with dark chocolate.

Once chocolate is melted, apply it with paintbrushes which will not lose their bristles. Paint directly onto mold, using one color at a time, then chilling it for a few minutes to harden. Continue painting and cooling until all the parts of the mold you wish colored are painted. Then fill mold completely with slightly cooled chocolate. Chill mold in freezer until it hardens slightly, then turn out candy.

Painting a mold.

## Three-Dimensional Molds

With three-dimensional molds, you can either make solid or hollow figures, as well as filled candy. For multicolored figures,

*Pictured opposite: Plastic Molds and finished chocolate painted molds.*

follow directions given for chocolate painting, coloring each half of the mold before completing figure.

Molds that clip together and have a hole in the base are very easy to use. For a solid piece of candy, use plenty of paper clips to fasten the two halves together and spoon chocolate into mold until it is full. Prop mold up in freezer so chocolate will not run out the bottom. Chill only until the chocolate hardens slightly. Remove from freezer; take paper clips off and carefully pull mold apart. If chocolate oozed into the seam, trim with a sharp knife.

To make hollow figures, fill mold only about one-half full, then turn mold from side to side until chocolate coats entire mold. Chill in freezer for a short time. Before chocolate hardens, remove and again turn from side to side to insure a thick layer of chocolate on the bottom. Repeat if necessary. Finally, remove from freezer and unmold as before. If you wish to have a soft candy center inside a hollow piece, fill figure before unmolding. Then cover bottom with chocolate so center will not be exposed to air.

There are many ways to use three-dimensional molds that come in sheets. If a solid figure is desired, prepare one half as for a solid, flat piece of candy. When this piece is made, fill other half with warm chocolate. Carefully position this piece over warm chocolate, making sure there is enough to make a good seal and the piece is aligned correctly. Chill in freezer for a few minutes, then unmold.

To make hollow figures, follow directions above, but instead of filling each half of the mold, use a paintbrush or spoon to make a thick layer of chocolate on mold. If you wish a soft center using this mold, paint each half of mold, and chill in freezer with halves apart. Then spoon the center inside the cavity. Paint fresh chocolate around edge of one mold. Leave this piece in the mold; remove other piece and position over first piece. Chill and unmold.

A hollow figure can also be made with these molds by filling one side of mold with soft chocolate, clipping the two halves together securely, and then rotating mold until completely covered. Chill for a short time, but remove before chocolate hardens. Rotate again for an even coat. Chill to harden and unmold.

# FONDANTS AND CENTERS

Fondant is the basis of a delicious creamy center dipped in chocolate, or it can be eaten without dipping. Most of the recipes in this chapter are easy to make, but there are a few tips which should aid in fondant making. Fondant should be cooked without stirring unless recipe indicates. Stir only enough to dissolve sugar, then cover and bring to a rolling boil. Remove lid, boil 2 or 3 minutes, cook to specified temperature, checking with a thermometer. Pour fondant, without scraping pan, on a marble, porcelain, or formica surface. On a surface other than marble, cool surface with cracked ice to chill quickly, then soak up moisture before pouring fondant. Do not move fondant while it is cooling.

When lukewarm, paddle fondant with a broad metal spatula or wooden paddle, moving forward under edges and backward over the surface, occasionally scraping off paddle. When fondant is thick, creamy, and white, it is ready to be formed into ½-inch to ¾-inch balls for dipping.

If, after paddling the fondant for about 15 minutes, it has not thickened, scrape onto a cookie sheet and place in a 250° to 300° oven for a few minutes until fondant is warm. Scrape back onto the slab and paddle again. It should thicken quickly; if not, repeat procedure.

If fondant becomes hard and crumbly during kneading, break off a small piece and knead with fingers until it is soft and smooth. Continue until all fondant is softened. Or cover fondant with a damp cloth for a few minutes, then knead. For a creamier, softer fondant with a light consistency, add ½ to 1 cup marshmallow creme per 4 cups sugar base during paddling.

Fondant may be kept several weeks wrapped in waxed paper and refrigerated or put in a cool place. If, during storage, it becomes too dry to use, cover with a damp cloth until you can knead it with your hands. If dipped fondants will be stored for more than a week, add a few drops to ½ teaspoon invertase and it will become creamier with time. If invertase is used, dip centers immediately.

When fondant is undercooked, it will get creamy but will not thicken. To save the candy, melt about ½ cup semisweet chocolate coating (or any other chocolate coating) and add to fondant (amount may vary). This makes a delicious chocolate cream center; vanilla and chopped nuts may also be added. The addition of dry fondant will also thicken undercooked fondant.

*Clear Fondant poured on marble slab.*

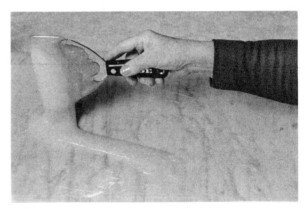

*Fondant worked with paddle.*

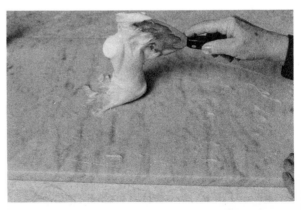

*Fondant becomes cloudy and thickens.*

Fondant forms firm white ball.

## WHIPPED CREAM CENTERS

*Another light center using your own homemade marshmallow stock to make candy smooth and light.*

### MARSHMALLOW STOCK FOR WHIPPED CREAM CENTERS

  1 c. sugar
  ½ c. light corn syrup
  ¼ c. hot water
  ½ c. egg whites

Combine sugar, syrup, and water in a saucepan with a tight-fitting lid. When syrup boils rapidly, remove lid. Cook to 248°. Turn off heat but leave pot on burner. Beat egg whites until they cling to the bottom and sides of the bowl, then beat for about ½ minute more. Pour hot syrup in a thin stream over the beaten egg whites. Beat about 5 minutes more after all the syrup has been added or until batch is lukewarm. For best results, use this stock as soon as possible.

### FONDANT FOR WHIPPED CREAM CENTERS

  4 c. sugar
  1 c. hot water
  ¼ t. cream of tartar
  3 to 5 c. Marshmallow Stock
    Dipping chocolate

Combine all ingredients except Marshmallow Stock in a saucepan with a tight-fitting lid. Cook until mixture boils; remove lid and cook to 240°. Pour out on a cold slab. When candy has cooled to lukewarm, paddle it until it begins to get cloudy. Add Marshmallow Stock to batch, continuing to paddle until it holds its shape. Turn out on waxed paper and cover with a wet towel. Wrap waxed paper and towel around candy and chill in refrigerator a couple of hours or until firm enough to form into centers. Do not let it get too firm. Gently form into ½-inch balls. Let stand an hour or so, then dip. Makes 150 to 200 centers.

## NO-COOK WHIPPED CREAM CENTERS

*This center is lighter in texture than the vanilla buttercream because of the addition of dry egg whites.*

4½ c. dry fondant, divided
  3 T. dry egg whites
  3 T. invert sugar
  ¼ t. salt
  ¼ t. vanilla
  ¼ t. invertase
  ¼ c. water

Place ½ cup dry fondant and remaining ingredients, except water, in a mixer bowl. Beat at slow speed, gradually adding only enough water to make a paste. When you have a smooth paste, gradually add remaining water, then whip at high speed until light. Add the remaining dry fondant, a little at a time, and mix at slow speed until smooth and light in texture. Form into ¾-inch balls and dip. Makes about 45 centers. *Note:* This mixture can be flavored and colored to taste.

# BASIC FONDANT

*An excellent all-purpose cream center, creamy off-white in color. Rich and smooth. Try all the suggestions below and use your own ideas to create other delicious centers with nuts, coconut, fruits, various flavorings and colors.*

- 5 c. sugar
- 1 c. whole milk
- 1 c. heavy cream
- 4 T. butter or margarine
- ½ t. cream of tartar
- 1 t. orange, vanilla, or almond flavoring (optional)
- 1 c. chopped nuts (optional)
- Dipping chocolate

In a large saucepan, combine all ingredients except flavoring and nuts. Stir until sugar is moistened. Place over high heat. Bring to a boil, then gradually lower candy thermometer into boiling syrup. Cook without stirring, lowering the heat slightly as mixture thickens. Cook to 236°. Pour out on a slab and cool to lukewarm. Work with spatula until fondant creams, then knead with hands until it is very smooth, adding a flavoring or chopped nuts, if desired. Form into a ball and let rest on the slab until it is completely cool. Form into ¾-inch balls and dip in chocolate. To store, wrap tightly in waxed paper or plastic wrap, place in a bowl and cover with a damp cloth. Makes about 125 centers.

## VANILLA FRENCH CREAMS

- 2 c. Basic Fondant
- 1 t. clear vanilla flavoring
- Dipping chocolate

Work the Basic Fondant on a slab until smooth. Add the vanilla; work until well blended. Place on waxed paper and let stand a few minutes. Form into ¾-inch balls; dip in chocolate, then roll in chopped nuts.

## CHOCOLATE FRENCH CREAMS

- 1 oz. dark chocolate coating
- 2 c. Basic Fondant
- Chocolate sprinkles

Melt the chocolate. Add to Basic Fondant which has been softened. Work until well blended. Form into ¾-inch balls and dip, rolling in chocolate sprinkles.

*Pictured opposite: Peppermint Patties, Orange Pecan Creams; Maple Creams, p. 21.*

## PEPPERMINT PATTIES

- 2 c. Basic Fondant
- ¼ t. oil of peppermint
- Few drops green food coloring
- Melted semisweet chocolate

Work Basic Fondant until softened. Add oil of peppermint and food coloring. Form into 1-inch balls and flatten each into patties. Dip in melted semisweet chocolate.

## ORANGE PECAN CREAMS

- 2 c. Basic Fondant
- ¾ t. oil of orange
- Few drops orange food coloring
- ½ c. finely chopped nuts
- Dipping chocolate

Work Basic Fondant until softened. Add oil of orange, food coloring and chopped nuts. Blend all together. Form into ¾-inch balls and dip in chocolate.

## MINT PATTIES

Melt Basic or Water Fondant in a double boiler until thin enough to drop. Add a few drops of food coloring and peppermint oil to taste. Do not stir more than necessary and do not get fondant too hot or spotting may occur. A little Simple Syrup may be added if fondant needs to be thinner to drop easily. Drop from a funnel or a teaspoon, one at a time on sheets of waxed paper.

## SIMPLE SYRUP

Combine equal parts of sugar and boiling water. Heat only enough to dissolve the sugar. Store in a covered jar in refrigerator.

# UNCOOKED FONDANT

*An easy flavored fondant. Good for stuffing dates and other simple confections. Flavor and color as desired.*

- ⅓ c. softened butter or margarine
- ⅓ c. light corn syrup
- 1 t. vanilla
- ½ t. salt
- 3½ c. (1 lb.) sifted confectioners' sugar

Blend butter, syrup, vanilla, and salt in a large mixing bowl. Add confectioners' sugar all at once. Mix together, first with a spoon, then with hands, kneading well. Turn out onto a board and continue kneading until mixture is well blended and smooth. Store wrapped in a tight container in a cool place. Makes about 25 centers.

## WATER FONDANT

*Use this in recipes calling for prepared fondant and in chocolate-covered cherry recipes using prepared fondant. Also good to flavor and color many ways. Pure white when finished.*

2 c. sugar
Dash of salt
2 T. corn syrup
¾ c. boiling water
½ t. vanilla

In a saucepan, combine all ingredients except vanilla. Mix well; cover and cook 3 minutes, then remove lid. Continue cooking without stirring to 240°. Pour fondant at once on a cold surface. Cool to lukewarm (about 110°). Work with spatula until white and creamy. Knead with hands until smooth; add vanilla. Knead until well blended. Let stand, uncovered, until cold, then wrap in waxed paper and store in a tightly covered jar in refrigerator or other cool place to ripen for at least 24 hours before using. Fondant may be kept for several weeks. Makes about 50 centers.

## CREAM FONDANT

*A rich fondant, good for vanilla and fruit-flavored creams. Off-white in color.*

2 c. sugar
Dash of salt
1 T. light corn syrup
½ c. heavy cream
¼ c. milk
½ t. vanilla

In a saucepan, combine all ingredients except vanilla. Mix well; place over medium heat. Cook without stirring to 240°. Pour fondant at once on a cold surface. Cool to lukewarm (about 110°). Work with spatula until white and creamy. Knead with hands until smooth. Add vanilla; knead until well blended. Let stand, uncovered, until cold, then wrap in waxed paper and store in a tightly covered jar in refrigerator or other cool place to ripen for at least 24 hours before using. Fondant may be kept for several weeks. Makes about 50 centers.

16

## SOUR CREAM CENTERS

*This is a rich, light brown center with a distinctly different flavor.*

3 c. light brown sugar
1 c. sour cream
½ c. butter
1 t. vanilla
Dipping chocolate
Chopped pecans (optional)

Cook brown sugar and sour cream to 240°. When temperature is reached, remove from heat; add butter and vanilla without stirring. Let stand until butter has melted, then pour out on cold slab. The butter will separate from the syrup. Cool to lukewarm, work with spatula or paddle. When mixture is creamy, and holds its shape, work in nuts if desired, and mound on slab. Let set until firm enough to shape into ¾-inch balls or pat into a buttered 8-inch square pan. Dip balls, or if candy has been put in a pan, cut into squares. Makes about 70 centers.

## CHEESEY BUTTERSCOTCH CREAMS

*A tangy taste treat.*

1 c. butterscotch coating, wafers, or chopped block
1 8-oz. pkg. cream cheese
1¾ c. confectioners' sugar
Dipping chocolate

In the top of a double boiler, melt butterscotch coating over hot, not boiling water. Add cream cheese, stirring to blend. Remove from hot water and add confectioners' sugar, stirring to blend. Spread in a buttered pan or on a buttered plate and chill. Remove from refrigerator, form into ¾-inch balls, dip in chocolate and drop into a small paper candy cup. Crushed graham cracker or a nut may be placed on top of candy while chocolate is still soft. The center will be quite soft when you work with it, but the creamy delicious results are well worth the trouble. Makes 30 pieces.

## TRUFFLES

*A delicious chocolate center with a light texture.*

4½ c. (about 1⅓ lbs.) real milk chocolate, finely chopped
⅓ c. heavy cream
⅓ c. half and half
1 t. vanilla
Dipping chocolate

Melt chocolate over hot water. Combine cream and half and half; heat to scalding. Cool cream mixture to 130°. Add to melted chocolate all at once, beating until smooth and well blended. Add vanilla and blend into mixture. Chill in refrigerator until candy is firm but pliable. Beat with mixer until candy is light and fluffy then return to refrigerator until firm. Form into ¾-inch balls and immediately dip in chocolate. Makes about 50 centers.

## WHIPPED CREAM TRUFFLES

*An excellent variation of the Truffle recipe. Rich and delicious.*

2½ c. (about ¾ lb.) real milk chocolate, finely chopped
1 c. heavy cream
¼ t. salt
¼ t. vanilla
Dipping chocolate

Melt milk chocolate. Cool to 98° and hold at this temperature. Whip cream until it holds a soft peak. Add warm chocolate, a little at a time, to whipped cream, stirring vigorously with a wooden spoon. When all chocolate is added, stir in salt and vanilla. Place in refrigerator to chill. When mixture is slightly firm, beat with a wooden spoon only until fluffy. Do not overbeat. Pack mixture into a pastry bag filled with a coupling without the ring. Squeeze out mounds on waxed paper. Chill mounds in refrigerator for several hours or overnight. Pat down any peaks after chocolate has been in refrigerator awhile. Dip in chocolate. Store candy in refrigerator. Makes about 40 centers.

## CRISPY PEANUT BUTTER CENTERS

*A crunchy variation of the all-time favorite peanut butter center.*

2 c. crunchy peanut butter
½ c. margarine
1 lb. confectioners' sugar
3 c. crisp rice cereal
Dipping chocolate

Combine peanut butter, margarine, and confectioners' sugar in a large bowl. Blend together well. Add rice cereal and blend into peanut butter mixture. Form into ¾-inch balls and dip in dipping chocolate. Makes about 75 centers.

## PEANUT BUTTER BALLS

*An extremely simple recipe and a family favorite.*

¼ lb. margarine
½ lb. peanut butter
¾ lb. confectioners' sugar
¼ c. light corn syrup
Dipping chocolate

Combine all ingredients, mixing well. Roll into ¾-inch balls and coat with dipping chocolate. Makes about 40 centers.

## ALMOND RUM PATTIES

*A very good, flavored center in patty form.*

4 c. sugar
⅓ c. brown sugar
⅓ c. light corn syrup
1 c. heavy cream
⅓ c water
½ c. butter
Pinch of salt
½ t. butter flavoring
1 or 2 t. rum flavoring
1 c. marshmallow creme
2 c. sliced, buttered roasted almonds
Dipping chocolate

Combine sugars, corn syrup, cream, water, butter, and salt in a saucepan. Cook to 240°. Pour out on a cold slab and cool to lukewarm. Work with spatula until almost firm, then add flavorings, marshmallow, and almonds. Continue working until set up. Form into 1-inch patties and dip in chocolate. Makes about 100 centers.

## VANILLA BUTTERCREAMS

*Special center with a fresh butter flavor. Good, good!!*

- 3 c. sugar
- 1 c. water
- ¼ t. cream of tartar
- ½ c. butter, broken into little pieces
- ¼ t. salt
- 1 t. vanilla
- Dipping chocolate

Combine sugar, water, and cream of tartar in a saucepan; cover with a tight lid and cook. When mixture boils rapidly, remove lid and cook to 238°. Pour out on cold slab and let stand until lukewarm. Place butter pieces, salt, and vanilla over the syrup and work with spatula or paddle until fondant is cool and thick. Move to a cooler part of the marble slab or other cold surface and let stand until candy is firm, holds its shape and is not sticky. Knead for a moment or two until creamy. Wrap in waxed paper and store in refrigerator until very firm, then shape into ¾-inch balls. Let stand about 30 minutes before dipping; for best results, dip within 2 hours. If kept longer than a week, wrap well and freeze. Makes 60 centers.

## ORIENTALS

*A light airy center. Entirely different in consistency than the former centers. Excellent if you like a candy less rich.*

- 5 c. sugar
- 2 c. water
- 1 T. glycerine
- 6 drops acetic acid
- 2 beaten egg whites
- Flavoring and coloring as desired
- Dipping chocolate

Place sugar, water, and glycerine in a saucepan with a tight lid. When mixture boils rapidly, remove the lid, insert thermometer, and add acetic acid. Cook to 238° in cold weather or to 240° in hot weather. Pour on cold slab. When mixture is lukewarm, add egg whites to the syrup on the slab. Work until creamy. Add flavoring and coloring. Turn out on waxed paper, cover with waxed paper and a damp towel and refrigerate for about 1 hour. Form into 1-inch balls, using flour to keep fingers from sticking. When centers are set on top (about an hour), roll them over so they will dry on the bottom, then dip in melted chocolate. Store where cool but do not refrigerate. Makes about 125 centers.

18

## COCONUT CENTERS FOR BONBONS

*If you like to make your own coconut bonbons, this is a very easy and good recipe.*

- ¼ c. corn syrup
- 6 large marshmallows, quartered
- 1 c. desiccated or macaroon coconut
- ½ t. vanilla

Melt syrup and marshmallows over medium heat. Remove from heat; add coconut and vanilla. Let set until cool enough to handle, then shape into ¾-inch balls. Makes about 20 centers.

## DIPPING BONBONS

Heat 1½ c. Water Fondant, (p. 16) slowly in upper part of double boiler until it melts to the consistency of heavy cream. Do not stir more than necessary. Keep fondant over hot water or work at the stove. With fork, coat bonbon centers. Drop on waxed paper. These do not keep long.

## COCONUT CANDY CENTERS

*Nice chewy coconut bonbons or almond coconut centers.*

- 1 c. sugar
- 1½ c. light corn syrup
- ½ c. water
- 4 c. desiccated coconut
- ½ t. almond flavoring
- Dipping chocolate
- Toasted almonds

Combine sugar, syrup, and water in a heavy saucepan. Cover; cook until boiling rapidly. Remove cover, insert thermometer and cook to 234°. Remove from heat, add coconut and flavoring. Pour out on slab or platter and let cool. When cool, shape into ¾-inch ovals or balls and put a toasted almond on top of each. Dip in chocolate. Makes about 50 centers.

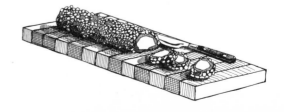

*Pictured opposite: Orientals and Turkish Delights, p. 37.*

## ORANGE CREAM CENTERS

*A rich, tangy, true orange flavored center. Delicious!*

3 c. sugar
½ c. heavy cream
⅔ c. orange juice
½ c. butter
Dipping chocolate

Combine all ingredients except chocolate and cook. As mixture thickens, gradually lower heat. Do not use spoon to stir, but stir a bit with the thermometer. When mixture reaches 240°, pour out on cold slab. When lukewarm, work as for fondant, form into ¾-inch balls and dip in chocolate. Makes about 70 centers.

## ORANGE CREAMS

*A good flavored orange center, getting creamier and softer as it ripens in the chocolate.*

3 c. sugar
¼ c. invert sugar
¾ c. water
⅛ t. salt
1 c. marshmallow creme
⅓ t. invertase
6 drops orange oil
Orange food coloring
1 t. grated orange rind (optional)
Dipping chocolate

Cook sugar, invert sugar, water, and salt in a tightly covered pan until mixture boils rapidly. Remove lid and cook to 240°. Pour on cold surface. Cool to lukewarm, work with a paddle until almost set up or until it is opaque. Add marshmallow, invertase, orange oil, food coloring, and orange rind if desired. Work until the mass becomes plastic-like. Let set until easy to handle. Form into ¾-inch balls and dip in chocolate. Makes about 70 centers.

## PENUCHE

*A super, creamy, rich flavored center, wonderful for those special occasions and at holiday time.*

3 c. sugar
1 c. firmly packed brown sugar
1 c. heavy cream
1 c. non-dairy coffee cream
¼ c. light corn syrup
⅛ t. salt
Dipping chocolate

Combine all ingredients except chocolate and blend well. Cook to 237°. Pour out on a marble slab or another cold surface. Cool to lukewarm. Paddle with spatula until candy holds its shape. Form into ¾-inch balls and dip in melted chocolate. This candy can be wrapped well and refrigerated several weeks, then made up into ¾-inch balls and dipped. Its flavor improves after ripening a few days. Makes about 100 centers.

## SOFT MAPLE CREAMS

*A rich maple-nut center. If you like maple, you'll love this center.*

3 c. brown sugar
½ c. water
½ c. butter
1 c. heavy cream
1 c. marshmallow creme
⅓ t. invertase
1 t. maple flavor
1 c. finely chopped nuts
Dipping chocolate

Cook brown sugar, water, and butter to 215°. Add heavy cream slowly so boiling does not stop. Cook to 238°. Pour on slab and let candy cool to warm lukewarm. (This fondant should be worked at a slightly warmer temperature than most fondants.) Work with spatula until cloudy and heavy. Add marshmallow, invertase, and maple flavor. Continue to work until almost set up and then add nuts. Let rest until it is easy to handle, then form into 1-inch balls and dip in melted chocolate. Makes about 75 centers.

## MAPLE CREAMS

*Very delicately flavored with real maple syrup. I suggest dipping only in a light coating of sweet milk chocolate so the coating does not overpower the maple flavor.*

- **1 c. coffee cream**
- **2 c. maple syrup**
- **Sweet milk chocolate, melted**

Cook cream and syrup to 238°. Pour on a cold slab; cool to lukewarm. Work with spatula or paddle until mass holds its shape. Form into ¾-inch balls and dip in melted chocolate. Makes about 25 centers.

## CHOCOLATE CREAM CENTERS

*A luscious, melt-in-your mouth filling, using heavy cream and real chocolate.*

- **2 lbs. milk chocolate**
- **½ pt. heavy cream**
- **Dipping chocolate**

Melt milk chocolate over hot water. Heat heavy cream to 130°. Combine chocolate and cream in a mixer bowl and whip 3 minutes on high speed of electric mixer. Cover with a damp cloth; chill in freezer for 5 minutes. Beat again for 3 minutes. Chill until firm enough to form centers or pour into an 8-inch buttered pan. When firm, form ¾-inch balls and dip, or cut into squares and dip. Makes about 100 centers.

## CHOCOLATE FONDANT

*A deliciously chocolate flavored center, quite firm.*

- **¾ c. water**
- **3 1-oz. squares baking chocolate**
- **2 c. sugar**
- **Dash of salt**
- **2 T. light corn syrup**
- **½ t. vanilla**

Combine water and chocolate in a deep 2-quart saucepan. Place over low heat and cook until blended, stirring constantly. Add sugar, salt, and syrup. Stir to mix ingredients thoroughly. Place a tight lid on pan and cook until mixture boils rapidly. Remove lid and cook without stirring to 236°. Pour on cold slab and cool to lukewarm. Work with spatula until creamy, then knead with hands until smooth. Add vanilla, working it in with spatula. Let stand, uncovered, until cold. Wrap in waxed paper and use as chocolate centers. Makes about 45 to 50 centers.

## FRENCH CHOCOLATE LOGS

*Note there are two parts to this recipe. It is a very pretty center with chocolate in the middle and the green marzipan around the chocolate. After being dipped, they are an unusual and attractive candy to bite into.*

### CHOCOLATE PUDDING

- **¾ lb. milk chocolate**
- **⅓ c. coffee cream**
- **¾ t. vanilla**

Line an 8-inch square pan with waxed paper. Melt chocolate and set aside. Scald cream and cool to 130°. Add warm cream to melted chocolate all at once; beat until smooth. Add vanilla; beat smooth and pour into prepared pan. Cool in refrigerator until firm.

### LOGS

- **¼ c. Water or Simple Fondant, p. 16, 22**
- **4 T. almond paste**
- **¼ t. vanilla**
- **Confectioners' sugar (enough to make a pie crust-like dough)**
- **Green food coloring**
- **Dipping chocolate**

Combine all ingredients except chocolate. Roll into a sheet about ¼-inch thick. Cut into strips about ¾-inch wide. Cut Chocolate Pudding into pencil-sized strips. Lay the chocolate pudding pieces on the green fondant strips; wrap fondant around chocolate, sealing the seam. Slice into ½-inch pieces and dip each piece in chocolate. Makes about 30 slices.

## CHOCOLATE FUDGE CENTERS

*Like chocolate? Then you will love these creamy, fudgey centers. For double chocolate, dip in semisweet chocolate.*

- **4 c. sugar**
- **1 c. heavy cream**
- **1 c. non-dairy coffee cream**
- **¼ c. light corn syrup**
- **⅛ t. salt**
- **3 1-oz. squares unsweetened chocolate, *or* 1 c. melted semisweet chocolate**
- **Dipping chocolate**

Combine all ingredients and blend well. Cook to 237°. Pour out on a marble slab or other cold surface. Cool to lukewarm. Paddle with spatula until candy creams up and holds its shape. Form into ¾-inch balls and dip. Makes about 90 centers.

The following recipes use Dry Fondant. The dry fondant and the liquid in each recipe is variable, so use the amount to get the consistency that you want.

## SIMPLE UNFLAVORED FONDANT

*Usually used for mint patties by melting in the top of a double boiler and adding color and flavoring oils, then dropping on waxed paper from a candy funnel.*

- 8½ c. dry fondant
- ⅓ c. light corn syrup
- ¼ c. water

Mix all ingredients together thoroughly and store in a covered container.

## NO-COOK CHERRY CENTERS

*A good, easy, time-saving center.*

- 9 c. dry fondant, divided
- 1 T. dry egg whites
- ½ t. invertase
- ¼ c. plus 3 T. water
- 3½ T. cherry preserves
- 1 t. cherry flavoring
- ⅛ t. citric acid
- ½ t. vanilla
- ¼ t. butter flavoring
  Dipping chocolate

Combine 4½ cups dry fondant with remaining ingredients. Mix at slow speed until blended, then beat at high speed for about 3 minutes. Add remaining dry fondant, beating at slow speed, until smooth. Form into ¾-inch balls and dip. Makes about 70 centers.

## DELUXE CENTERS

*A rich, delicious center for creams and Easter eggs.*

- 1 c. sweetened condensed milk
- 1 c. butter
- 2 c. dry fondant
- 4 c. pecans
- 4 c. desiccated coconut
  Dipping chocolate

Cream together all ingredients until well blended. Chill 2 hours and form into ¾-inch balls; chill, then dip in chocolate. Store in refrigerator, dip centers as needed. Makes about 2¾ lbs. or 125 centers.

## BASIC CREAMS

*A good, easy basic cream which is very versatile.*

- 5 c. dry fondant
- ⅔ c. marshmallow creme
- 3 T. water
- ½ t. salt
- ¼ t. invertase
- ¼ to ½ t. vanilla
  Dipping chocolate

Combine 1½ cups dry fondant and remaining ingredients in a large mixing bowl. With a spoon, mix until creamy and smooth. Gradually add remaining dry fondant. Mix with a spoon and then knead with hands until it forms a smooth ball. Make into ¾-inch balls and dip. Makes about 40 centers.
*Variations:* Instead of vanilla flavoring, use one of these combinations.
Orange oil, orange color, grated orange rind, chopped pecans
Lemon oil, yellow color, grated lemon rind
Black walnut flavoring, chopped walnuts
Peppermint oil, green color
Finely chopped candied cherries, red color, almond flavoring

## NO-COOK VANILLA BUTTERCREAMS

*A very good and rich center, with no cooking.*

- 7½ c. dry fondant, divided
- ½ c. (scant) light corn syrup
- ⅓ c. plus 1 T. water
- ½ t. invertase
- ½ t. salt
- ½ t. vanilla
- ½ c. butter
  Dipping chocolate

In a mixing bowl, combine 3¾ cups dry fondant with remaining ingredients. Mix at slow speed to blend. Slowly add remaining dry fondant, mixing at slow speed until smooth. Form into ¾-inch balls and dip. Makes about 50 centers.
*Note:* For a richer center, use 1 cup butter and refrigerate overnight before forming centers.

*Pictured opposite: Mexican Orange Fudge, Pineapple Fudge, and Layered Fudge Squares, p. 28; Cocoa Fudge, p. 24.*

# FUDGE

Many kinds of fudge are included in this section, some very easy and some requiring more work. Do not stir fudge once the boiling starts, unless the recipe specifically requires it; unnecessary stirring may cause graining.

Beating fudge is very important. While fudge is cooling, it is necessary to make the fudge creamy and smooth. Beating must be started while the fudge is comfortably warm and continued until it is almost firm. For fudges that require cooling and beating, beat hot fudge in pan or pour the hot fudge on a marble slab or formica; cool to lukewarm, then paddle with a spatula, until of the right consistency to spread.

Marshmallow creme may be mixed into many of these recipes just before the fudge sets up to make a softer, lighter fudge. If fudge is overcooked, marshmallow creme will help it from becoming hard and dry.

## COCOA FUDGE

*A good basic chocolate fudge. The use of whipping cream or non-dairy cream substitute makes stirring unnecessary. This makes a very creamy fudge.*

- ⅔ c. cocoa
- 3 c. sugar
- ⅛ t. salt
- 1½ c. heavy cream or non-dairy liquid cream substitute
- ¼ c. butter
- 1 t. vanilla

Combine cocoa, sugar, salt, and heavy cream in a large saucepan. Bring to a rolling boil; then reduce heat to medium and cook to 234° without stirring. Remove from heat and add butter and vanilla. Do not stir. Cool to lukewarm (about 110°). Beat by hand or with mixer until fudge thickens and loses some of its gloss. Quickly spread fudge in lightly buttered 8-inch square pan. When cool, cut into squares. Makes about 49 pieces.

## SUPER FUDGE

*Unusual, delicious fudge, requiring a minimum of beating.*

- 2 c. firmly packed brown sugar
- 1 c. sugar
- 1 c. non-dairy liquid cream substitute
- ½ c. butter or margarine
- 2 c. marshmallow creme
- 1½ c. finely chopped semisweet chocolate
- 1½ c. finely chopped butterscotch coating
- 2 c. chopped nuts
- 1 t. vanilla

Combine brown sugar, sugar, cream substitute, and butter in a large saucepan. Cook to 234°. Remove from heat, let bubbles subside. Add marshmallow creme, semisweet chocolate and butterscotch coating. Stir until well blended. Stir in nuts and vanilla. Pat into a buttered 9-inch square pan. Cut into squares when cool. Makes about 64 pieces.

## DATE NUT ROLL

*A family favorite. Creamy and rich with dates and nuts. Store a long time in airtight containers.*

- 2 c. sugar
- 1 c. heavy cream
- 1 c. milk
- 1 c. chopped dates
- 1 c. chopped nuts
- 1 t. vanilla

Cook sugar, cream, and milk to 230°. Slowly add chopped dates so boiling does not stop. Occasionally, stir mixture so the dates do not settle to the bottom of the pan and scorch. Cook to 238°. Cool in the pan or pour out on a marble slab. When a little warmer than lukewarm, around 150°, stir and work with your hands or a spatula until creamy. Work nuts and vanilla into the candy. Form into rolls, wrap tightly in waxed paper or plastic wrap until firm. Store in a tightly covered container. Makes about 30 pieces.

## SIMPLE, EASY FUDGE

*A very good fudge with no cooking or thermometer watching.*

- 3 c. chopped chocolate or chocolate wafers (sweet, semisweet, or a combination)
- 1 can sweetened condensed milk
  Pinch of salt
- 1 t. vanilla
- ½ c. chopped nuts

Melt chocolate in the top of a double boiler over hot, not boiling, water. Remove from heat and stir in remaining ingredients. Spread in a generously buttered 8-inch square pan. Chill 2 hours or until firm. Turn fudge out onto a cutting board, cut into squares. Store in tightly covered containers. Makes 49 pieces.

## FRENCH CREAM ALMONDINE

*A quick, easy, and delicious fudge with almonds to add crunchiness.*

- 5 c. chopped milk chocolate
- ½ c. milk
- ¾ c. marshmallow creme
- 2½ c. chopped toasted almonds, divided

Melt milk chocolate to 110°. Scald milk. Add hot milk and marshmallow to melted chocolate, beating until smooth. Stir in 1½ cups almonds. Spread in a buttered 8-inch square pan. Sprinkle remaining almonds over top and press in. When set, cut into squares. Makes about 49 pieces.

## SUE'S EASY 15-MINUTE PEANUT BUTTER FUDGE

*A cooked peanut butter fudge, very good and simple to make.*

- 1 c. sugar
- 1 c. light brown sugar
- ¼ t. salt
- ½ c. milk
- 1 c. miniature marshmallows
- ½ c. peanut butter
- 1 t. vanilla

In a saucepan, combine sugars, salt, and milk. Cook to 240°. Remove from heat and add marshmallows, peanut butter, and vanilla. Beat with a wooden spoon several minutes until thick and creamy and gloss disappears. Spread in a buttered 8-inch square pan. Cut into squares. Makes about 48 pieces.

## CHOCOLATE WALNUT CREAMS

*This is especially good with black walnuts—giving an old-fashioned flavor to the fudge.*

- 2¼ c. sugar
- ½ c. light corn syrup
- 2 c. heavy cream, or non-dairy liquid coffee cream
- 1 lb. semisweet chocolate, melted (about 3½ c.)
- 2 c. marshmallow creme
- 1 c. Water Fondant, p. 16
- 1 t. vanilla
- 2 c. English or black walnuts

Combine sugar, corn syrup, and heavy cream and cook to 244°. Remove from heat and add semisweet chocolate, marshmallow, Fondant, and vanilla. Beat by hand or in a mixer until thick and creamy. Add walnuts. Spread in a 9 x 13-inch pan. Cut into squares when mixture holds its shape. Makes about 80 pieces.

## COFFEE FUDGE

*A mildly flavored fudge for coffee lovers, topped with chocolate and nuts.*

- 3 c. sugar
- ¾ c. milk
- 2 T. instant coffee powder
- ½ c. non-dairy liquid coffee cream
- 1 T. light corn syrup
- 2 T. butter
- 1 t. vanilla
- 1½ c. (6 oz.) chopped chocolate coating or wafers
- ¼ c. finely chopped nuts.

Combine sugar, milk, instant coffee, coffee cream and syrup in a 3-quart saucepan. Cover and bring to a boil. Uncover and place thermometer in pan; cook without stirring to 236°. Remove from heat; add butter and vanilla without stirring. Cool to lukewarm. Beat until candy begins to thicken; pour into a buttered 8-inch square pan. Melt the chocolate coating over hot, not boiling, water in a double boiler. Spread evenly over fudge, sprinkle nuts over chocolate. Cut into squares before candy becomes firm. Makes about 49 pieces.

## BUTTERSCOTCH NUT FUDGE

*Melted brown sugar and sour cream give this fudge its unusually good flavor.*

- ¼ c. butter
- 1 c. brown sugar
- 1 c. sugar
- ¾ c. sour cream
- 1 t. vanilla
- ½ c. chopped walnuts
  Walnut halves

Melt butter in a heavy saucepan. Add brown sugar and heat to boiling. Add sugar and sour cream. Cook over medium heat until sugar dissolves, then slightly higher heat to 236°. Without stirring cool at room temperature to lukewarm. Beat until mixture holds its shape and loses its gloss. Quickly add vanilla and nuts. Spread immediately in a buttered 8-inch square pan. Cool and cut into squares. Garnish with walnut halves. Makes about 49 pieces.

## CARAMEL FUDGE

*The flavor of this golden brown fudge comes from the caramelized sugar.*

- 6 c. sugar, divided
- 2 c. light cream
- ¼ t. baking soda
- ½ c. butter or margarine
- 8½ c. (2 lbs.) pecans, broken

Combine 4 cups sugar and cream in a heavy 4-quart saucepan. Set aside. Melt 2 cups sugar in a heavy 10-inch skillet over medium heat. Stir sugar constantly until it begins to melt. Heat sugar-cream mixture over medium heat. Continue melting sugar in skillet, stirring and watching closely so it does not scorch. As soon as it is completely melted, pour liquid sugar in a thin stream into boiling sugar-cream mixture, stirring constantly. Do not let sugar remain over heat after completely melted; this will produce a scorched taste. Cook combined mixtures to 246°. Remove from heat and add baking soda and butter. Stir in and let candy stand for 30 minutes. Add nuts. Stir to mix; pour into buttered 9-inch square pans. Cool slightly and cut into squares. Makes about 78 pieces.

*Pictured opposite: Butterscotch Nut Fudge and White Fudge.*

## WHITE FUDGE

*Excellently flavored, easy to make, creamy white fudge.*

- 1⅓ c. sugar
- ½ c. butter or margarine
- ⅔ c. non-dairy liquid coffee cream
- ⅛ t. salt
- ½ lb. white chocolate coating (wafers or block chocolate, finely chopped)
- 2 c. miniature marshmallows
- ½ t. vanilla
  Dipping chocolate (optional)

Cook first 4 ingredients without stirring to 238°. Remove from heat and add the next 3 ingredients. Blend well. Pack into a 9-inch square pan. When partially cool, cut into squares. Other colors of chocolate (pink, green, yellow, butterscotch) can be added instead of white, adding appropriate flavoring, fruits or nuts. The fudge can be packed in pans and cut in squares or bars, or rolled in a log and sliced, then dipped in chocolate. Makes about 64 pieces.

## GOLDEN FUDGE

*Try this beautiful fudge for easy making and delicious, unusual flavor.*

- 2½ c. (1 lb.) firmly packed brown sugar
- 1 c. sugar
- ½ c. butter or margarine
- 1 c. non-dairy liquid coffee cream
- 2¼ c. butterscotch wafers or chopped butterscotch blocks
- 4½ c. marshmallow creme
- 1 c. chopped pecans or other nuts
- ½ c. raisins
- ½ t. vanilla
- 1 t. butter-rum flavoring

Combine sugars, butter, and coffee cream in a heavy 2½-quart saucepan. Place on medium heat and stir until butter is melted. Cook without stirring to 238°, about 15 minutes. Remove from heat; add butterscotch and marshmallow. Stir until thoroughly blended. Add nuts, raisins, and flavorings. Pour into 2 greased 8-inch square pans. Let set several hours until firm. Cut into squares. Keep in closed container. Makes about 98 pieces.

## MEXICAN ORANGE FUDGE

*Golden color and rich flavor is achieved by the caramelization of the sugar, and the addition of orange rind.*

3 c. sugar, divided
¼ c. boiling water
1 c. non-dairy liquid coffee cream
¼ t. salt
2 t. grated orange rind
1 c. chopped pecans or walnuts

Melt 1 cup sugar in a heavy 3-quart saucepan, stirring constantly so it does not burn. Very carefully, add boiling water, stirring to mix. Add remaining sugar, coffee cream, and salt. Place over medium heat and stir until all ingredients are blended together and mixture boils. Cook to 238° without stirring. Remove from heat and cool to lukewarm. When lukewarm, beat until candy loses its gloss and holds its shape. Fold in grated orange rind and nuts. Spread in a buttered 8-inch square pan. Cut into squares. Makes about 48 pieces.

## PINEAPPLE FUDGE

*An excellent, unusually flavored fudge.*

2 c. sugar
1 c. brown sugar
1 8½-oz. can crushed pineapple and juice
½ c. milk
1 T. corn syrup
¼ t. salt
2 T. butter
24 large marshmallows
1 t. vanilla
1 c. chopped pecans or walnuts

Combine sugars, pineapple and juice, milk, corn syrup, salt, and butter in a 2-quart saucepan. Cook to 238°, stirring occasionally. Remove from heat and add marshmallows and vanilla. Mix together to melt marshmallow, then beat until mixture becomes heavy and creamy. Add nuts. Spread in a buttered 8-inch square pan. Cut into squares when cool and firm. Makes about 49 pieces.

## LAYERED FUDGE SQUARES

*A two-part recipe. Make the fondant first and set aside, then the fudge layer.*

### FONDANT LAYER

2 c. sugar
Dash of salt
2 T. light corn syrup
¾ c. boiling water
½ t. vanilla
½ c. marshmallow creme

Combine sugar, salt, corn syrup, and boiling water in a 2-quart saucepan. Cover and bring to a rolling boil. Remove lid and place thermometer in pan; cook without stirring to 240°. Pour out on marble slab. Cool to lukewarm and work with spatula until creamy and white, then knead smooth with hands. Add vanilla and marshmallow. Work into the fondant. Let fondant stand, uncovered, until completely cold. For Layered Fudge Squares, pat and roll fondant into an 8-inch square between two pieces of waxed paper. Set aside.

*Note:* To store fondant, wrap in waxed paper and place in a tightly covered jar. Keep in refrigerator.

### FUDGE LAYER

5 c. (1½ lbs.) chopped milk chocolate or sweet coating
¼ c. light cream
¼ c. half and half
1½ t. vanilla
¾ c. chopped nuts

In the top of a double boiler, melt milk chocolate or sweet coating over hot, not boiling, water. Heat cream, half and half, and vanilla to scalding. Remove from heat and cool to about 130°. *Do not allow temperature to drop below 125°.* Add warm cream mixture to melted chocolate all at once and beat until smooth and well blended. Remove from hot water and let cool until pliable. Beat with an electric mixer until candy is light and fluffy. Spread half in an 8-inch square pan which has been lined with lightweight foil. Place the fondant square over the fudge; spread the remaining fudge over the fondant. Sprinkle with nuts, and press the nuts into the fudge. Cut into squares when firm, and wrap in waxed paper. Makes about 48 pieces.

## STRAWSTACKS

*A fudge-type candy in different form, adding nice variety to a plate of assorted fudges.*

- 2 c. brown sugar
- 1 c. non-dairy liquid coffee cream
- 1 T. butter
- 1 c. coconut

In a saucepan mix all ingredients except coconut; cook without stirring to 238°. Remove from heat, cool 30 minutes, and beat until mixture thickens. Add coconut, blend in well. Drop by spoonsful onto waxed paper in the shape of strawstacks. Makes about 60 pieces.

## COCONUT FUDGE

*A coconut lover's delight.*

- 3 c. sugar
- 1 T. light corn syrup
- 1 c. milk
- 1 8-oz. pkg. shredded coconut

Place all ingredients in a 2-quart saucepan. Cook, stirring occasionally, to 237°. Cool in the pan or pour out on a marble slab to cool. When warm, beat in pan or work with a spatula on slab until candy turns dull and creamy. Spread in an 8-inch square pan. Cut into squares. Makes about 49 pieces.

## PEANUT BUTTER FUDGE

*A no-cook fudge, using confectioners' sugar.*

- ½ c. butter
- ⅓ c. chunky peanut butter
- 1 lb. confectioners' sugar
- ⅓ c. dry powdered milk
- ⅓ c. light corn syrup
- 1 T. water
- 1 t. vanilla
- ½ to 1 c. chopped peanuts

In top of double boiler, combine butter and peanut butter and melt. Sift together confectioners' sugar and dry powdered milk; set aside. Add corn syrup, water, and vanilla to the peanut butter mixture. Stir in about half the dry ingredients, blend well, then add the remaining dry ingredients. Blend until very smooth. Stir in chopped peanuts. Turn into a buttered 8-inch square pan. Cut into squares. Makes about 48 pieces.

## THREE LAYER FUDGE

*An easy, attractive candy with a white center layer.*

- ¾ c. butter, divided
- 1 1-oz. square baking chocolate
- 1¼ c. sugar
- 2 t. vanilla, divided
- 1 egg
- 2 c. crushed graham crackers
- 1 c. flaked coconut
- ½ c. nuts
- 2 T. light cream
- 2 c. confectioners' sugar
- 6 oz. (1 generous cup, unmelted) semi-sweet chocolate
- 3 T. paramount crystals (optional)

Melt ½ cup butter and baking chocolate. Blend in sugar, 1 teaspoon vanilla, egg, graham crackers, coconut, and nuts. Mix well with a spoon, then with hands. Press mixture in an ungreased 11½ x 7½ x 1½-inch pan; refrigerate. Mix together ¼ cup butter, light cream, confectioners' sugar, and 1 teaspoon vanilla; beat well. Spread over chocolate mixture in pan; chill. Melt semisweet chocolate and paramount crystals over hot, not boiling, water. Spread melted chocolate over white filling; chill. Cut into 1-inch squares. Store in refrigerator. Makes about 56 pieces.

## CHRISTMAS FUDGE

*Candied fruit makes this fudge attractive and good.*

- 3 c. sugar
- 1½ c. non-dairy liquid coffee cream
- 1 c. light corn syrup
- 1 t. salt
- 2 t. vanilla
- 2 c. candied pineapple and cherries
- 1 c. sliced almonds
- 1½ c. broken pecan pieces

Combine sugar, cream, syrup, and salt in a heavy saucepan. Stir to dissolve sugar; cook to 236° without stirring. Remove from heat. Add vanilla and beat with electric mixer until mixture is creamy and begins to hold its shape. Stir in pineapple, cherries, almonds, and pecans by hand. Press into two buttered 8-inch square pans and chill until firm enough to cut. Let stand in refrigerator 24 hours before serving. Makes about 80 pieces.

# MINTS

## MINTS MADE FROM ICECAP COLORED COATINGS

*Mints made in this way are simple to make and very delicious.*

Melt 1 lb. colored chopped coating over hot (not boiling) water in a double boiler. When melted and smooth, add 2 or 3 drops of peppermint oil to the chocolate (vary the amount according to taste.) By using a spoon or a candy funnel fill the cavities of a mold (using soft rubber and clear plastic molds). Be careful not to overfill and tap mold to release air bubbles. Place mold in freezer for a few minutes, then remove candy. It is not necessary to grease or prepare the molds in any way. Any flavoring oil can be added to the chocolate to make good candies other than peppermints. Makes 50 roses and 75 to 80 leaves.

## MINT PINWHEELS

*A colorful way to serve party mints.*

1 recipe Water Fondant, p. 16
    Green food coloring and oil of wintergreen flavoring
    Red food coloring and peppermint oil flavoring

Divide Water Fondant into 4 equal parts. Color one portion light green and flavor with oil of wintergreen. Roll between 2 pieces of waxed paper to a rectangle about 14 x 5-inches. Remove top piece of waxed paper. Roll 1 portion of white fondant between 2 pieces of waxed paper to same size. Remove top piece of waxed paper. Lift white fondant by paper, invert on top of green. Press layers together. Remove top piece of waxed paper. Roll tightly, jelly-roll fashion, removing waxed paper as you roll. Wrap roll in waxed paper. Chill about 1 hour until firm but not hard. Cut into ¼-inch slices. Repeat process with other two portions, coloring one part pink and flavoring with peppermint oil. In a cool place, store candy between layers of waxed paper in covered containers. Makes 50 to 60 mints.

*Pictured opposite: Mints made from Icecap Colored Coatings, Mint Pinwheels, Bavarian Mints, Cream Cheese Mints.*

## BAVARIAN MINTS

*Light flavored and light textured, melt-in-your mouth chocolate mints.*

1¼ lbs. chocolate coating (sweet, semi-sweet, or a combination)
4½ c. dry fondant
2½ T. light corn syrup
1 c. evaporated milk
½ t. invertase
⅛ t. peppermint oil

Melt chocolate in a double boiler. Combine dry fondant, corn syrup, evaporated milk, invertase, and peppermint oil, and beat on high speed of electric mixer 12 to 15 minutes. Gradually add the melted coating, beating at medium speed. When all is added, whip at high speed for 30 seconds, then spread out in a 10 x 15-inch buttered pan to set. Cut into squares. Makes about 90 pieces.

## EASY CHOCOLATE COVERED MINTS

*Use chocolate wafers and make mints with almost no work.*

Place any chocolate flavored wafer in a container with an airtight lid. Place a few drops of peppermint oil on a piece of cotton and place in container with chocolate pieces. Cover tightly. Stir chocolate pieces every hour or so to distribute peppermint. Cover flavored chocolate pieces with melted chocolate or serve plain.

## CREAM CHEESE MINTS

*Good creamy soft mints.*

1 3-oz. pkg. cream cheese, room temperature
    Color and flavor as desired
2½ c. confectioners' sugar
    Granulated sugar

Beat cream cheese until softened, add color and flavor. Gradually beat in confectioners' sugar. Knead the mixture until of a pie dough consistency ( a soft or firmer candy can be made by adding or decreasing the amount of sugar). Pinch off a small piece, form into a small marble-sized ball and roll in granulated sugar. Press the candy into a soft rubber mold, and shape. Remove excess and unmold at once onto waxed paper. Makes about 40 to 50 mints.

## BUTTER MINTS

*A creamy, buttery, simple-to-make mint pattty.*

2 T. butter
3 T. milk
1 15¼-oz. pkg. creamy white frosting mix
3 drops peppermint oil (or other flavoring)
Green food coloring (or other coloring)

Melt together butter and milk. Stir in frosting mix. Heat to about 150°. (Do not overheat.) Blend in flavoring and coloring. Drop from the tip of a teaspoon or from a candy funnel onto waxed paper. When mints are firm, store in a tightly covered container in refrigerator. Use within a few days. Makes 50 mints.

## MINT SANDWICH

*Chocolate-green-chocolate layered mints. Very pretty and good, too.*

3½ c. semisweet chocolate coating, finely chopped or wafers
2 c. green chocolate coating, finely chopped or wafers
2 T. coconut oil or vegetable shortening, divided
Few drops of peppermint oil

Melt chocolates in separate double boilers over hot, not boiling, water. Add 1 tablespoon coconut oil to each pot of chocolate. Flavor green chocolate with peppermint oil. Cool both coatings down to between 85° to 90°; keep warm water in the bottom of the double boilers. Thinly spread one-half of the dark chocolate over waxed paper. Wait until layer is just about firm, then spread the entire pot of green chocolate thinly over all of the chocolate layer. Again, wait until green layer is almost firm, then spread remaining semisweet chocolate over the top. Let the candy harden, then cut with a sharp knife dipped in hot water and dried. Can build up several layers if desired, and different colors can be used. Makes about 60 squares.

## CREAM MINTS

*Dropped, creamy fondant mints.*

½ c. water
¼ t. plain gelatin
¼ c. sugar
1¼ lbs. Simple or Water Fondant, p.16, 22
Flavoring
Coloring

Put water and gelatin in a heavy saucepan and heat over low heat until gelatin is dissolved. Add sugar; continue heating until sugar is dissolved. Add fondant. Continue heating to 155° to 160°. Add flavoring and coloring as desired. Drop from a spoon or candy funnel onto waxed paper. Remove from waxed paper when dry. (In humid weather add ¼ pound more fondant.) When tops are dry, turn mints over to dry on bottom. When completely dry but creamy inside, store in a covered container. Makes about 100 patties.

## MELTAWAY MINTS

*Peppermint-flavored square chocolate mints to be dipped.*

1½ lbs. dipping chocolate, finely chopped (milk, semisweet, or mixture)
⅔ c. melted vegetable shortening
3 or 4 drops oil of peppermint (or to taste)
Dipping chocolate

Melt 1½ lbs. of dipping chocolate over hot water in a double boiler. Beat until smooth. Add shortening, beating until just blended. Pour into a small bowl and chill in refrigerator until the consistency of soft custard. Occasionally scrape from the sides and bottom of the bowl. Beat with an electric mixer about 30 seconds. Do not overbeat. It will appear lighter in color and texture. Mix in peppermint and pour out on a waxed paper-lined 10 x 13-inch pan. Place a piece of waxed paper on top of batch and level off. Let stand in a cool place until firm but not hard. Cut into squares; leave in the pan until ready to dip. Makes about 80 pieces.

# CARAMELS

### CARAMELS

*Old-fashioned chewy caramels, rich and buttery.*

- 2 c. sugar
- ½ t. lecithin
- ½ c. butter
- ¾ c. light corn syrup
- 2 c. heavy cream, divided

In a saucepan, combine sugar, lecithin, butter, corn syrup, and 1 cup of cream. Bring to a rolling boil. Slowly add the remaining cup of cream so boiling does not stop. Reduce heat as the temperature increases. Cook to 250° for a very firm caramel, or a few degrees less for a softer candy. Pour into a buttered 8-inch square pan. Do not scrape the candy out of the saucepan as this may cause the candy to crystalize. Makes about 48 pieces.

### MOLASSES PEANUT CHEWS

*These have a distinctive molasses flavor and make very fine dipped candies.*

- 1 c. molasses
- 1 c. light corn syrup
- 1 c. sugar
- 2 T. water
- ⅓ c. invert sugar
- 2 T. butter
- 1 lb. peanuts, chopped or crushed
- ½ t. salt
- ½ t. baking soda
  Dipping chocolate

In a large saucepan, combine molasses, corn syrup, sugar, water, invert sugar, and butter and cook to 256°. Remove from heat and add peanuts, salt, and soda. Mix thoroughly and spread in a greased 9 x 13-inch pan. Cool, then turn out on a greased marble slab; stretch to desired thickness. Cut in small bars and dip in chocolate. Makes about 20 to 25 bars.

## CHOCOLATE CARAMELS

*For the chocolate lover.*

- 3 c. sugar
- ½ c. light corn syrup
- ½ lb. honeycomb
- 1 c. coffee cream
- 3 T. butter
  Pinch of salt
- 1 c. heavy cream
- 4 1-oz. squares baking chocolate, melted
- 2 t. vanilla
  Nuts, if desired

In a saucepan, combine sugar, corn syrup, honey, coffee cream, butter and salt. Cook to 230°. Add heavy cream and heat to 230°. Add baking chocolate and cook to 248° in the summer; 245° in the winter. Remove from heat, stir in vanilla and nuts. Pour into a buttered 9-inch square pan. Makes about 64 pieces.

## CREAM NUT CARAMELS

*Nut-filled and chewy.*

- 1 c. heavy cream
- 1 c. coffee cream
- 2 c. sugar
- 1 c. light corn syrup
- ¼ c. butter
- ½ t. salt
- 1 t. vanilla
- ½ c. chopped pecans

In a small saucepan, combine heavy cream and coffee cream, and warm. Place one cup of the cream mixture into a 4-quart saucepan, add sugar and syrup. Cook for about 5 minutes. Very slowly add the remaining cream mixture so that boiling does not stop. Cook about 5 more minutes. Add butter, small amounts at a time; and cook slowly to 244° to 246°. Watch thermometer during cooking; when it reaches 230° lower heat to prevent scorching. If a heavy saucepan is used, no stirring should be necessary. When thermometer reaches 244° to 246°, remove candy from heat and let stand 10 minutes. Carefully stir in salt, vanilla and pecans. Pour into a well greased 8-inch square pan. Let stand until firm, then cut into squares and wrap. Makes about 49 pieces.

## PENNY'S TIME-SAVING CARAMELS

*An excellent caramel, quick-cooking with the flavor of brown sugar and butter.*

1 c. butter
2¼ c. (1 lb.) brown sugar, firmly packed
⅛ t. salt
1 c. light corn syrup
1 15-oz. can sweetened condensed milk
1 t. vanilla

In a saucepan, melt butter. Stir in sugar and salt, then add corn syrup and mix well. Add sweetened condensed milk, stirring constantly. Continue stirring and cook to 245°. Remove from heat and stir in vanilla. Pour into a 9-inch buttered pan. When cold, cut into squares and wrap. Makes about 49 pieces.

## CARAMEL-COCONUT ROLL-UPS

*A delicious combination of flavors, attractive and simple.*

⅓ c. invert sugar
1 c. light corn syrup
2¼ c. liquid non-dairy coffee cream, divided
1¼ c. heavy cream
2¼ c. sugar
5 T. butter
½ t. salt
1 t. vanilla
1½ lbs. prepared Coconut Bonbon recipe, p. 18

Combine invert sugar, syrup, ¼ cup coffee cream, heavy cream, sugar, and butter in a saucepan. Bring to a rolling boil. Add remaining coffee cream slowly so boiling does not stop. Cook without stirring to 245°. Turn heat down a little as mixture thickens. Remove from heat and stir in salt and vanilla. Pour into a 9 x 13-inch pan. When cool and firm, turn out on a greased marble slab. Distribute prepared Coconut Bonbon evenly over the top of the caramel. Roll tightly together. Stretch the roll to the desired diameter. Slice and wrap the pieces. Makes about 70 pieces.

34

## HONEY CARAMELS

*A very unusual caramel, not as sweet as some, with a different texture and flavor. Very good.*

1¼ c. sugar
1½ c. heavy cream
½ c. honey
6 T. flour
6 T. butter
1 t. vanilla
1 c. chopped nuts

In a large saucepan, combine sugar, heavy cream, honey, flour and butter. Cook stirring constantly, to 245°. Remove from heat; stir in vanilla and nuts. Pour out into a buttered 8-inch square pan. Cut into squares when cool. Makes about 30 pieces.

## BLACK WALNUT CARAMELS

*These will remind you of winter days on the farm when you sat around the fire picking out black walnut goodies.*

3 c. brown sugar, packed
2 c. light corn syrup
1 c. butter
¾ c. sweetened condensed milk
½ t. vanilla
1⅓ c. black walnuts

Combine sugar, corn syrup, butter, and condensed milk in a heavy pan. Cook over medium heat, stirring constantly, until sugar is dissolved and mixture boils. Continue cooking to 248°, stirring now and then to prevent scorching. Remove from heat and stir in vanilla and walnuts. Pour into two buttered 8-inch square pans. When firm, cut and wrap in waxed paper squares. Best stored in refrigerator. Makes about 98 pieces.

*Pictured opposite: Honey Caramels, Black Walnut Caramels, Caramel-Coconut Roll-ups.*

# MISCELLANEOUS

## SEA FOAM

*A beige, delicately flavored, smooth and creamy candy. Store airtight.*

1¾ c. light brown sugar
¾ c. sugar
½ c. hot water
¼ c. light corn syrup
¼ t. salt
2 egg whites
1 t. vanilla
1 t. pecan flavoring
¼ c. pecan pieces

Combine sugars, water, corn syrup, and salt in a heavy 2-quart saucepan. Cook, covered until mixture boils rapidly. Remove lid, place thermometer in pan, and cook without stirring to 260°. Remove from heat. Beat 2 egg whites until stiff. Pour hot syrup in thin stream over egg whites, beating constantly with electric mixer on high speed. Add vanilla and pecan flavoring. Continue beating until soft peaks form and candy starts to lose its gloss. Stir in pecans and drop by spoonfuls on waxed paper. Makes about 50 pieces.

## DIVINITY

*Smooth, creamy, pure white candy. Store airtight.*

2½ c. sugar
½ c. light corn syrup
½ c. water
¼ t. salt
2 egg whites
1 t. vanilla
½ c. finely chopped nuts

Cook sugar, corn syrup, water, and salt to 248°. Cover and boil for 3 minutes. Uncover and place thermometer in pan. Beat egg whites until stiff but not dry. When syrup is 248° slowly pour about one-half of the syrup over the egg whites, beating constantly with the mixer. Cook remaining syrup to 272°. Pour the remaining syrup over the candy very slowly, beating constantly. Beat until mixture begins to lose its gloss and soft peaks form. Mix in vanilla and nuts. Drop by teaspoonfuls on waxed paper.
Makes about 50 pieces.

## NO-COOK DIVINITY

*A new quick method for an old favorite.*

1 7-oz. pkg. fluffy white or cherry icing mix
⅓ c. light corn syrup
1 t. vanilla
½ c. boiling water
1 lb. confectioners' sugar
½ c. finely chopped nuts

Combine icing mix, corn syrup, vanilla, and water in a small mixing bowl and beat at high speed until stiff peaks form. Transfer beaten mixture to a larger bowl and at low speed, beat in confectioners' sugar. Fold in nuts. Drop by teaspoonfuls onto waxed paper and top with additional nuts if desired. Allow to dry on top, then turn and dry bottoms. Dry 12 hours, turning pieces over once or twice. Store in an air-tight container. Makes about 45 pieces.

## HOLIDAY DIVINITY

*Fluffy, colorful candy, flavored and colored with gelatin.*

3 c. sugar
¾ c. light corn syrup
¾ c. water
¼ t. salt
2 egg whites
1 3-oz. pkg. flavored gelatin
1 t. vanilla
½ c. flaked coconut
½ c. finely chopped pecans

Place sugar, corn syrup, water and salt in a 2-quart saucepan. Cover with a tight lid and bring to a boil. Remove lid, place thermometer in pan, and cook to 250° without stirring. Remove from heat, set aside. Beat egg whites until soft peaks form. Add gelatin and beat into egg whites. Pour hot syrup slowly over flavored, beaten egg whites, beating constantly on high speed of electric mixer until soft peaks form and hold. Add vanilla, coconut, and nuts. Drop from teaspoon onto waxed paper. Makes about 70 candies.

## ANOTHER DIVINITY

*An exceptionally fine divinity, with just a touch of butterscotch flavor.*

- 2 c. sugar
- ½ c. water
- 3 T. light corn syrup
- 3 egg whites, room temperature
  Dash of salt
- ½ t. butterscotch flavor
- ½ t. vanilla
- 1 c. chopped pecans or walnuts

Cook sugar, water, and corn syrup in a covered saucepan until mixture boils rapidly. Remove lid and place thermometer in pan. Cook to 236°. Whip egg whites until stiff. Pour 1/3 cup cooked syrup slowly over the beating egg whites. Continue beating at medium speed. When remaining syrup cooks to 264° add it to beaten egg white mixture, pouring in a small stream and beating constantly. Beat 12 to 15 minutes longer, until batch loses gloss. Remove beater; add salt, flavorings and nuts. Drop by spoonfuls on waxed paper. Store in tight container. Makes about 40 pieces.

## GUMDROPS

*An easy, chewy, and inexpensive candy. Use a cherry flip mold to mold this candy into attractive pieces.*

- 1 1¾-oz. pkg. powdered fruit pectin
- ¾ c. water
- ½ t. baking soda
- 1 c. sugar
- 1 c. light corn syrup
- 3 to 4 drops peppermint oil (or other flavoring oil)
  Red or green food color

Lightly grease candy molds. In a small saucepan combine fruit pectin, water and baking soda; set aside. In a 2-quart saucepan combine sugar and corn syrup, mixing well. Cook both mixtures, stirring alternately until foam subsides in soda mixture, about 5 minutes. Pour pectin mixture in a slow steady stream into the boiling sugar mixture, stirring constantly. Boil and stir one minute more. Remove from heat and stir in flavoring and food color. Pour into prepared molds. Let set 24 hours. Take out of molds. Let stand at least a day before packaging. Makes about 20 pieces.

## TURKISH DELIGHTS

*An easy flavorful jelly candy.*

- ½ c. water
- 2 c. sugar
- 2½ T. gelatin
- ¼ c. cold water
- ½ c. orange juice
- ¼ c. lemon juice
  Food coloring as desired
  Confectioners' sugar

Cook ½ cup water and sugar to 255°, remove from heat. Soften gelatin in ¼ cup cold water for 5 minutes. Add gelatin mixture to cooked syrup. Add juices and food coloring. Stir and strain through a fine sieve. Pour into a buttered 8-inch square pan. Let stand until firm. Turn out, cut into squares and roll in confectioners' sugar. Makes about 49 pieces.

## RASPBERRY JELLIES

*This colorful candy is a nice addition to a box or plate of candy.*

- 2⅔ c. sugar
- ⅓ c. pectin
- 2½ c. cool water
- 1⅔ c. light corn syrup
- 1 12-oz. jar raspberry jam
- 1 T. liquid citric acid *or* ½ t. citric acid and 1 T. hot water
- 1 c. walnuts
  Red food coloring
  Confectioners' or granulated sugar

Combine sugar and pectin in a 4-quart saucepan and mix well. Slowly add cool water, stirring until smooth. Bring to a boil, stirring constantly. Add syrup, which has been heated to boiling. Cook rapidly to 220°, stirring occasionally. Add mashed raspberry jam and a few drops red food coloring. Cook to 224° stirring constantly. Remove candy from heat and add liquid citric acid. Fold in nuts. Pour into a buttered 9-inch square pan. When cool and firm enough, cut and roll in confectioners' or granulated sugar. Makes about 64 pieces.

## MARZIPAN 1

*A favorite marzipan recipe. Rubbed to a soft sheen, it gives molded articles a lovely finish.*

- 1 lb. almond paste
- ⅓ c. light corn syrup
- 1 t. vanilla
- 1¼ c. marshmallow creme
- 4 to 6 c. confectioners' sugar
- Food coloring

Combine almond paste, corn syrup, vanilla, and marshmallow creme; mix well. Gradually add confectioners' sugar. Knead until uniform and smooth. Color as desired. Makes about 50 pieces.


## MARZIPAN 2

*This is especially nice for strawberries.*

- 1 12-oz. pkg. macaroon coconut
- 1 c. sweetened condensed milk
- 2 3-oz. pkgs. strawberry or cherry gelatin

Combine ingredients. Shape as desired. Makes about 75 pieces.


## MARZIPAN 3

*A good, pliable recipe for molding or filling tarts and cakes.*

- 1 c. almond paste
- 2 egg whites, unbeaten
- 3 c. confectioners' sugar, divided
- ½ t. vanilla or rum flavoring
- Paste food color

Place almond paste in a bowl and knead until soft. Add egg whites and mix well. Add confectioners' sugar one cup at a time. Continue kneading and add flavoring; marzipan should feel like heavy pie dough. Use confectioners' sugar when dusting table to prevent marzipan from sticking. Color with paste color. Mold by hand. Touch up with paste food color where necessary. Makes about 30 pieces.
*Note:* Use yellow color for bananas and pears, orange for carrots and pumpkins, red for strawberries and apples, and purple for plums and grapes. Make potatoes white and dust with cocoa.

## BROWN AND WHITE BALLS

*Attractive as well as good.*

- 1 lb. semisweet chocolate
- 1 15-oz. can sweetened condensed milk
- Chocolate decorettes
- 1 egg white
- 2 T. evaporated milk
- 1 T. cold water
- 1 t. vanilla
- 5 c. confectioners' sugar

Melt semisweet chocolate in the top of a double boiler over hot, not boiling, water. Add sweetened condensed milk. When mixture is completely melted and blended together, cool. Roll mixture into 1½-inch balls, then roll each ball in chocolate decorettes and chill. Beat together egg white, evaporated milk, cold water, and vanilla. When well blended, add confectioners' sugar very slowly. Knead until smooth. Cover with waxed paper and a damp cloth; let stand about one hour. Form into 1½-inch balls and chill. Cut both chocolate and white balls into quarters. Alternate dark and white quarters to form new balls, so each ball will have 2 white and 2 dark sections. Chill again. Makes about 40 balls.

## TAFFY

*Plain, old-fashioned taffy to flavor and color many ways.*

- 2 c. sugar
- 2 T. cornstarch
- 1 c. light corn syrup
- ¾ c. water
- 1 t. salt
- 2 T. margarine
- ¼ t. any flavoring oil
- Food color as desired

In a heavy saucepan, mix together sugar and cornstarch. Stir in corn syrup, water, salt, and margarine. Place over medium heat and stir until sugar dissolves. Cover pan and bring to a boil for 2 or 3 minutes. Uncover, place thermometer in pan and cook to 266°. Remove from heat and add flavoring and food color. Stir gently, pour on a greased marble slab or a shallow greased pan to cool. When cool enough to handle, grease hands and pull until light in color and has a satiny gloss. Pull into a long rope, cut with scissors and wrap in waxed paper squares, twisting ends. Makes about 50 pieces.

*Pictured opposite: Marzipan and Taffy; Molded Chocolate Covered Cherries, p. 40.*

## MOLASSES TAFFY

*Try this distinctively molasses-flavored taffy with peanut butter as suggested.*

    1 12-oz. jar molasses
    ¾ c. sugar
    2 T. butter
    2 t. cider vinegar
      Peanut Butter Balls (optional), p. 17

Combine molasses, sugar, butter and vinegar in a heavy saucepan. Cover tightly, bring to a boil two or three minutes. Remove lid, place thermometer in pan and cook to 264°, stirring occasionally. Pour hot candy into a shallow buttered pan or onto a buttered marble slab. As it starts to cool, pull edges toward middle. Work with a spatula until the candy is quite firm, then pull with buttered hands until it becomes golden colored. Roll in long strips and cut in 1-inch pieces. Wrap in waxed paper. Or roll Peanut Butter in ropes instead of balls; placed in center of a band of taffy and wrap taffy around peanut butter. Cut into 1-inch pieces and wrap. Makes about 30 pieces.

## MOLDED CHOCOLATE COVERED CHERRIES

      Milk or semisweet chocolate coating
    1 c. dry fondant
      Liquid from cherries
    90 small maraschino cherries

Melt sweet or semisweet chocolate flavored coating in a double boiler. Using a half-inch, good quality brush, brush molds with chocolate, checking for weak spots by holding the molds toward a light. Chill the chocolate lined molds in a freezer. While they are hardening, mix a small amount of juice from the maraschino cherries with dry fondant to form a heavy liquid. Fill the chocolate covered molds about half full of the liquid. Drop a cherry into the liquid, and seal with more melted chocolate. Make sure before you seal the molds with chocolate, there is a small rim of chocolate not covered by the liquid. Makes 90 cherries.

## ROLLED CHOCOLATE COVERED CHERRIES

    3 c. dry fondant
    90 maraschino cherries
      Liquid from cherries
    3 drops invertase
      Dipping chocolate (optional)

Place dry fondant in the bottom of a flat sheet cake pan. Put drained maraschino cherries on the fondant and roll to coat with fondant. Place cherries in another pan and spray with maraschino cherry juice and a few drops of invertase. Roll cherries again in dry fondant. Mist and roll cherries several times until they are well-coated with dry fondant and to the size you desire. Either dip the fondant covered cherries in prepared chocolate or drop in chocolate-lined molds, seal with melted chocolate and chill in freezer until set. Makes 90 cherries.

## FONDANT DIPPED CHOCOLATE COVERED CHERRIES

    3 c. dry fondant
    1 T. water
    2 T. liquid from cherries
    1 T. light corn syrup
    3 drops invertase
    90 small maraschino cherries
      Dipping chocolate

Mix together dry fondant, water, cherry liquid, and corn syrup; heat in a double boiler to 165°. Add invertase. Dip cherries in the hot fondant. Cool and dry on waxed paper. (For a heavier fondant coating, dip cherries a second time, and dry on waxed paper.) Dip in chocolate. Makes 90 cherries.

## CEREAL CANDY

*A longtime favorite of our family.*

    5 c. cornflakes
    3½ c. crisp rice cereal
    2 c. salted peanuts
    1½ c. sugar
    1 c. heavy cream
    1 c. light corn syrup

Combine cereals and nuts in a large bowl; set aside. In a large pan, combine sugar, cream, and syrup; bring to a boil and cook to 250°. Pour over cereal and nut mixture, stirring until completely coated. Press mixture into a buttered 9 x 13-inch pan. Cut into squares. Makes 48 pieces.

## CRISPY CEREAL CANDY

*Super easy, use any cereal. A great way to use leftover dipping chocolate.*

Melt chocolate flavored coating over hot, not boiling, water. Stir any natural cereal into the melted chocolate. Drop by spoonfuls on waxed paper.

## CRAZY QUICK CANDY

*This candy has a surprising consistency—crunchy and layered.*

- 1 c. light corn syrup
- ¾ c. peanut butter
  Melted sweet chocolate

Place corn syrup in a small 1-quart saucepan. Boil until syrup turns golden brown. Pour hot corn syrup over peanut butter, beating on medium speed of mixer until ingredients are combined. Immediately turn out on a buttered cookie sheet and pat out to about ¼-inch thickness. When cool, spread one side with melted sweet chocolate, let chocolate harden, then turn candy over and spread other side with chocolate. Break or cut into pieces. Makes about 40 pieces.

## PECAN ROLLS

*Another favorite recipe. Just delicious!*

- 2½ c. sugar
- ½ c. light corn syrup
- ½ c. water
- 2 c. marshmallow creme
  Flavoring and coloring as desired
- ⅓ c. vegetable shortening
  Dipping chocolate or Caramel Coating, p. 45
  Chopped pecans

In a saucepan, cook sugar, syrup, and water to 256° or to 254° for a softer roll. Remove from heat; add marshmallow creme. Do not stir; let marshmallow creme set on the syrup for 10 minutes. After 10 minutes, stir well and beat. Add flavoring and coloring as desired. Beat with mixer at medium speed until mixture will break off when beaters are lifted. Add shortening. Add nuts and/or fruit if desired. Pour batch out on marble slab sprinkled with confectioners' sugar. When cool enough to handle, form into rolls. Dip in Caramel Coating. Roll in pecans. Makes about 20 rolls.

## PEANUT PATTIES  1

*Chewy, opaque patties.*

- 2 c. sugar
- 1 c. brown sugar
- ½ c. margarine
- 3½ c. light corn syrup
- 2 t. salt (less if peanuts are salted)
- ½ c. water
- ¼ t. baking soda
- 5 c. (2 lbs.) roasted Spanish peanuts

In a large pan, combine sugars, margarine, corn syrup, salt, and water; mix thoroughly. Cover tightly and bring to a boil; uncover and place thermometer in pan. Cook, without stirring, to 244°. Remove from heat and stir in soda. Add nuts and mix in well. Drop from a spoon onto a well-greased cookie sheet. Cool and wrap in waxed paper or plastic wrap. Makes 50 patties.

## PEANUT PATTIES  2

*Clear, chewy, and nutty.*

- ⅔ c. light corn syrup
- ½ c. sugar
- 3½ T. butter
- 1½ c. coarsely chopped peanuts

Butter 24 muffin cups. Combine corn syrup, sugar, and butter in a saucepan and cook to 238°. Remove from heat and stir in nuts. Drop approximately 1 tablespoon candy into each muffin cup. Let cool completely; remove patties, wrap in individual plastic wrap, and store in a tightly covered container. Makes 24 patties.

## STUFFED DATES

*Attractive and flavorful addition to a box of candy.*

- 1 T. butter
- 1¾ c. sifted confectioners' sugar
- 2 T. orange juice
- 1 8-oz. pkg. dates
  Granulated sugar (optional)

Thoroughly cream butter and confectioners' sugar together. Add orange juice. Blend together and form mixture into long thin rolls. If mixture is too thin, add a little more confectioners' sugar; if too thick, add more orange juice. Cut rolls in lengths to fit into pitted dates and stuff dates. Roll in granulated sugar if desired. May be garnished with nut slivers, candied cherries, or slivered gumdrops. Makes about 32.

## FRUIT AND NUT EASTER EGG

*This can be made long before needed. Improves as it ripens.*

2¼ c. sugar
1 c. light corn syrup
¾ c. hot water
½ lb. marshmallow creme
½ c. shortening, melted
¼ c. confectioners' sugar
2 c. candied fruit (cherries and pineapple)
Nuts
Dipping chocolate

In a saucepan, cook sugar, syrup, and water to 265°. Add marshmallow creme and beat until almost firm. Add melted shortening, confectioners' sugar, candied fruit, and nuts. Mix well, shape eggs by hand and dip. Will keep 6 to 8 months. Makes 10 eggs.

## CREAMY EASTER EGGS

*Excellent also for candy bars. Just pat candy into a square on waxed paper, cut into bars and dip in chocolate.*

3 T. invert sugar
⅓ c. chopped candied cherries and pineapple
⅓ c. chopped walnuts or pecans
3 c. sugar
2 T. light corn syrup
Dash of salt
½ c. water
½ t. vanilla
1 c. plus 2 T. marshmallow creme
Dipping chocolate

In a small saucepan, combine invert sugar, fruit, and nuts. Stir and boil 2 to 3 minutes; drain, reserving liquid. Combine liquid, sugar, corn syrup, salt and water in a 2-quart saucepan. Cover tightly, and bring to a boil. Uncover and place thermometer in pan; cook to 250°. Pour candy out on a marble slab and cool to lukewarm. Work candy with a spatula until it is opaque. Add vanilla and marshmallow creme. Continue to paddle candy until creamy. Add prepared fruit and nuts; knead into candy. Form into egg shapes and let stand for a couple of hours. Dip in chocolate. Makes 16 medium-size eggs.

*Pictured opposite: Fruit and Nut Easter Egg, and Sugared Marshmallow Bunnies and Chicks; Rock Candy Sucker, p. 59; Green Coconut Nests, p. 48; Painted Chocolate Molds, p. 11.*

## SUGARED MARSHMALLOW BUNNIES AND CHICKS

*This chewy marshmallow can be formed in any mold.*

¼ c. water
3½ T. plain gelatin
¼ c. water
1¼ c. sugar
¾ c. invert sugar
⅜ c. light corn syrup
½ t. vanilla
Flavoring and coloring, if desired
Colored sugar

In a mixing bowl soak gelatin in water. In a saucepan, combine water, sugar, and invert sugar. Heat but do not boil; pour hot syrup into gelatin, beating slowly. Gradually add corn syrup and vanilla, beating on medium-high speed of mixer until mixture is fluffy, white, and doubled in bulk. Color and flavor marshmallow as desired. Keep mixing bowl in a larger bowl of very hot water to keep marshmallow from hardening. Butter Easter molds and spoon candy into molds. Set aside about 1 hour; remove from molds and roll in colored sugar. Dry candy for a few hours, then pack in tightly covered containers. Makes 12 to 15 molds.

## CANDIED ORANGE PEEL

*Good for eating, garnishing, or adding to baked items.*

Orange peel from 3 oranges
1 T. salt
4 c. water
2 c. sugar
½ c. water
Granulated sugar

Cut orange peel into sixths by running a knife from top to bottom of orange to form petals. Loosen petals with bowl of a spoon. Place orange peel in a bowl and add salt and 4 cups water. Weight peel down with a plate and let stand overnight. Drain and wash thoroughly. Cover peel with cold water in a saucepan. Bring to a boil, then drain. Repeat three times to take away the bitter taste of the peel. Cut peel into long strips. Put 2 cups prepared peel, sugar, and ½ cup water in a heavy saucepan. Cook slowly, stirring occasionally, until peel is translucent (about 30 minutes). As mixture thickens, lower heat. Drain and roll peel in granulated sugar. Makes 2 cups.

## FAIRY CANDY

*Light, airy chocolate-covered candy.*

1 c. sugar
1 c. dark corn syrup
1 T. vinegar
1 T. baking soda
1 T. vanilla
Sweet chocolate for dipping

Mix sugar, syrup, and vinegar in a large saucepan. Cover tightly and bring to a boil. Uncover and place thermometer in pan. Without stirring, cook over medium heat to 300°. Gradually lower heat as mixture thickens to prevent scorching. Remove from heat and quickly stir in baking soda and vanilla. Turn into a buttered 9 x 13-inch pan. Do not spread as candy will spread itself. Cool. Break into pieces. Dip pieces into prepared sweet chocolate. Place on waxed paper to harden. Makes about 35 pieces.

## CHOCOLATE PUDDING SANDWICHES

*A deluxe center for a box of mixed chocolates.*

4 egg yolks
⅔ c. heavy cream
⅔ c. sugar
1⅔ c. (9-oz.) chopped semisweet dipping chocolate
1 t. vanilla
Pecan halves
Milk chocolate (optional)

Beat egg yolks until thick and lemon colored. Add cream and sugar. Cook in the top of a double boiler until very thick. Melt chopped dipping chocolate. Cool chocolate a little, then add to the hot custard. Add vanilla; beat well and chill mixture. Form chilled pudding into small oblong shapes. Press between two pecan halves then dip the sandwiches in milk chocolate or serve as is. The pudding makes an excellent chocolate cream center for dipped chocolates, also. Makes about 80 sandwiches.

## COCONUT KISSES

*Little white fluffy mounds with chocolate bases.*

3 T. water
2½ lbs. dry fondant
2½ c. marshmallow creme
2 drops invertase
4 c. desiccated coconut
½ t. salt
1 t. vanilla
Dipping chocolate

Combine water, dry fondant, and marshmallow and beat with a mixer or by hand with a wooden spoon. Transfer to a heavy saucepan. Cook over very low heat to 120° to 125°, stirring occasionally. Add remaining ingredients except dipping chocolate. Blend together thoroughly. Drop from a teaspoon onto waxed paper. When firm, dip bottom half of each candy in dipping chocolate. Makes about 75 kisses.

## DELIGHT BARS

*Try this chewy, homemade coconut candy for a special treat.*

3 c. light corn syrup
¼ t. salt
1 c. water
2 c. sugar
5⅔ c. desiccated coconut
¾ c. chopped candied cherries and pineapple
¾ c. raisins
¾ c. chopped pecans
Milk chocolate

In a saucepan combine corn syrup, salt, water, and sugar. Cover tightly and bring to a rolling boil. Remove lid, place thermometer in pan and cook to 236°. Place coconut, candied fruit, raisins, and pecans in a large bowl and mix well. Pour cooked syrup over fruit and nuts; mix thoroughly. Pour out on buttered marble slab and pack into a ⅜-inch thick square shape. Cool, slice into bar shapes. Let dry, then dip in sweet chocolate. Makes about 60 bars.

## CANDY BAR FILLING

*Mildly flavored chocolate nougat. Easy to make.*

1 c. sugar
1 c. brown sugar
1 c. light corn syrup
1 c. water
¼ c. dry egg whites
3 T. water
4 T. melted semisweet chocolate
1 t. vanilla

Combine sugars, syrup, and 1 cup water in a saucepan. Cover pan and bring to a boil. Remove the lid and cook to 238°. In a mixer bowl soak dry egg whites and 3 tablespoons water. Just before the syrup reaches 238°, start whipping the egg white mixture. Add the syrup to the partially beaten egg whites in a slow stream. Continue beating until candy is thick and fluffy. Fold in semisweet chocolate and vanilla. Butter or moisten hands; roll candy into centers or form into logs. Place in chocolate lined candy bar molds. Or wrap the candy in waxed paper, then plastic wrap, and store it. Makes about 30 candy bars.

## ALMOND NOUGAT

*A delicious chewy candy which can be wrapped or dipped in chocolate.*

2 c. sugar
½ c. light corn syrup
½ c. water
2 T. butter
⅓ c. liquid non-dairy coffee cream
1 t. vanilla
1 c. blanched toasted almonds
2 T. marshmallow creme
Confectioners' sugar
Dipping chocolate (optional)

Combine sugar, syrup and water in heavy saucepan. Cover tightly and bring to a rolling boil. Remove lid, place thermometer in pan and cook to 270°. Remove from heat; add butter and coffee cream. Cook to 240°. Cool to about 160°; add vanilla. Beat by hand or on low speed of mixer until creamy. Add nuts and marshmallow creme. Mix together and pour into a buttered 9-inch square pan, which has been dusted with confectioners' sugar. Cover top with confectioners' sugar and let stand in a cold place. Cut and wrap, dip in chocolate, or flavor and color as desired. Makes about 64 pieces.

## HONEY NOUGATS

*Chewy, with a honey-nut flavor.*

2 c. sugar
½ c. honey
1 c. light corn syrup
½ c. water
4⅓ c. marshmallow creme or frappe
3 T. shortening
⅓ c. confectioners' sugar
1⅓ c. finely chopped nuts
Dipping chocolate

Cook sugar, honey, syrup, and water to 272°. Remove from heat and let stand for 10 minutes. Add marshmallow creme and shortening; beat until well blended. Fold in confectioners' sugar and nuts. Spread into a buttered 9-inch square pan and let stand for 24 hours. Cut and wrap individual pieces or dip in chocolate. Makes about 80 pieces.

## NOUGAT ALMONDINE

*This nut log has a fruit-nut nougat center and a caramel almond coating.*

2 c. sugar
¾ c. light corn syrup
1 c. water
2 egg whites
¼ c. Simple or Water Fondant, p. 16, 22
¼ c. vegetable shortening
½ c. chopped, roasted almonds
1½ c. candied cherries and pineapple
1 t. vanilla
Caramel Coating

Cook sugar, corn syrup, and water to 240°. Beat egg whites. Pour about one-half of the syrup over the whipped egg whites. Cook the remaining syrup to 280°; pour it into egg white mixture, continuing to beat. Add Fondant, shortening, and almonds while mixing at slow speed. Fold in cherries, pineapple, and vanilla. Put in a paper-lined pan and cut into bars when set. Dip in caramel and roll in chopped, toasted almonds.

### CARAMEL COATING

2½ c. sugar
2 c. light corn syrup
½ c. vegetable shortening
Dash of salt
2½ c. heavy cream, divided

Cook sugar, corn syrup, shortening, salt, and 2 cups heavy cream to 235°. Add remaining heavy cream slowly so as not to stop the boiling. Cook to 245°.

# MARSHMALLOW

*A standard good marshmallow recipe.*

- 2 c. sugar
- ¾ c. hot water
- 1 c. light corn syrup
- ½ c. water
- 2 T. unflavored gelatin
- 2 t. vanilla
  Confectioners' sugar (optional)
  Dipping chocolate (optional)

In a saucepan combine sugar, hot water, and corn syrup. Cover and bring to a rolling boil; uncover and cook to 240°. In a mixer bowl soak gelatin in water. Slowly pour cooked mixture into gelatin mixture, beating constantly. When mixture begins to thicken, add vanilla. Beat until marshmallow sticks to beaters (about 10 minutes). Pour into a buttered 8-inch square pan. When cool, turn out on a surface dusted with confectioners' sugar; cut into squares with wet shears. Dip or use as they are. Otherwise, cover each square with confectioners' sugar. Makes about 80 pieces.

## NO-COOK MARSHMALLOW

*This is a more tender marshmallow, which stays soft longer.*

- ½ c. cold water
- 4 T. unflavored gelatin
- ½ c. warm water
- 2½ c. sugar
- 1½ c. invert sugar
- ¾ c. light corn syrup
- 1 t. vanilla

Soak gelatin in cold water and set aside. In a saucepan, combine warm water, sugar, and invert sugar. Heat, but do not boil. Pour into a mixing bowl and add gelatin, corn syrup, and vanilla. Whip until white and doubled in bulk. Pour into a buttered 12 x 18-inch pan and let set 24 hours before cutting. Squares may be rolled in toasted coconut, dipped in chocolate, made into Rocky Road Candy (p. 53) or rolled in confectioners' sugar. Makes about 100 pieces.

*Pictured opposite: No-cook Marshmallow; Almond Nougat, p. 45; Butter Nut Crunch, p. 59.*

# MARSHMALLOW CREME OR FRAPPÉ

*An excellent make-it-yourself marshmallow creme.*

- 2¼ c. invert sugar, divided
- 4½ T. dried egg whites
- 2¼ c. light corn syrup
- 1 t. vanilla

In a mixing bowl, combine 1⅛ cups of the invert sugar with egg whites; whip at low speed of electric mixer to blend. Set aside. In a saucepan, combine remaining 1⅛ cups invert sugar and corn syrup. Heat to approximately 210°. Slowly add heated syrup to egg white mixture and beat until light. Add vanilla. Store in covered container and use in any recipe calling for marshmallow creme. Makes about 3½ quarts.

## APPLE-WALNUT JELLIES

*This firm jelly candy uses applesauce for flavor and makes a good center for dipping in chocolate.*

- 2⅔ c. sugar
- ⅓ c. pectin
- 2½ c. cool water
- 1⅔ c. light corn syrup
- 1 15-oz. jar applesauce
- 1 T. liquid citric acid *or* ½ t. citric acid plus 1 T. very hot water
- 1 c. chopped walnuts
  Confectioners' or granulated sugar

In a 4-quart saucepan combine sugar and pectin. Mix well; slowly add cool water, stirring until smooth. Bring to a boil, stirring constantly. Heat syrup just to the boiling point and add to sugar mixture. Continue to stir until boiling begins and cook rapidly to 220°; stirring occasionally. Add applesauce and cook to 224°, stirring constantly. In a separate container, combine citric acid and water or liquid citric acid. Stir well until dissolved; add to the cooked candy. Fold in nuts. Pour into a well-buttered 9-inch square pan. When cool and firm enough, cut and roll each piece in confectioners' or granulated sugar. Makes about 64 pieces.

47

# EASY CANDIES

## COCONUT PUFFS

*A colorful candy made in a few minutes with no cooking.*

Tint coconut by placing it in a jar, adding a few drops of food coloring. Cover the jar and shake until the coconut is uniform in color. Dip marshmallows in slightly beaten egg white, then roll in tinted coconut.

## GREEN COCONUT NESTS

*An Easter treat, easy to make.*

1 lb. green chocolate coating
1 7-oz. pkg. flaked or shredded coconut
Water

In the top of a double boiler, melt coating over hot, not boiling, water. Add coconut and mix together well. Add very small amounts of water to coconut mixture until it thickens enough to hold shapes. Form into small nests by making mounds and then hollowing them out with the bowl of a spoon. Fill nests with jelly beans or molded chocolates. Makes 8 nests.

## DRY FONDANT FUDGE

*Easy old-fashioned flavored fudge, very rich chocolate taste.*

6½ c. dry fondant
½ c. evaporated milk
½ t. salt
2 T. invert sugar
2 t. light corn syrup
¼ c. butter
6 1-oz. squares baking chocolate
1 t. vanilla
½ c. marshmallow creme
1 c. chopped black or English walnuts

Combine fondant, milk, salt, sugar, and syrup in a double boiler or a heavy saucepan over very low heat. Heat to 175° to 180°, stirring occasionally. Remove from heat, add butter and baking chocolate. Mix until completely blended. Add vanilla, marshmallow creme, and nuts. Mix together well; spread in a buttered 9 x 13-inch pan. When cool, cut into squares. Makes about 80 pieces.

## SNOW DROPS

*Yummy, chocolate-cream cheese combination.*

4 c. chopped semisweet chocolate
½ c. dark corn syrup
2 T. water
1 c. chopped nuts
1 8-oz. pkg. cream cheese, softened
⅔ c. confectioners' sugar
1 t. vanilla

In the top of a double boiler, combine chocolate, syrup, and water over hot, not boiling, water; heat until mixture is smooth. Stir in nuts. With teaspoon, drop in small mounds onto waxed paper-covered cookie sheets. Chill in refrigerator 5 minutes. In a bowl, combine cream cheese, sugar, and vanilla; beat until creamy. Top each chocolate drop with cream cheese mixture. Garnish with nuts, if desired. Return to refrigerator and chill until firm. Refrigerate in airtight container. Makes about 50 pieces.

## TING-A-LINGS

*Cereal candy made in a jiffy.*

½ lb. semisweet chocolate
1 c. cornflakes
½ c. coconut
1 t. vanilla
½ c. crushed salted peanuts

In the top of a double boiler, melt chocolate over hot, not boiling, water. Stir in remaining ingredients. Drop by spoonfuls onto waxed paper. Refrigerate until firm. Makes 30 pieces.

## CORNFLAKES DELIGHT

*Delicious chewy bars.*

1 c. maple-flavored pancake syrup
1 c. sugar
1 c. peanut butter
8 c. cornflakes
1 c. peanuts (optional)
Dipping chocolate

In a saucepan bring syrup and sugar to a boil. Remove from heat, add peanut butter. Stir until melted. Pour over cornflakes and peanuts. Mix until well coated. Turn out on a waxed paper lined 9 x 13-inch pan and spread with a spoon. When cool, break in small pieces and dip in chocolate, or spread chocolate over candy before breaking into pieces. Makes about 70 pieces.

## BUTTERSCOTCH CHEWS

*Combines chewy raisins and crunchy cereal.*

- **1 lb. butterscotch coating**
- **1 15-oz. can sweetened condensed milk**
- **4 c. bite-size wheat cereal or crisp rice cereal**
- **1 c. golden raisins**

In the top of a double boiler, melt together butterscotch coating and condensed milk over boiling water. Cook, stirring occasionally, until mixture is thickened and smooth, about 5 to 10 minutes. Remove from heat and set aside. In a large bowl, combine cereal and raisins. Pour butterscotch mixture over cereal and mix to coat well. Drop by teaspoonfuls onto waxed paper. Chill for several hours. Cover and store in a cool place. Makes about 60 clusters.

## BUTTERSCOTCH MIX BARS

*Chow mein noodles add crunch to this candy.*

- **6 oz. butterscotch coating**
- **2 T. coconut oil or vegetable shortening**
- **½ c. confectioners' sugar**
- **1 c. salted peanuts**
- **1 c. chow mein noodles, slightly crushed**
  **Dipping chocolate**

In the top of a double boiler, melt dipping chocolate over hot, not boiling, water. Spread on waxed paper to a thin layer about 8 inches square. Refrigerate until almost firm. In the top of another double boiler, melt butterscotch coating and shortening over hot, not boiling, water. Stir in confectioners' sugar. Add peanuts and noodles. Cool to lukewarm. Remove chocolate layer from refrigerator and spread prepared butterscotch mixture over the top, making a smooth, even layer. Cover with chocolate, cool until firm and cut into bars. Wrap individually. Makes 30 pieces.

## EASY BUTTERSCOTCH CENTERS

*A super easy, butterscotch-flavored center for chocolates.*

- **1 lb. butterscotch coating**
- **3 T. water**
- **¾ c. marshmallow creme**
  **Butterscotch or milk chocolate coating**

Melt coating over hot, not boiling, water. Add water and marshmallow creme. Beat until thoroughly mixed, then allow to stand until mixture is slightly firm. Form into ¾-inch balls and let stand one hour. Dip in butterscotch or milk chocolate coating. Makes about 60 centers.

## TWO-TONE SQUARES

*A chocolate-butterscotch flavor combination.*

- **2 c. finely chopped butterscotch coating, or wafers**
- **2 T. shortening, divided**
- **1 c. chopped nuts**
- **2 c. miniature marshmallows**
- **2 c. finely chopped semisweet coating, or wafers**
- **½ c. chopped nuts**

In a saucepan, combine butterscotch coating and 1 tablespoon shortening. Melt over hot, not boiling, water and stir to blend. Add 1 cup nuts. Spread in a greased 9-inch square pan. Sprinkle marshmallows over top, pressing in gently. Melt semisweet coating and remaining shortening over hot, not boiling, water. Spread over marshmallows. Sprinkle top with remaining nuts. Chill until firm. Let stand at room temperature to soften slightly before cutting. Makes about 64 pieces.

## PECAN CHEWS

*A special flavor treat. Makes a great gift box of candy.*

- **½ lb. soft caramels**
- **2 T. heavy cream**
- **1¼ c. pecan halves**
  **Dipping chocolate (optional)**

In a double boiler, melt the caramels and heavy cream over hot, not boiling, water. Scatter nuts thickly in the bottom of a pan. Let the caramel mixture cool a few minutes, then drop spoonfuls of the caramel partially over the nuts, letting the nuts stick out around the caramel. Let stand until firm, then cover or dip each piece with chocolate. If dipping, let the tips of the nuts show. Makes about 20 pieces.

## THREE-CORN KRUNCH

*Easy chocolate snack. More chocolate can be added if preferred.*

- 8 c. popped corn
- 3 c. crunchy corn puffed cereal
- 2 c. broken corn chips
- ½ lb. each butterscotch coating and semi-sweet coating, *or* 1 lb. any coating

In a large bowl mix together popped corn, cereal, and corn chips. In the top of a double boiler melt butterscotch and semisweet coatings. Pour coating over popcorn mixture. Stir until evenly coated. Let coating harden. Makes about 50 servings.

## MARBLED BARK CANDY

*A very attractive, easy candy made with two colors of coating.*

- 1 lb. chocolate coating
- 2 T. coconut oil, divided
- 1 lb. tinted white chocolate coating
- 3 or 4 drops peppermint oil (or other flavoring oil)

In the top of a double boiler, melt chocolate coating. Add 1 tablespoon coconut oil. In the top of another double boiler, melt tinted chocolate coating. Add remaining coconut oil. Add peppermint oil (or other flavoring oil) to *one* of the melted coatings. Spread darker chocolate thinly on waxed paper. Dribble the tinted chocolate over the dark chocolate in a swirled pattern. With a knife or spatula, cut through both colors, marble-izing the chocolates. Let candy harden, then cut or break into serving-size pieces. Makes about 75 pieces.

## ALMOND BARK CANDY

*A long time favorite of many.*

Toast almonds (blanched or unblanched) in a low oven. Place in bottom of buttered cookie sheet. Melt real chocolate in double boiler as for dipping, and temper it. Pour the chocolate over the almonds. You may also use the chocolate flavored coating in which case you need not temper your chocolate, just cool the chocolate slightly after melting it, and pour over the nuts. A good way to use leftover chocolate.

## SWEET 'N SALTY

*Easy bark candy.*

- 1 lb. white chocolate
- 1¼ c. blanched salted peanuts
- 2½ c. pretzel sticks

In the top of a double boiler, melt chocolate over hot, not boiling, water. Set aside. Crush peanuts to medium-sized pieces and break pretzel sticks into small pieces. Mix together chocolate, peanuts, and pretzels until well coated. Spread on waxed paper and cool. When firm, break into pieces. Makes about 50 pieces.

## SUGARPLUMS

*Fruity candy, a nice addition to a box of mixed candy.*

- 1 c. Simple or Water Fondant, p. 16, 22
- ½ t. vanilla
  Dash of salt
- ¼ c. chopped candied cherries
- ¼ c. chopped candied pineapple
- 1 12-oz. can pitted prunes
  Pecan halves
  Sugar

Mix fondant, vanilla, and salt together. Fold in cherries, and pineapple. Mix together well. Cut prunes in half or slot one side and fill each piece with fondant mixture. Place a pecan half on top; roll in granulated sugar. Let dry on waxed paper; place in paper cups. Makes about 60 pieces.

## FRUIT-NUT BARS

*Easy and very good.*

- 2 c. chopped semisweet chocolate
- 1 14-oz. can (1 1/3 c.) sweetened condensed milk
- 1 t. vanilla
- 4 c. miniature marshmallows
- 1 c. chopped pecans
- 1 c. finely chopped candied fruit

In the top of a double boiler melt chocolate, condensed milk, and vanilla over hot, not boiling, water. Remove from heat and set aside. Combine marshmallows, pecans, and candied fruit in a large bowl. Pour chocolate mixture over fruit and nuts and mix well. Spread in buttered 9-inch square pan. Chill until firm. Cut into squares. Makes about 64 pieces.

*Pictured opposite: Marbled Bark Candy, Sugarplums, and Fruit-Nut Bars; Christmas Fudge, p. 29; Brown and White Balls, p. 38.*

## DATE CHEWS

*Just grind and combine. Very nutritious.*

1 c. dates
1 c. black walnuts
½ c. coconut
2 t. light cream
3 t. vanilla
2 c. brown sugar
½ c. confectioners' sugar
Brown sugar
Confectioners' sugar

Grind dates, nuts, and coconut together. Mix together cream, vanilla and sugars; blend with date-nut mixture. Coat with brown sugar, then with confectioners' sugar.

## FRUITCAKE SQUARES

*The cake makes a surprise filling.*

6 oz. semisweet chocolate coating
16 1½-inch cubes fruitcake
½ c. chopped nuts

In the top of a double boiler, melt chocolate coating over hot, not boiling, water. Cool a little and dip squares of fruitcake into chocolate; sprinkle tops with nuts. Serve when chocolate is firm. Makes 16 cubes.

## DATE BALLS

*Crunchy chocolate balls with chewy, flavorful dates added.*

½ c. butter
4 c. miniature marshmallows
¼ c. milk
2 c. milk chocolate coating
4 c. crisp rice cereal
1 8-oz. pkg. chopped dates
1 c. chopped nuts

In large saucepan melt butter over low heat. Add marshmallows and milk and cook until melted, stirring constantly. Stir in chocolate coating and heat until melted and mixture is smooth. Remove from heat. Cool until mixture thickens, then blend in rice cereal, dates, and nuts. Roll into 1-inch balls. Store in refrigerator. Makes between 70 to 80 balls.

## FIG-DATE-NUT BALLS

*Very good health-food candy.*

½ c. ground dried figs
½ c. ground dates
1 c. ground nuts
Dash of salt
4 t. lemon juice
½ t. grated lemon rind
Confectioners' sugar (optional)

Combine figs, dates, nuts, salt, lemon juice, and lemon rind. When well blended, shape into ¾-inch balls. Roll in confectioners' sugar or use as centers and dip. Makes 3 dozen balls.

## FRUIT-NUT DROPS

*Apricots give this candy a tangy taste.*

1 lb. white chocolate coating
1 c. chopped dried apricots
1 c. natural cereal
½ c. coarsely chopped salted peanuts
½ c. raisins

In the top of a double boiler, melt chocolate coating over hot, not boiling, water. Add remaining ingredients and stir until mixture is well coated. Drop by teaspoonfuls onto waxed paper. Refrigerate until firm, about 20 minutes. Makes about 40 candies, or 1¾ pounds.

## FRUIT SLICES

*A nutritious treat.*

1½ c. seeded raisins
1 c. dried apricots
1 c. dried figs
1½ c. pitted dates
1 c. candied orange peel
12 candied cherries
1½ c. English walnuts
5 T. orange juice
⅓ c. finely chopped English walnuts

Put fruit and 1½ cups walnuts through a food grinder using the coarse blade, and making a paste. Add orange juice to hold fruit and nuts together. Mix together thoroughly and shape into a 1½-inch roll. Roll in chopped walnuts. Wrap in waxed paper and chill. Cut into ½-inch slices. Makes 24 pieces.

## MARSHMALLOW CUPS

*These are just luscious!*

Melt semisweet or milk chocolate coating. With a good quality 1-inch brush, line candy cups or baking cups with chocolate. Quickly chill in freezer. If you want a thicker chocolate cup, brush cup with a second coat of chocolate and chill again. Remove from freezer as soon as chocolate is firm. Fill with marshmallow creme to within an eighth of an inch from the top. Cover the top with melted chocolate, starting at the outside in a circular motion and finishing in the center. Chill again; wrap in foil or put in a cellophane bag.

## ROCKY ROAD

*Chocolate-marshmallow mixture. One of the best flavor combinations you can imagine.*

**Milk chocolate or chocolate coating**
**Coconut oil or vegetable shortening**
**(2 T. per lb. chocolate)**
**Marshmallows**
**Coarsely chopped, roasted almonds**

Melt chocolate coating and shortening in the top of a double boiler. If milk chocolate is used, temper it. Cool the chocolate to about 84°, mix marshmallows and almonds with the chocolate. Ladle out into a 9 x 13-inch or 8 x 8-inch buttered pan about 2 inches deep. Do not cut into pieces until ready to use, as marshmallow dries out. Makes about 50 pieces.

## MALTED MILK BALLS

*Crunchy malted centers.*

1 c. white chocolate coating
1 c. malted milk powder

In the top of a double boiler, melt chocolate coating over hot, not boiling water. Set aside. Measure malted milk powder into a small bowl. Add 5 to 6 tablespoons of the melted chocolate to the powder, or enough powder to form balls. Make into ½-inch balls and chill. Dip balls in remaining melted chocolate.
*Note:* To make Malted Milk Cups, do not chill malted milk mixture, but pack into small candy cups lined with firm melted chocolate. Cover and seal with melted chocolate; chill until covering chocolate is firm. Makes 20 pieces.

## CANDY HASH

*Children love to make this recipe.*

¼ c. toasted sliced almonds
1 c. (scant) dry roasted peanuts
1 c. sugared crunch cereal
1 c. crisp rice cereal
1 c. white miniature marshmallows
1 lb. white chocolate

In a large bowl, combine all ingredients except white chocolate. Melt the white chocolate and pour over cereal, nuts, and marshmallows. Drop by spoonfuls onto waxed paper. Makes about 50 candies.

## CHEWY CHOCOLATE ROLLS

*Children love them.*

2 T. butter
½ c. light corn syrup
2 1-oz. squares chocolate, melted
1 t. vanilla
¾ c. powdered dry milk
¼ t. salt
3 c. (1lb. 7-oz.) confectioners' sugar

Mix together butter, syrup, chocolate, vanilla, powdered milk, and salt. Gradually add confectioners' sugar; mix and knead. Roll out in ¾-inch rolls, cut into 2½-inch lengths. Let stand for about one hour, then wrap in plastic wrap. Makes about 18 rolls.

## NEAPOLITANS

*A colorful, not-so-sweet, candy.*

⅔ c. mashed potatoes
1 to 1½ lbs. confectioners' sugar
1 t. vanilla
   Butter flavoring
6 drops peppermint oil
   Red and green food coloring

Combine mashed potatoes and sugar in a mixing bowl to make a thick mixture. (Instant mashed potatoes will take more confectioners' sugar than freshly cooked.) Divide mixture into thirds. Add vanilla and butter flavoring to one third. Add 3 drops peppermint oil to each of the other two thirds. Color one peppermint-flavored third green, the other pink. Place in layers with the white vanilla layer between the two colored layers in a buttered 6 x 3 x2-inch loaf pan. Chill until firm. Slice down the center lengthwise, and then slice in thin pieces crosswise. Makes 48 pieces.

## PEANUT CLUSTERS

*Whip these up quickly for a great snack.*

    6 oz. semisweet chocolate-flavored
        coating
    ⅔ c. sweetened condensed milk
    1 t. vanilla
    1½ c. Spanish peanuts

In the top of a double boiler, melt chocolate coating over hot, not boiling, water. Remove from heat and add remaining ingredients. Mix together well; drop by spoonfuls onto waxed paper. Makes about 35 clusters.

## EASY PECAN ROLLS
### (Uncooked)

*An easy variation of the well-liked pecan roll.*

    2 c. (7½-oz.) marshmallow creme
    3½ c. (1 lb.) confectioners' sugar
    1 t. vanilla
    ¼ t. butter flavoring
    1 14-oz. pkg. caramels
    2 T. heavy cream
        Chopped pecans

Combine marshmallow creme, confectioners' sugar, vanilla, and butter flavoring. Knead until all sugar is thoroughly blended. Shape into 8 rolls. Wrap each in plastic and freeze. Melt caramels and heavy cream in the top of a double boiler. Dip frozen candy rolls in melted caramel and roll in chopped pecans. Store covered in a cool, dry place. Makes 8 rolls.

## ALMOND SUGAR SQUARES

*The combination of almond paste and chocolate lends an interesting texture and flavor.*

    2⅝ c. (¾ lb.) finely chopped semisweet
        chocolate coating
    3½ c. (1 lb.) finely chopped milk chocolate
    1 8-oz. can plus 2 T. almond paste
    1 t. pineapple flavoring
    2 c. marshmallow creme
        Dipping chocolate

Melt chocolate coating and milk chocolate in separate double boilers. Combine melted chocolates, almond paste, and flavoring. Beat together until completely blended. Blend in marshmallow creme. Spread in a 10-inch square pan. When firm, cut into squares and dip in semisweet chocolate. Makes about 80 pieces.

## MOLDED PEANUTS

*They melt in your mouth.*

    1 lb. butterscotch or pastel coating
    ½ c. peanut butter

In the top of a double boiler, melt coating over hot, not boiling, water. Add peanut butter and blend together. Scantily fill peanut molds or any other mold; chill quickly in freezer. As soon as candy is firm, turn out. Makes about 40 peanuts.

## PEANUT BUTTER BARS

*These are delicious plain, but especially good with a slice of caramel on top and dipped in chocolate.*

    3 c. crisp rice cereal
    1 c. salted peanuts
    ½ c. sugar
    ½ c. light corn syrup
    ½ c. peanut butter
    ½ t. vanilla
        Dipping chocolate (optional)

Mix together cereal and peanuts, then set aside. In a saucepan, combine sugar and corn syrup. Cook, stirring constantly, until mixture comes to a full rolling boil. Remove from heat. Stir in peanut butter and vanilla. Immediately pour the syrup over the cereal mixture, stirring to coat. Pat evenly into buttered 8-inch square pan. Cool. Cut into bars. Makes about 35 bars.

## SUGGESTIONS FOR EASY AND DELICIOUS CANDY OR COOKIES

Melt milk chocolate-flavored coating over hot, not boiling, water. Dip one of the following into the chocolate:

    Graham crackers
    Pretzels
    Vanilla wafers
    Club-type soda crackers

Or make petit fours from sugar wafers stacked two high with chocolate in between, then cut in half and dip in chocolate.

Or crush graham crackers into crumbs and add to melted chocolate. Drop on waxed paper, into paper cups, or mold in candy bar or other shapes. Any of the coatings may be used in the same way.

*Pictured opposite: Molded Peanuts; Fairy Candy, p. 44; Crunchy Nuts and Peanut Brittle, p. 57; Peanut Patties 2, p. 41.*

# CRUNCHES

## COCONUT FLAKE CANDY 1

*The following three coconut peanut brittle recipes are all good old-time favorites.*

  2½ c. sugar
  ⅔ c. water
  ⅓ c. vinegar
  ½ t. salt
  1 T. butter
1¼ c. salted peanuts, roasted
  3 c. raw chip coconut

Cook sugar, water, and vinegar to 300°. Remove from heat; add salt and butter, stirring until butter is melted. Quickly stir in peanuts and coconut. Spread as thinly as possible on heavily greased cookie sheets or on a well greased marble slab. Let cool a few minutes, then turn over. When cool, break into pieces and store in a tight container. Makes about 40 pieces.

## COCONUT FLAKE CANDY 2

  3 c. sugar
1¾ c. light corn syrup
  1 c. water
  2 T. butter
  ¾ T. baking soda
  1 t. salt
1¾ c. salted peanuts, roasted
  4 c. raw chip coconut

Cook sugar, corn syrup, and water to 295°. Remove from heat, add butter, stirring until melted. Stir in soda and salt, blending well. Quickly stir in peanuts and coconut chips. Turn out on a buttered marble slab or well greased cookie sheet. Spread as thinly as possible. Turn over after a few minutes. Let cool completely and break into small pieces. Store tightly covered. Makes about 40 pieces.

## COCONUT FLAKE CANDY 3

  1 c. water
  3 c. sugar, divided
1¾ c. light corn syrup
  2 T. butter
  1 t. salt
  ¾ T. butter
1¾ c. salted peanuts, roasted
  4 c. raw chip coconut

Bring water to a boil. In a heavy saucepan, heat 1 cup sugar until fluid and golden brown, stirring constantly. Very carefully add the boiling water to the caramelized sugar. Let the mixture boil until the sugar is completely dissolved. Add remaining sugar and syrup and cook to 295°. Remove from heat, add 2 tablespoons butter and stir until dissolved. Add salt and remaining butter and stir again until dissolved. Quickly stir in peanuts and coconut. Turn out on a buttered marble slab or well greased cookie sheet. Spread as thinly as possible. Turn over after a few minutes. Let cool completely and break into small pieces. Store tightly covered. Makes about 40 pieces.

## GLACE NUTS

*Buttery, sugar-coated deluxe nuts.*

  4 c. mixed nuts (no peanuts)
1½ c. sugar
  1 c. light corn syrup
  ⅓ c. water
  2 T. butter
  ½ t. salt
  1 t. vanilla
  Dipping chocolate (optional)

Warm nuts in a 350° oven. Generously butter a 17 x 14-inch cookie sheet. Combine sugar, syrup, and water in a saucepan. Cover and bring to a boil. Remove cover; place thermometer in pan and cook, without stirring, to 290°. Remove from heat and stir in warm nuts, butter, salt, and vanilla. Pour out on a generously buttered cookie sheet and spread as thinly as possible. Cool completely and break into pieces. Can be eaten as is or dipped in chocolate. Store in an airtight container. Makes about 5 cups.

## CRUNCHY NUTS

*A nice party snack.*

1½ c. (½ lb.) almonds
 2 c. (½ lb.) English walnut halves
 2 egg whites
   Dash of salt
 1 c. sugar
 ½ c. butter or margarine

Toast nuts in a 325° oven until light brown. Set aside. Beat egg whites and salt until soft peaks form. Beat sugar into meringue until stiff peaks form. Fold nuts into meringue; set aside. Melt butter in a 15 x 10 x 1-inch jelly roll pan. Spread nut mixture over butter. Bake in a 325° oven for about 30 minutes, stirring every few minutes, or until nuts and coating are browned, and no butter remains in pan. Cool. Makes about 4 cups.

## HOLIDAY CRUNCH

*Sweetened popcorn with a special flavor.*

 8 c. popped corn
 2 c. bite-size shredded wheat squares
 1 c. toasted whole or slivered almonds
1½ c. sugar
 1 c. light corn syrup
 ½ c. butter
 1 t. vanilla
 6 or 7 drops cinnamon oil (or other concentrated flavoring)

Combine popped corn, wheat squares, and almonds in a large buttered saucepan. Heat mixture in a 250° oven. In a large saucepan, combine sugar, syrup, and butter. Cook over medium heat, stirring constantly until mixture comes to a boil. Cook to 290° without stirring. Remove from heat and stir in vanilla and flavoring. Pour syrup slowly over corn mixture, stirring constantly until all is well coated. Spread onto 2 buttered cookie sheets. Cool and break into pieces. Store in a tightly covered container.

## PEANUT BRITTLE

*A family favorite.*

 3 c. sugar
1¾ c. light corn syrup
 1 c. water
 5 c. (1½ lbs.) raw peanuts
 2 T. butter
 ¾ T. baking soda
 1 t. salt

Cook sugar, corn syrup, and water to 240° and add peanuts. Cook to 295° stirring constantly. Remove from heat, add butter and stir until dissolved. Add soda and salt, stirring vigorously. Pour out on a buttered slab and spread as thinly as possible. Break or cut into pieces when cool. Makes about 50 pieces.

## PECAN BRITTLE

*This is an excellent gift item. Put it in an apothecary jar and tie with a ribbon.*

 2 c. sugar
 ⅓ c. light corn syrup
 1 c. butter
 ½ t. salt
 1 t. baking soda
 1 t. vanilla
 5 c. pecans

Toast pecans in a 200° oven until warm. Set aside. In a large saucepan, combine sugar and corn syrup and cook to 310°, stirring constantly. Add butter; continue cooking, stirring constantly, to 290°. Remove from heat; stir in salt, soda, vanilla, and nuts. Beat quickly, and spread out on a greased marble slab or on a heavily greased cookie sheet. Break apart when cool. Can be used as is or coated with chocolate. Makes about 30 pieces.

## LOLLIPOPS

*Fun to make for the children or grandchildren.*

- 2 c. sugar
- ⅔ c. light corn syrup
- 1 c. water
- ⅛ t. salt
- ⅛ t. oil of peppermint
- Red food color, as desired

Place lollipop sticks at intervals on a heavily oiled cookie sheet or on silicone paper. Combine sugar, corn syrup, water, and salt in a 2-quart saucepan. Stir well and cover with a tight lid. Cook to a rolling boil; remove lid and place thermometer in pan. Cook without stirring to 310°. Remove from heat. Add peppermint and food color, stirring only enough to mix. Working quickly, drop hot syrup by spoonfuls in mounds, covering one end of the sticks. When hardened and cool, wrap individually and store in an airtight box. Makes 8 to 12 lollipops.

## ROCK CANDY

*Flavorful, colorful, hard candy. Use for suckers or cut into small pieces.*

- 1¾ c. sugar
- ½ c. water
- ½ c. light corn syrup
- Dash of salt
- Food coloring as desired
- ¼ t. flavoring oil
- Confectioners' sugar

In a small saucepan, combine sugar, water, corn syrup, and salt and stir until sugar dissolves. Cover and bring to a rolling boil. Remove lid, place thermometer in pan and cook to 250°. Add food coloring and continue cooking to 300°. (Remove from heat at 285° to 290° as temperature will continue rising to 300°.) Let cool a few minutes. Add flavoring oil and cover 5 more minutes. Pour into a buttered 7 x 10-inch pan. Cut with shears into strips as soon as cool enough to handle. Then cut into squares or diamond shapes. When cold, dust with confectioners' sugar to keep from sticking. Makes about 50 small pieces.
*Note:* To form suckers, spray rubber molds with vegetable coating and pour hot syrup in. Unmold when cool.

*Pictured opposite: Lollipops and Rock Candy; Gumdrops, p. 37; Crispy Cereal Candy, p. 41; Cornflakes Delight, p. 48; Marzipan, p. 38; Painted Chocolate Molds, p. 11.*

## BUTTER NUT CRUNCH

*An excellent toffee, crunchy sweet. Try it with pecans or pecan substitutes.*

- 1 c. sugar
- ½ t. salt
- ¼ c. water
- ½ c. butter
- ½ t. lecithin
- ½ c. nuts
- 3 c. sweet chocolate, melted

Combine sugar, salt, water, butter, and lecithin in a heavy skillet or saucepan. Cook to 285°. Add nuts. Pour onto well greased cookie sheet; cool. Spread half of sweet chocolate on the cooled candy. Sprinkle with nuts. When the chocolate is firm, turn the candy over on waxed paper and spread with remaining melted chocolate. Sprinkle with remaining nuts. Break into pieces when firm. Makes about 20 pieces.

## OPAL'S BEST BUTTERSCOTCH

*Try dropping from a candy funnel to get uniform melt-in-your-mouth butterscotch patties. When making these, work fast as candy hardens rapidly.*

- 2½ c. sugar
- ½ c. light corn syrup
- ¾ c. water
- ¼ c. honey
- 1 c. butter
- ½ t. salt
- ½ t. rum flavoring

In a heavy saucepan, combine sugar, syrup, and water. Cover tightly and bring to a rolling boil. Remove cover, place thermometer in pan and cook without stirring to 270°. Add honey, butter, salt, and flavoring. Cook to 290°, stirring constantly. Remove from heat and pour into a 12 x 16-inch buttered jelly roll pan. Set aside to cool to a soft set. Remove to a buttered flat surface and score in 1-inch squares. When hard, break into pieces. Store airtight. Makes about 192 small pieces.

# POPCORN CRUNCH

*A deluxe popcorn-nut mixture.*

- 2 qts. popped corn
- 1½ c. pecan halves
- ⅔ c. whole almonds
- 1⅓ c. sugar
- ½ c. light corn syrup
- 1 c. margarine
- Dipping chocolate (optional)

Mix together popped corn and nuts. In a saucepan, combine sugar, corn syrup, and margarine. Bring to a boil, and boil 10 to 15 minutes, stirring constantly. When mixture turns light caramel in color, remove from heat, and stir in popcorn and nuts. Spread out on a lightly greased cookie sheet. Break apart when cool. Can be dipped or spread with chocolate, if desired. Makes about 40 pieces.

# SISTER MABEL'S SUPER CARAMEL CORN

*Excellent flavor and baking makes it super crunchy.*

- 2 c. light brown sugar
- ½ c. light corn syrup
- 1 c. butter or margarine
- ¼ t. cream of tartar
- 1 t. salt
- 1 t. baking soda
- 6 qts. popped corn

In a saucepan, combine sugar, corn syrup, butter, cream of tartar, and salt. Boil rapidly on medium high heat, stirring constantly, until mixture reaches 260°. Remove from heat. Stir in soda, stirring to mix thoroughly. Immediately pour over popped corn in a large bowl, stirring until well coated. Place coated corn in a large buttered roasting pan or sheet cake pan. Bake caramel corn for 1 hour in a preheated 200° oven, stirring 3 or 4 times. Keep in a tightly covered container. If it becomes sticky, place in oven again for a little while. Makes about 6 quarts.

# POPCORN BALLS

*Sweet sugary popcorn.*

- 5 qts. popped corn
- 2 c. sugar
- ½ c. light corn syrup
- 1½ c. water
- ½ t. salt
- 1 t. vinegar
- 1 t. vanilla

Measure popped corn into a large heat-proof bowl. Place in a 300° to 325° oven to keep hot and crisp. Combine sugar, corn syrup, water, salt, and vinegar in a small saucepan. Cook, covering with a tight lid the first few minutes of cooking to dissolve sugar, then remove lid and place thermometer in pan. Cook to 250°. Add vanilla. Slowly pour syrup over hot popped corn. Mix well until all the corn is well coated. Shape into balls. Makes 15 to 20 balls.

# POPCORN SURPRISES

*Chocolate on popcorn? Try it, you'll like it!*

- 8 c. popped corn
- 1 c. sugar
- ⅓ c. light corn syrup
- ⅓ c. hot water
- ⅛ t. salt
- ½ t. vanilla
- 1 lb. chocolate coating

Measure popped corn into a large bowl. In a small saucepan, combine sugar, syrup, water and salt. Cover tightly and bring to a rolling boil. Remove lid and add thermometer. Cook to 270°; remove from heat and stir in vanilla. Pour cooked syrup over the popped corn, stirring to coat corn. Cool completely, then run through a food chopper. Melt chocolate coating in top of double boiler. Stir ground popcorn into chocolate, using as much popcorn as the chocolate will hold. Pack into chocolate lined molds or roll out between waxed paper and cut into shapes with cookie cutters or knives. Makes about 50 pieces.

# DIETETIC CANDIES

## DIETETIC CANDIES

Sweet chocolate and white chocolate is available in sugar-free form. This chocolate is *not* for people on reducing diets, but rather for people who must restrict their sugar consumption. The chocolate may be used in the same way as the chocolate-flavored coatings, and may be combined with fruit, nuts, cereals, or other centers.

## DIETETIC CANDY CUPS

**1 lb. milkcote coating**

In the top of a double boiler, melt milkcote over hot, not boiling, water. Paint sides and bottoms of candy cups or small baking cups with melted coating, using a good quality 1-inch brush. Freeze until firm. Remove from freezer and fill to within 1/16-inch from the top with dietetic jellies, peanut butter filling, nut meats, raisins, or any filling a diabetic may eat. Add milkcote to cover top and seal edges. Chill again until top is firm. Store candies in their paper cups.

## DIETETIC MELT-AWAY MINTS

**1½ lbs. finely chopped milkcote chocolate coating**
**⅔ c. melted vegetable shortening**
**3 or 4 drops peppermint oil**
**Milkcote chocolate**

In the top of a double boiler, melt milkcote coating over hot, not boiling, water. Add shortening and peppermint, a little at a time, beating well after each addition. Chill chocolate mixture in refrigerator until of a soft custard consistency. Place in a mixing bowl and beat for 30 seconds. *Do not overbeat.* Pour into a waxed paper-lined 10 x 13-inch pan. Cover with waxed paper and tap pan to level mixture. Place in refrigerator until firm but not hard. Cut into squares. Dip in melted and cooled milkcote coating. Makes about 100 pieces.

## DIETETIC PEANUTS

**1 lb. whitecote chocolate coating**
**½ c. peanut butter**

In the top of a double boiler, melt coating over hot, not boiling, water. Add peanut butter and blend until smooth. Fill peanut molds almost full and chill in freezer until firm. Turn over and tap peanuts from molds. Makes about 75 peanuts.

## DIETETIC CREAM CHEESE BALLS

**1 8-oz. pkg. cream cheese**
**¾ c. finely chopped pecans**
**Milkcote or whitecote chocolate**

Cream the cream cheese and add pecans. Chill until cheese will form balls. Dip balls into melted whitecote or milkcote chocolate coating. Makes about 25 balls.

## DIETETIC BARK CANDY

**1 lb. milkcote or whitecote chocolate coating**
**1 c. crunchy cereal**
**Watermelon seeds or any other crunchy food**

In the top of a double boiler, melt coating over hot, not boiling, water. Add cereal and seeds. Blend together thoroughly, then pour onto waxed paper and spread thinly. Let stand until firm. Break into pieces.

## OTHER DIETETIC SUGGESTIONS

Raisins, dates, or half pecans or walnuts may be dipped in dietetic chocolate coating, separated and placed on waxed paper and chilled until firm.

Clusters may be made by mixing the melted coatings with raisins, nuts, or cereals. Place on waxed paper, chill until firm.

Strawberries may be partially or entirely dipped in coatings. Serve the same day as dipped.

# GLOSSARY

**Acetic Acid** A strong vinegar concentrate obtained from a pharmacist.

**Almond Paste** A smooth, heavy dough made of ground almonds. Used in candies and pastries.

**Brown Sugar** Light brown sugar is milder in flavor and better than dark for most candy recipes. Pack brown sugar firmly when measuring.

**Chocolate Coatings** Man-made chocolate which eliminates the tempering process necessary for real chocolate.

**Citric Acid** Helps prevent sugaring and improves flavors, especially in fruit candies. Comes in liquid or crystal powder form. Crystals can be mixed with an equal amount of water to form liquid citric acid.

**Coconut Oil** One of the ingredients in man-made chocolate. Used to thin chocolate or soften finished candy and make it less brittle.

**Corn Syrup** Light corn syrup should be used in candy.

**Cream** For these recipes, use heavy cream (whipping cream) unless otherwise noted.

**Desiccated (Macaroon) Coconut** A finely cut, dry, unsweetened coconut.

**Dry Corn Syrup** Corn syrup which has been dried to a powder. Do not reconstitute. To substitute for liquid corn syrup, add 5 parts dry corn syrup to 1 part water, by weight. Heat over low heat until dissolved.

**Dry Egg Whites** Reconstitute by adding 8 ounces dry egg whites to 1 pint water. Mix at slow speed until well blended. Gradually add 2½ pints water and mix well. Use 2 tablespoons reconstituted egg white for each egg white in the recipe.

**Dry Fondant** A commercial powdered cane sugar product that needs to be reconstituted with liquids to make a simple fondant.

**Frappe** Marshmallow creme. An excellent recipe is included in this book.

**Glucose** Concentrated corn syrup.

**Invert Sugar** Cane sugar in liquid form. Improves the quality and keeping properties in candy. If it crystallizes, place over hot water until it liquifies.

**Invertase** A yeast derivative, used in fondant centers to make them creamier as the fondant ripens. Usually only a few drops are necessary. Can be omitted from any recipe.

**Lecithin** An emulsifier made from soybeans and used to keep oils from separating.

**Non-dairy Liquid Coffee Cream** The frozen liquid type is excellent in candy. Use in place of milk or cream in fudges.

**Oils and Flavorings** Oils have a more potent flavor and do not thin candy. To flavor hard candies or chocolate, always use oils or very concentrated flavorings.

**Paramount Crystals** Vegetable oils, mostly coconut oil, in small solid pieces and used as coconut oil.

**Paste Food Color** Very concentrated food coloring obtained from cake decorating stores.

**Raw Chip Coconut** Unsweetened coconut in wide strips, used to make excellent brittle.

**Sugar** Granulated cane sugar.

*Pictured opposite: Popcorn Crunch, Sister Mabel's Super Caramel Corn, and Popcorn Surprises, p. 60.*

# Book II Index

# Book III

# Cookie
# COOKBOOK

by Darlene Kronschnabel

# CONTENTS

## Book I Nice & Easy Desserts Cookbook

## Book II Candy Cookbook

## Book III Cookie Cookbook

*Pictured opposite*
*Three-Way Peanut Butter Cookies, page 4*

# ALL-AMERICAN COOKIES

## THREE-WAY PEANUT BUTTER COOKIES

½ c. butter
⅓ c. peanut butter
½ c. sugar
¼ c. brown sugar
1 egg
2 T. milk
1 t. vanilla
2¼ c. flour
¼ t. baking powder
¼ t. salt
2 1-oz. squares unsweetened chocolate, melted
Salted peanuts, chopped
Semisweet chocolate chips

Cream butter and peanut butter. Gradually add sugars, beating until light and fluffy. Add egg, milk and vanilla; beat well. Combine flour, baking powder and salt; gradually blend into creamed mixture. Divide dough into two parts, one slightly larger than the other. Add cooled chocolate to the smaller portion. Mix until evenly blended.

### LAYER BARS

Divide chocolate dough in half; repeat for peanut butter dough. Roll out each dough between 2 sheets of waxed paper to form an 8-inch square. Invert one square of peanut butter dough on top of one square of chocolate dough, removing waxed paper. Invert remaining chocolate dough on top, then remaining peanut butter dough, to form four layers. Cover and chill several hours or overnight. Cut into thirty-two 2-inch bars. Place on cookie sheets. Bake in 350° oven 12 to 14 minutes. Drizzle with melted chocolate chips if desired. Makes 32 bars.

### PINWHEEL LOLLIPOPS

Roll out each half of dough between two sheets of waxed paper to form a 14 x 8-inch rectangle. Invert chocolate dough on top of peanut butter dough, removing waxed paper. Roll up along 14-inch side as for jelly roll. Cover and chill several hours or overnight. Cut into ¼-inch slices. Place 5-inch wooden sticks or skewers on cookie sheets. Press one cookie on end of each stick to form lollipops. Bake in 350° oven 10 to 12 minutes. Makes 56 lollipops.

### TWO-TONE COOKIES

Roll out peanut butter dough between two sheets of waxed paper to form a 14 x 6-inch rectangle. Shape chocolate dough to form a 14-inch log. Roll up peanut butter dough around chocolate log, removing paper. Cover and chill several hours or overnight. Cut into ¼-inch slices. Sprinkle with chopped peanuts, packing lightly. Place on cookie sheets. Bake in 350° oven 10 to 12 minutes. Makes 56 cookies.

> Don't bake cookies too long; they will become hard.

## OLD-FASHIONED GINGERSNAPS

| | |
|---|---|
| 2¼ c. flour | 1 egg, |
| ½ t. cinnamon | well beaten |
| 1 t. ginger | ½ c. light |
| ¼ t. salt | molasses |
| ⅓ c. shortening | 2 t. baking soda |
| ¾ c. sugar | 2 t. hot water |

Sift flour, cinnamon, ginger and salt. Set aside. Cream shortening and sugar until light. Add egg and molasses. Dissolve soda in hot water; add to creamed mixture. Stir in dry ingredients. Chill for ease in handling. Roll out on a lightly floured board to ⅛-inch thickness and cut with a 2-inch round cookie cutter. Place on greased baking sheet. Bake in 350° oven 10 to 12 minutes. For a crackled surface, brush each cookie with water before baking. Makes about 6 dozen cookies.

## THE WORLD'S GREATEST COOKIE

1 c. butter or margarine
1 c. crunchy peanut butter
1 c. sugar
1 c. brown sugar
2 eggs
2 c. flour
1 t. baking soda
1 6-oz. pkg. semisweet chocolate chips

Cream butter and peanut butter. Gradually add sugars and cream until blended. Add eggs, one at a time, and beat until smooth. Sift together flour and soda and add to creamed mixture. Stir in chocolate chips. Drop from a teaspoon onto a greased baking sheet. Slightly flatten cookie dough with back of spoon. Bake in 325° oven for 15 minutes. Makes 6 dozen 2-inch cookies.

---

Hermits are traditionally spicy rich and plump with raisins. As the recipe originated in Cape Cod, it is not surprising they went to sea on Clipper Ships. Records show that hermits were still seafarers in World War II. A recipe for hermits was found posted in the galley of the USS *North Carolina*, now a state memorial anchored at Wilmington, North Carolina.

---

## CINNAMON HERMITS

3½ c. flour
4½ t. baking powder
1½ t. salt
2 c. light brown sugar
½ c. shortening
1½ t. cinnamon
½ t. cloves
3 large eggs
2 T. milk
2 c. raisins

Sift together the first 3 ingredients and set aside. Cream sugar, shortening and spices. Beat in eggs. Blend in milk and raisins. Gradually stir in sifted flour mixture. Drop from a teaspoon onto lightly greased cookie sheet. Bake in a 375° oven 15 to 18 minutes. Makes 6 dozen cookies.

## DOUBLE CHOCOLATE CHIP COOKIES

2½ c. flour
1 T. baking powder
1 t. baking soda
1 t. salt
1 c. butter, softened
¾ c. sugar
½ c. light brown sugar
2 eggs
1 t. vanilla
3 1-oz. squares unsweetened chocolate, melted
1 6-oz. pkg. semisweet chocolate chips

Sift together flour, baking powder, soda and salt. Cream butter and sugars until fluffy. Add eggs and vanilla; beat well. Stir in chocolate. Add flour mixture and blend until smooth. Fold in chocolate chips. Drop by rounded teaspoons onto lightly greased baking sheets. Bake in 350° oven 10 to 12 minutes. Remove from baking sheets and cool on wire racks. Makes about 6½ dozen.

---

## GRANDMA'S COOKIE JAR

When I went to visit Grandma
I was always thrilled
For I knew she kept
A cookie jar well filled.

Quickly I removed my wraps
And Grandma led the way
Into a pungent kitchen
With treasures on display.

Peanut butter cookies,
Gumdrops tart and sweet,
Macaroons and gingersnaps
And brownies for a treat.

With a glass of buttermilk
I tasted everything,
With Grandma looking on at me
As though I were a king.

I love to visit Grandma;
It's a trip I most enjoy,
Though manhood's now replaced
That eager little boy.

*Bernice Peers*

---

## PUMPKIN COOKIE FACES

¼ c. shortening
⅔ c. brown sugar
½ c. mashed pumpkin
¾ c. light molasses
3 c. flour
1 t. baking soda
½ t. salt
½ t. ginger
½ t. cinnamon
½ t. nutmeg
½ t. allspice
   Icing, raisins, gumdrops and other
   candies

Cream sugar and shortening; stir in pumpkin and molasses. Sift together flour, soda, salt and spices; blend into pumpkin mixture. Cover and chill 2 to 3 hours. Roll dough ¼ inch thick on lightly floured board. Cut with floured pumpkin-shaped cookie cutter. Gently place on lightly greased baking sheets; bake at 375° for 8 to 10 minutes. Cool. Decorate with icing, raisins and candies. Makes 2 dozen 3-inch cookies.

## OLD-FASHIONED OATMEAL COOKIES

1 c. butter
1½ c. brown sugar
2 eggs
2 c. flour
2 t. baking powder
¼ t. baking soda
1 t. salt
1 t. cinnamon
1 t. nutmeg
½ c. milk
2 c. uncooked oats
2 c. raisins
½ c. chopped walnuts

Cream butter and sugar until light and fluffy. Add eggs; mix well. Combine flour, baking powder, soda, salt and spices. Add to creamed mixture alternately with milk. Stir in oats, raisins and nuts. Drop by heaping teaspoons onto buttered cookie sheets. Bake at 375° for 9 to 11 minutes or until set. Makes about 8 dozen.

Each Colonial homemaker had her own favorite recipe for jumbles, or jumbals. These early cookies, or biscuits as they were known, received their name from the method of mixing.

In the days before accurate measurements, cooks added a pinch of salt, lard the size of an egg, a handful of flour and "jumbled" the mixture together. Hence the name.

## OLD-FASHIONED CINNAMON JUMBLES

2 c. flour
½ t. baking soda
½ t. salt
½ c. butter, softened
1¼ c. sugar
1 egg
¾ c. buttermilk
1 t. vanilla
1 t. cinnamon

Sift together flour, baking soda and salt. Set aside. Cream butter, 1 cup sugar and egg until light and fluffy. Blend in buttermilk and vanilla. Stir in dry ingredients. Mix well. Chill dough. Drop by rounded teaspoons 2 inches apart on greased baking sheets. Sprinkle with remaining sugar mixed with cinnamon. Bake in 400° oven 8 to 10 minutes until set but not brown. Makes 4 dozen 2 inch cookies.

## PEANUT BUTTER CRISPIES

2½ c. self-rising flour
½ c. butter, softened
1 c. chunky peanut butter
1 c. brown sugar
⅓ c. water

Cream butter, peanut butter, and sugar until smooth. Add flour alternately with water, mixing well after each addition. Shape into two rolls, 2 inches in diameter. Chill several hours or overnight. Slice ¼-inch thick. Place on ungreased baking sheet and bake in 400° oven 8 to 10 minutes. Makes 3½ dozen cookies.

*Pictured opposite*
*Pumpkin Cookie Faces*

## BAR COOKIES

### ROCKY ROAD BARS

¼ c. flour
¼ t. baking powder
⅛ t. salt
⅓ c. brown sugar
 1 egg
 1 T. butter
½ t. vanilla
½ c. finely chopped walnuts
  Rocky Road Topping

Sift flour, baking powder and salt. Add remaining ingredients except walnuts, and beat until smooth. Stir in walnuts. Turn into greased 9-inch square pan. Bake at 350° for 15 minutes, or just until top is lightly browned and springs back when touched lightly. Remove from oven and immediately cover with Rocky Road Topping. Return pan to oven for 2 minutes only, just until chocolate is softened. Remove from oven and swirl chocolate over marshmallows and walnuts. Cool until chocolate is set before cutting. Makes fifteen 1¾ x 3-inch bars.

#### ROCKY ROAD TOPPING

 1 c. miniature marshmallows
½ c. chopped walnuts
 1 6-oz pkg. semisweet chocolate chips

Place ingredients in order listed over the baked layer.

To store bar cookies, do not cut into bars but wrap entire square in foil and store in cool place. To remove from pan without cutting, line the bottom and two sides of the pan with foil before baking. Grease pan. Grease foil. When square has cooled, loosen sides and lift out, using foil as handles.

### MARY'S MARBLE SQUARES

½ c. butter or margarine
¼ c. + 2 T. sugar
¼ c. + 2 T. brown sugar
 1 t. vanilla
 1 egg
 1 c. flour
½ t. baking soda
½ t. salt
½ c. sunflower seeds or coarsely chopped
   walnuts
 1 6-oz. pkg. semisweet chocolate chips

Cream butter, sugars, and vanilla. Beat in egg. Sift together flour, soda and salt and blend into creamed mixture. Stir in sunflower seeds or nuts. Spread in greased and floured 13 x 9 x 2-inch pan. Sprinkle chocolate chips over top. Place in preheated 375° oven 1 minute. Remove from oven and run knife through dough to marbleize. Return to oven and bake 12 to 15 minutes or until golden brown. Remove from oven and cool. Cut into 2-inch squares. Makes 2 dozen bars.

### BUTTERSCOTCH-COFFEE-SPICE BARS

 1 c. brown sugar
½ c. shortening
 1 egg
½ c. hot water
 1 t. instant coffee
1½ c. flour
 1 t. baking powder
½ t. baking soda
½ t. salt
½ t. cinnamon
 1 c. butterscotch chips
½ c. chopped nuts

Combine sugar, shortening and egg; beat until creamy. Mix hot water and instant coffee; blend into creamed mixture. Sift together flour, baking powder, soda, salt and cinnamon; gradually stir into creamed mixture. Add butterscotch chips and chopped nuts; mix well. Spread in greased and floured 13 x 9 x 2-inch pan. Bake in 350° oven about 20 to 25 minutes. Cool. Cut into 3 x 1½-inch bars. Makes 2 dozen bars.

# CALIFORNIA DREAM BARS

## CRUST

½ c. brown sugar
1 c. flour
½ c. butter, melted

Combine ingredients. Press firmly into bottom and sides of an ungreased 7 x 11 x 2-inch pan. Bake at 375° about 15 minutes. Remove from oven. Add topping.

## TOPPING

2 eggs, slightly beaten
1 c. brown sugar
1 c. nuts, coarsely chopped
1 c. flaked coconut
2 T. flour
½ t. baking powder
¼ t. salt

Combine ingredients, blending well. Spread over baked crust. Return to oven. Bake at 375° for 15 minutes longer. Remove from oven and cool. Cut into bars or squares. Makes about 30.

# BUTTERSCOTCH-SUNFLOWER NUT BARS

1 c. butter
1½ c. brown sugar
½ c. granulated sugar
3 eggs, separated
1 t. vanilla
2 c. flour
1 6-oz. pkg. butterscotch chips
¾ c. salted sunflower nuts

Cream butter with granulated sugar and ½ cup brown sugar until smooth. Add well-beaten egg yolks and mix well. Add vanilla and flour and blend well. Press into a greased jelly roll pan or 10 x 15-inch cookie sheet. Sprinkle butterscotch chips over top. Beat egg whites until stiff. Fold in remaining brown sugar. Spread mixture over crust and chips. Sprinkle sunflower nuts over the top. Bake in a 350° oven for 25 minutes or until lightly browned. Cool and cut into 3 dozen bars. For variation, use chocolate chips and salted peanuts.

# SPICY JUMBO BARS

3 c. flour
1 t. baking soda
½ t. salt
1 t. cinnamon
½ t. nutmeg
1 c. brown sugar
1 c. granulated sugar
¾ c. butter, softened
1 egg
3 t. vanilla
½ c. sour cream
1 6-oz. pkg. semisweet chocolate chips
1½ c. raisins
½ c. chopped nuts

Sift together flour, soda, salt and spices. Set aside. Cream sugars and butter. Add egg and vanilla, mixing thoroughly. Alternately add dry ingredients and sour cream to creamed mixture. Stir in raisins, chips and nuts. Spread in a 15 x 10-inch pan lined with waxed paper. Chill at least 3 hours in refrigerator or 1 hour in freezer. Invert pan and remove chilled cookie dough. Peel off waxed paper and cut into 2 x 1½-inch rectangles. Place 2 inches apart on ungreased baking sheet. Bake at 400° for 10 to 12 minutes. Remove from baking sheet and cool on rack. Makes 50 bars.

# COCONUT MOUNDS

16 graham crackers, finely crushed
⅓ c. butter
2 T. confectioners' sugar
1 17-oz. can flaked coconut
1 14-oz. can sweetened condensed milk
1 12-oz. pkg. semisweet chocolate chips
2 T. butter

Combine graham cracker crumbs, ⅓ cup butter, and sugar. Pat mixture into a greased 13 x 9-inch pan. Bake at 350° for 5 minutes. Remove from oven. Stir together coconut and milk. Pour over crust. Return pan to oven and continue to bake at 350° for 15 minutes. Remove from oven and cool for 5 minutes. Melt chocolate chips with remaining butter over low heat. Pour melted mixture over all. Allow to cool before cutting into slender bars.

*Lemon Cheese Balls*
*Rich Butter Cookies*

## RICH BUTTER COOKIES

| | | |
|---|---|---|
| ¾ c. butter | ½ t. vanilla | |
| ½ c. sugar | ½ t. almond or | |
| 1 egg | lemon extract | |
| 2¼ c. flour | 1⅓ c. flaked coconut | |

Cream butter and sugar until fluffy. Add egg and beat well. Add flour, a small amount at a time, mixing thoroughly after each addition. Blend in vanilla, almond extract and coconut. Divide dough in two portions and wrap each in waxed paper. Chill 30 minutes.

Roll chilled dough ⅛ inch thick. Cut into shapes with lightly floured 2-inch cookie cutters. Bake on ungreased baking sheets at 400° for about 6 minutes, or until edges just begin to brown. Makes about 5 dozen cookies.

# BUTTER AND DAIRY COOKIES

## TWO-WAY BUTTER COOKIES

### BASIC DOUGH

1 c. butter
1½ c. confectioners' sugar
1 egg
1 t. vanilla
2½ c. flour
1 t. baking soda
1 t. cream of tartar
¼ t. salt

Cream butter and sugar until fluffy. Beat in egg and vanilla. Sift together flour, soda, cream of tartar and salt. Gradually add to creamed mixture. Use half of dough for Butter Fingers and half for Molasses Spice-Eez.

### BUTTER FINGERS

½ Basic Dough
½ c. nuts, chopped
¼ c. candied cherries, chopped

Add nuts and cherries to dough. Chill 30 minutes. Shape into oblongs the size of a little finger. Place on ungreased baking sheets. Bake in 400° oven 7 to 8 minutes. Remove to wire rack to cool. Makes 3 dozen.

### MOLASSES SPICE-EEZ

½ Basic Dough     ½ t. ginger
2 T. molasses     ¼ t. nutmeg
1 t. cinnamon

Combine all ingredients. Chill at least 30 minutes. On floured surface, roll dough to ⅛-inch thickness; cut into desired shapes. Place on ungreased baking sheets. Bake in 400° oven 5 to 6 minutes. Remove to wire rack to cool. Makes 4 dozen.

## SOUR CREAM ORANGE COOKIES

½ c. butter
1½ c. brown sugar
2 eggs
1 t. vanilla
1 t. baking soda
2¼ c. flour
1 t. salt
1 c. sour cream
1 c. chopped walnuts
Creamy Orange Frosting

Cream butter and sugar; add eggs and vanilla. Alternately add sifted dry ingredients with sour cream, beginning and ending with dry ingredients. Blend well. Stir in nuts. Drop from teaspoon onto greased cookie sheets. Bake at 350° for 10 to 12 minutes. While warm, frost with Creamy Orange Frosting. Makes 6 dozen cookies.

### CREAMY ORANGE FROSTING

2 c. confectioners' sugar
1 t. vanilla
2 T. butter
1 t. grated orange rind
1 to 3 T. orange juice

Combine confectioners' sugar, vanilla, butter and orange rind. Blend in orange juice to spreading consistency.

## LEMON CHEESE BALLS

½ c. butter
1 3-oz. pkg. cream cheese, softened
½ c. sugar
1 T. grated lemon rind
½ t. lemon extract
1 c. flour
1 t. baking powder
¼ t. salt
1¾ c. cornflakes, coarsely crushed

Cream butter and cream cheese; add sugar gradually. Add rind and extract. Sift together flour, baking powder and salt and add to mixture. Chill several hours. Shape rounded teaspoons of dough into balls. Roll in cornflake crumbs. Place on ungreased cookie sheet. Bake at 350° about 12 minutes. Makes about 3 dozen cookies.

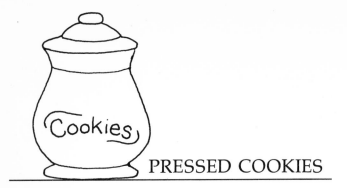

## PRESSED COOKIES

### FENNEL COOKIES

1 c. butter
½ c. sugar
1 egg, well beaten
2½ c. flour
½ t. baking powder
1 t. vanilla
1 t. fennel seed

Cream butter and sugar until fluffy. Add egg gradually, beating thoroughly. Stir in flour and baking powder. Blend in vanilla and fennel seed. Force through a cookie press. Bake on ungreased cookie sheet at 350° for 12 minutes. About 5 dozen cookies.

Don't place dropped cookies too close together on baking sheet. Allow them room to spread.

### CREAM CHEESE SPRITZ

½ c. butter
1 3-oz. pkg. cream cheese
⅓ c. sugar
1 egg yolk
1½ t. orange extract
1½ c. flour
½ t. salt
Food colors and decorators

Cream together butter and cheese until soft. Add sugar gradually and mix until light and fluffy. Add egg yolk and orange extract. Stir in flour and salt. Color dough as desired with food coloring. Force dough through a cookie press onto ungreased cookie sheets. Sprinkle with decorators. Bake at 375° for about 10 minutes. Do not overbake. Makes about 4 dozen.

### SPRITZ

1 c. butter
½ c. plus 1 T. sugar
1 egg
¾ t. salt
1 t. vanilla
½ t. almond extract
2½ c. flour
Colored sugar, candies for decorating

Cream butter and sugar. Blend in egg, salt, extracts and flour. Knead dough in hands until soft and pliable. Force dough through cookie press onto ungreased cookie sheets. Decorate as desired. Bake at 400° for 8 to 10 minutes. Makes about 6 dozen cookies.

### BROWN SUGAR SPRITZ

1 c. butter
¼ c. sugar
⅓ c. light brown sugar
1 egg yolk
½ t. vanilla
¼ t. salt
¼ t. almond extract
2¼ c. flour

Cream butter with sugars. Add egg yolk, vanilla, salt and almond extract. Beat until fluffy. Blend in flour. Knead dough in hands until it is soft and pliable. Force dough through cookie press onto ungreased cookie sheets. Decorate if desired. Bake at 350° about 8 minutes. Makes about 8 dozen.

### NORWEGIAN ALMOND COOKIES

¾ c. butter
½ c. confectioners' sugar
1 c. finely ground almonds
1 t. lemon juice
1 egg
1½ c. flour

Cream together butter and sugar until light and fluffy. Force almonds through a coarse sieve and add to creamed mixture. Add lemon juice and egg, mixing well. Gradually blend in flour. Force cookies through cookie press on ungreased cookie sheets. Bake in 400° oven 7 to 10 minutes. Remove at once to cooling rack. Decorate with frosting, if desired. Makes 5 to 6 dozen.

# REFRIGERATOR COOKIES

## PECAN REFRIGERATOR COOKIES

| | |
|---|---|
| 1 lb. butter | 4 c. flour |
| 1 lb. light brown sugar | 1 t. cinnamon |
| | 1 t. baking powder |
| 2 eggs | 1 t. salt |
| 2 t. vanilla | 1 lb. chopped pecans |

Cream butter and sugar together until light and fluffy. Beat in eggs, one at a time. Add vanilla. Sift dry ingredients together and add to butter mixture, mixing thoroughly. Stir in pecans. Chill dough for one to two hours. Divide into 6 portions; shape into rolls about 1¾ inches in diameter. Wrap the rolls in waxed paper and chill overnight or longer. Slice about ¼ inch thick. Bake on greased cookie sheet in 375° oven for 10 minutes or until cookies are delicately browned. Makes 14 dozen.

## APPLESAUCE FREEZER COOKIES

1 c. butter
1½ c. brown sugar
1 egg, slightly beaten
4 c. flour
1 t. salt
½ t. baking soda
1 t. cinnamon
¼ t. cloves
1 c. thick applesauce, unsweetened
½ c. chopped walnuts

Cream butter and brown sugar until fluffy. Add egg; blend well. Sift together flour, salt, soda, cinnamon and cloves. Add alternately to the creamed mixture with the applesauce. Add chopped walnuts. Form into 4 rolls, 1½ inches in diameter. Wrap in waxed paper; freeze until firm. Slice thinly. Bake on greased cookie sheets at 375° for 15 minutes. Makes 7 dozen cookies.

## CHERRY N' CHOCOLATE COOKIES

1 c. butter
1½ c. sugar
1 egg
2 t. vanilla
2½ c. flour
1½ t. baking powder
¾ t. salt
½ c. candied cherries, diced
⅓ c. chopped walnuts
1 square unsweetened chocolate
Hot milk

Sift together flour, baking powder and salt. Cream butter and sugar gradually. Beat in egg and vanilla. Blend in sifted dry ingredients. Divide dough into 2 equal portions. Mix cherries into one portion, walnuts and melted chocolate into remaining portion. Work dough with hands until pliable. Shape each portion of dough into 2 bars 9 x 1½ inches. Wrap in waxed paper; chill until firm. Cut each bar in half lengthwise; brush cut side of bar with milk. Press one cherry and one chocolate bar together. Press firmly. Wrap in waxed paper. Chill until firm. Cut into ¼-inch slices. Bake at 350° about 10 minutes. Makes about 10 dozen.

## ORANGE PEANUT REFRIGERATOR COOKIES

2 c. flour
¼ t. baking soda
¼ t. salt
1 c. butter or margarine
½ c. brown sugar
½ c. sugar
1 egg
3 T. frozen orange juice concentrate
1 T. grated orange rind
½ c. chopped peanuts

Sift together flour, baking soda and salt. Cream butter with sugars; beat in egg. Blend in undiluted orange concentrate, orange rind and dry ingredients. Stir in peanuts. Chill dough. Shape into 2 rolls 2 inches in diameter; wrap in waxed paper. Refrigerate several hours or overnight. Cut into ¼-inch slices. Place on ungreased baking sheet. Bake in 400° oven 10 to 12 minutes or until lightly browned. Makes about 4 dozen.

## OATMEAL REFRIGERATOR COOKIES

| | |
|---|---|
| ½ c. peanut butter | 1¾ c. flour |
| ½ c. butter | 2 t. baking soda |
| 2 c. brown sugar | ¾ t. salt |
| 1 t. vanilla | 1½ c. uncooked oats |
| 2 eggs | ½ c. chopped nuts |

Cream together peanut butter and butter. Add sugar gradually and cream together until light and fluffy. Add vanilla and eggs and beat well. Mix in flour, sifted together with soda and salt. Then add oats and nuts. Shape dough into rolls about 2 inches in diameter. Wrap in waxed paper. Chill in refrigerator. Slice ⅛ inch thick. Place on greased cookie sheet and bake in 350° oven for about 15 minutes. Makes 6 to 6½ dozen.

---

Real vanilla comes from the fruit of a tropical orchid, mostly grown in the Madagascar region.

---

## REFRIGERATOR SANDWICH COOKIES

| | |
|---|---|
| ¾ c. butter | 1 egg yolk |
| ¼ c. light brown sugar | 1 t. vanilla |
| | 1¾ c. flour |
| ¼ c. sugar | Pecan halves |

Cream butter and sugars and beat until blended. Beat in egg and vanilla; gradually add flour. Chill for ease in handling. Form into 2 rolls, each 7 inches long and 1½ inches in diameter. Wrap in waxed paper; chill several hours or overnight. Cut into ⅛-inch slices and place on lightly greased baking sheets. Bake in 350° oven 8 to 10 minutes. Remove to wire rack to cool. Put 2 cookies together with vanilla frosting and top with a dollop of frosting and a pecan half. Makes about 3 dozen.

### VANILLA FROSTING

| | |
|---|---|
| ¼ c. butter | 1 egg white |
| 2½ c. confectioners' sugar | ½ t. vanilla |
| | Food color |

Cream butter. Add sugar alternately with egg white, beating until light and fluffy. Blend in vanilla and food coloring. Makes 1 cup.

## ORANGE-COCONUT REFRIGERATOR COOKIES

½ c. butter
½ c. light brown sugar
¾ c. sugar
1 egg
2 t. grated orange peel
1 t. vanilla
1¾ c. flour
2 t. baking powder
½ t. salt
⅓ c. flaked coconut

Cream butter and sugars. Beat in egg, orange peel and vanilla. Sift together flour, baking powder and salt; gradually add to creamed mixture. Blend in coconut. On lightly floured surface, form into rolls 1½ inches in diameter. Wrap in waxed paper. Chill several hours or overnight. Cut rolls into ⅛-inch slices and place on baking sheets. Bake in 400° oven 5 to 6 minutes. Remove to wire rack to cool. Makes about 11 dozen.

*Note:* The rolls can be placed in protective wrapping and refrigerated up to 1 week or frozen up to 3 months. If frozen, thaw in refrigerator and bake.

## PEANUT BUTTER LEMON ICEBOX COOKIES

| | |
|---|---|
| 2 c. flour | 1 c. light brown sugar |
| 1 t. baking soda | |
| ½ t. salt | 1 egg |
| 1 c. peanut butter | 1 T. grated lemon rind |
| 1 c. butter or margarine | 2 T. lemon juice |

Sift together flour, soda and salt. Blend together peanut butter and butter. Add sugar gradually, beating until light and fluffy. Beat in egg, lemon rind and juice. Stir in flour mixture, mixing just enough to blend. Shape into two 12-inch rolls—1½ inches in diameter. Wrap in waxed paper. Chill overnight. When ready to bake, cut, using a sawing motion, into ⅛-inch slices. Place on ungreased baking sheet. Bake in 375° oven 8 to 10 minutes. Cool on cookie sheet about 2 minutes before removing to wire rack. Makes 9 dozen cookies.

*Pictured opposite*
Fabulous Filbert Bars, page 16

# COOKIE CONFECTIONS

## BUTTERSCOTCH STACKS

1 12-oz. pkg. butterscotch chips
1 1½-oz. can potato sticks
1 c. dry roasted peanuts

Melt butterscotch chips; stir in potato sticks and peanuts. Drop by teaspoons onto waxed paper. Let stand at room temperature until set, about one hour. Makes about 3 dozen.

## CHOCOLATE MELTAWAYS

½ c. butter
1 square unsweetened chocolate
¼ c. sugar
1 t. vanilla
1 egg, beaten
2 c. graham cracker crumbs
1 c. flaked coconut
½ c. chopped walnuts

Melt butter and chocolate in saucepan. Blend in sugar, vanilla, egg, crumbs, coconut and nuts. Mix well. Press into a 11½ x 7 x 2-inch pan. Refrigerate until set. Prepare topping and spread over chilled crust.

### TOPPING

¼ c. butter
1 T. cream
2 c. confectioners' sugar
1 t. vanilla
1½ squares unsweetened chocolate

Combine butter, cream, sugar and vanilla. Beat until creamy. Spread over crumb mixture. Chill. Melt chocolate and spread evenly over frosting. Chill again. When chocolate is set, but not firm, cut into tiny squares.

## COCOA CONFECTIONS

1½ c. vanilla wafer crumbs
½ c. confectioners' sugar
2 T. cocoa
¾ c. finely chopped walnuts
1½ T. corn syrup
3 T. frozen orange juice concentrate
½ t. rum extract
¼ c. finely chopped raisins
Confectioners' sugar
Finely chopped nuts
Cookie crumbs

Combine wafer crumbs with remaining ingredients in large bowl. Shape into 1-inch balls and roll in additional confectioners' sugar, nuts or cookie crumbs. If desired, dip in chocolate coating. Makes about 3 dozen.

## FABULOUS FILBERT BARS

1 c. chopped filberts
1 c. butter
1 c. creamy peanut butter
2 6-oz. pkgs. butterscotch chips
5 c. pastel miniature marshmallows
1¾ c. flaked coconut

Toast chopped filberts in 350° oven 5 to 8 minutes. Melt butter, peanut butter, and butterscotch chips together over low heat. Cool slightly. Add marshmallows, filberts and ¾ cup coconut. Mix well. Pat mixture into a buttered 9 x 13-inch pan. Sprinkle on remaining coconut. Cool until firm in refrigerator. Cut into small bars.

## GRAHAM SNACKERS

24 graham cracker squares
½ c. butter, melted
½ c. brown sugar
1 c. chopped walnuts

Line an ungreased 15½ x 10½ x 1-inch jelly roll pan with graham cracker squares. Combine butter with brown sugar and spoon over graham crackers. Sprinkle with walnuts. Bake at 350° about 12 minutes. Break into squares. Makes 2 dozen cookies.

## NO-BAKE WALNUT BALLS

1 6-oz. pkg. semisweet chocolate chips
1 6-oz. pkg. butterscotch chips
¾ c. confectioners' sugar
½ c. sour cream
1 t. grated orange rind
¼ t. salt
1¾ c. chow mein noodles, crushed
¾ c. ground walnuts

Melt chocolate and butterscotch chips together over hot water in a double boiler;
remove from heat. Add rest of ingredients
except nuts; mix well. Chill dough 20 minutes. Shape into 1-inch balls; roll in ground
walnuts. Store in a tightly covered container. Makes 3½ dozen.

---

If you don't have time to mix and bake
cookies all at once, store the batter in the
refrigerator. Bake them later—when it's
convenient. Or let the kids do the baking.
Cookie batter will keep refrigerated in a
tightly covered container for up to a week.

---

## ORANGE CONFECTION BALLS

2¾ c. graham cracker crumbs
1 c. confectioners' sugar, sifted
1 c. finely chopped walnuts
2 T. butter, melted
¼ c. light corn syrup
½ c. frozen orange juice concentrate,
    thawed
1 3½-oz. can flaked coconut

Combine all ingredients except coconut; mix
well. Shape into balls about ¾ inch in diameter. Dip top of each ball into Orange Glaze,
then into coconut. Store in air-tight container. Flavor improves with storage. Makes
3½ to 4 dozen.

### ORANGE GLAZE

1 c. confectioners' sugar
4 T. frozen orange juice concentrate,
    thawed

Mix sugar and undiluted orange concentrate
together.

## CRISPY FRESH ORANGE-GUMDROP COOKIES

1¾ c. flour
½ t. baking soda
¼ t. salt
½ c. shortening
1 c. sugar
1 egg, beaten
1½ T. grated orange peel
⅓ c. fresh orange juice
1 c. gumdrops, cut up
½ c. coarsely chopped walnuts

Sift together flour, soda, and salt. Cream
together shortening and sugar until light.
Add egg; mix until thoroughly blended. Alternately add sifted dry ingredients and
orange juice, beating until smooth. Stir in
grated peel, gumdrops and walnuts, blending well. Drop from a teaspoon onto a
greased cookie sheet. Bake in a 375° oven, 10
to 12 minutes, or until lightly browned. Remove from oven and let stand about 1 minute before removing to a rack to cool.
Cookies will be very crisp. Makes 4 dozen
cookies.

## CHOCO-PEANUT RING COOKIES

½ c. butter
½ c. sugar
½ c. brown sugar
1 egg
½ t. vanilla
1½ c. flour
½ t. baking soda
½ t. salt
15 small (about 1-inch) peanut butter cup
    candies, sliced in half crosswise

Beat butter until creamy. Add sugars gradually and beat thoroughly. Beat in egg, then
vanilla. Sift together flour, soda and salt;
add to creamed mixture. Form into 1¼-inch
balls and place on greased cookie sheets;
flatten slightly. Press one peanut butter cup
candy half in center of each cookie, peanut
butter side up. Bake in 375° oven 10 to 12
minutes. Cool on wire racks. Makes 2½
dozen cookies.

## COOKIES
## FROM A MIX

### MASTER MIX

9 c. flour
¼ c. baking powder
1 to 1½ T. salt
1½ c. shortening

Stir the baking powder and salt into the flour. Sift three times into a large bowl or pan. Cut in shortening with a pastry blender until the mixture resembles tiny peas or until it is as fine as cornmeal. Store in tightly covered container or in a cool, dry place. Put the mix in a large glass jar or a coffee can lined with a moisture proof plastic bag until baking. Measure into single portions to use. Makes about 13 cups.

### BASIC DROP COOKIES

2 c. Master Mix
⅔ c. sugar
1 egg, beaten
1 t. vanilla
½ c. cream (or ⅓ c. milk and 2 T. melted butter)

Stir the sugar into the Master Mix. Combine cream, egg and vanilla. Blend wet and dry ingredients well. Drop by teaspoons onto greased baking sheet. Bake in 375° oven 10 to 12 minutes. Makes 2 to 2½ dozen cookies.

*VARIATIONS:* Use brown sugar instead of white sugar.

Use 1 tablespoon grated orange or lemon rind in place of vanilla

For chocolate cookies, add 1 square melted chocolate.

Add ½ cup coconut and ½ cup raisins or dates.

Certainly the chocolate chip cookie is an all around winner. This classic American invention first appeared as the original Toll House cookie, named after the famous Toll House Inn at Whitman, Massachusetts. Toll House cookies were introduced to homemakers in 1939 on the radio series Famous Foods from Famous Places.

One story claims this all-American cookie was discovered by accident. One day a home economist used chopped chocolate in her cookie dough instead of raisins. The idea caught on and became popular across the nation. An entirely new industry was created with the invention of the machinery to make the little chocolate pieces.

### CHOCOLATE CHIP COOKIES

2 c. Master Mix
½ c. butter or margarine
1 c. brown sugar
1 egg
½ c. chopped nuts
1 6-oz. pkg. semisweet chocolate chips

Mix butter or margarine, sugar and egg together. Stir in rest of ingredients. Drop by teaspoons about 2 inches apart on ungreased baking sheet. Bake in 375° oven 10 minutes or until lightly browned. Makes 4 dozen 1½-inch cookies.

### OATMEAL DROP COOKIES

| | |
|---|---|
| 1 c. Master Mix | 1 egg, beaten |
| ½ c. sugar | 3 T. water |
| ¾ c. uncooked oats | ¼ c. raisins |
| ½ t. cinnamon | ¼ c. chopped nuts |
| ⅛ t. cloves | |

Combine dry ingredients. Add water to beaten egg. Combine liquid with dry ingredients and mix thoroughly. Add raisins and nuts. Stir until well mixed. Drop by teaspoons onto greased baking sheet. Bake in a 400° oven for 10 to 12 minutes, or until browned. Makes 2 dozen medium-sized cookies.

*Pictured opposite*
*Date-Orange Toppers, page 21*

19

## TUTTI-FRUTTI COOKIE SQUARES

1 pkg. coconut-pecan snack
  cake mix
2 T. butter, melted
1 T. water
1 t. vinegar
1 8-oz. pkg. cream cheese
1 egg
2 T. sugar
½ c. flaked coconut
¼ c. maraschino cherries, chopped
½ c. crushed pineapple, well drained
¾ c. semisweet chocolate mini-chips

Measure 1½ cups cake mix into a bowl. Stir in butter, water and vinegar; blend well. Pat into greased 9-inch square pan. Bake at 350° about 12 minutes or until firm and lightly browned around edges. Cool about 10 minutes. Thoroughly combine cream cheese, egg and sugar in small bowl. Stir in coconut and cherries; spread over cooled layer in pan. Combine pineapple with remaining cake mix until all cake mix is moistened; add chocolate mini-chips. Crumble onto top of cream cheese layer, covering completely. Bake at 350° for 30 to 35 minutes or until lightly browned. Cool and chill. Cut into 25 squares.

---

When you store cookies, make sure soft cookies remain soft; crisp cookies keep crisp. The two types cannot be stored together.

---

## CHEERY CHERRY BARS

1 pkg. spice or apple-spice cake mix
2 eggs
⅓ c. water
6 T. butter, softened
¾ c. dried apricots, chopped
1 3½-oz. can flaked coconut
½ c. maraschino cherries, chopped

In large mixing bowl, beat together cake mix, eggs, water and butter for length of time specified on cake mix. Stir in apricots, coconut and cherries, mixing just until combined. Spread evenly into buttered 15½ x 10½ x 1-inch jelly roll pan. Bake in 375° oven 18 to 20 minutes. Cool in pan on wire rack before cutting. Makes 5 dozen bars.

## APPLE RAISIN CRUNCHIES

½ c. butter or margarine
¼ c. milk
1 13¾-oz. pkg. coconut-almond
  frosting mix
2 c. granola
½ c. currants or raisins
½ c. shredded, or finely chopped, apple

In large saucepan, heat butter and milk until butter is melted. Stir in remaining ingredients. Drop by rounded teaspoons 1 inch apart, onto greased cookie sheets. Bake in 325° oven 15 to 20 minutes. Cool 5 minutes before removing. Makes 3 dozen cookies.

## CRUNCHY LEMON BARS

1 13¾-oz. pkg. coconut-pecan frosting
  mix
1 c. flour
1 t. baking powder
⅔ c. butter or margarine, softened
1 14-oz. can sweetened condensed milk
1 T. grated lemon peel
½ c. lemon juice

In large mixing bowl, combine dry frosting mix, flour, baking powder and butter; mix until crumbly. Press half of the mixture in an ungreased 8 to 9-inch square baking pan. Combine sweetened condensed milk, lemon peel and juice. Pour over crumb layer. Sprinkle remaining crumbs over filling. Bake in 350° oven for 30 to 40 minutes until golden brown. Cool. Cut into 2 dozen bars.

## LEMON COCONUT BARS

½ c. butter
1 lemon cake mix
1 13¾-oz. pkg. lemon fluff frosting mix
1 c. shredded coconut
1 c. chopped walnuts

Cut butter into the dry cake mix. Press and flatten mixture with hand into bottom of ungreased 15½ x 10½-inch pan. Bake at 350° for 5 minutes. Meanwhile, prepare frosting mix as directed on package. Fold in coconut and nutmeats. Spread mixture over baked base. Bake at 350° for 25 minutes or until done. Cool slightly. Cut into bars. Makes 2½ dozen.

## EASY BUTTERSCOTCH CRISPIES

½ c. sugar
1 t. baking powder
1 pkg. butterscotch pudding mix
1 c. butter or margarine
1 t. vanilla
2 c. flour
½ c. chopped nuts

In large bowl, combine first five ingredients. Blend thoroughly at medium speed. By hand, stir in flour and nuts. Divide dough into 3 balls. Place each on ungreased cookie sheet. Press into a 9-inch circle; with thumb, press a 1-inch hole in center. Bake in 325° oven 15 to 20 minutes or until edges are lightly browned. Cut each circle into 12 to 16 wedges. Cool 5 minutes. Remove from sheets. Makes about 3 dozen cookies.

*Note:* Dough may be pressed into a 15 x 10-inch jelly roll pan and cut into squares after baking.

---

Short of cookie sheets? Try using the aluminum 9 x 13-inch cake pan cover. Or cut pieces of waxed paper the size of your cookie sheets. Place cookie dough on waxed paper. Replace paper with each new batch of cookies.

---

## DATE-ORANGE TOPPERS

1 c. dates, chopped
⅓ c. water
⅓ c. sugar
¼ c. nuts, chopped
1 roll refrigerated slice and bake cookies, any flavor
1 T. orange peel, grated

In saucepan, combine dates, water and sugar. Cook over medium heat, stirring constantly, until mixture thickens. Remove from heat; add nuts. Set aside. Slice cookie dough into 36 slices ¼ inch thick. Place 27 slices on cookie sheets. Place 1 teaspoon of date-nut mixture on top of each slice. Cut remaining 9 slices into thirds. Place each third on top of date-nut mixture. Sprinkle tops with orange peel. Bake in a 350° oven for 10 to 13 minutes or until golden brown. Remove from cookie sheet. Cool. Makes 27 cookies.

## CHOCODILES

1 roll refrigerated slice and bake cookies, any flavor
1 6-oz. pkg. milk chocolate or semisweet chocolate chips
1½ c. cornflakes, crushed
½ c. crunchy peanut butter

Slice cookie dough ¼ inch thick and overlap slices in bottom of greased 8- or 9-inch square pan. Bake at 375° for 15 to 20 minutes until lightly brown. (Cookies will be puffy when removed from oven.) Cool slightly. In medium saucepan, melt chocolate pieces. Stir in cornflakes and peanut butter. Spread over cookie base. Cool. Makes 24 bars.

## PEPPERMINT REFRESHERS

1 roll refrigerated slice and bake cookies, any flavor
2 egg whites
½ c. sugar
⅛ t. peppermint flavoring
2 T. peppermint stick candy, crushed

Slice cookie dough ¼ inch thick and overlap slices in bottom of greased 8- or 9-inch square pan. Bake at 350° for 15 minutes. (Cookies will be puffy when removed from oven.) Beat egg whites until foamy. Gradually add sugar and continue beating until stiff peaks form. Stir in peppermint flavoring. Spread over baked cookie dough; sprinkle with crushed peppermint candy. Return to oven and bake for 10 minutes. Makes 24 bars.

## FRECKLED MALT COOKIES

2 c. flour
1 13¾-oz. pkg. coconut-pecan frosting mix
1 c. malted milk balls, crushed
1 c. butter or margarine, softened
½ t. baking soda
2 eggs, beaten

In large bowl, combine all ingredients; stir until well mixed. Drop by rounded teaspoons, 1 inch apart, onto greased cookie sheets. Bake in 375° oven 8 to 14 minutes or until golden brown. Makes 4 to 5 dozen cookies.

# MERINGUE COOKIES

Old-fashioned "kisses" were invented by the thrifty homemaker facing a bowl of leftover egg whites. Today meringue cookies are versatile mouth-watering confections. Tinted or fruit laden, they add an airy festive touch to parties and dinners the year around.

## RAISIN KISSES

4 egg whites
¼ t. salt
1 c. sugar
1 t. vanilla
2 c. cornflakes
1 c. raisins, coarsely chopped
½ c. flaked coconut

Beat egg whites with salt until peaks form. Gradually add sugar, beating until very stiff but not dry. Beat in vanilla. Fold in cornflakes, raisins and coconut. Drop mixture by teaspoons onto lightly greased cookie sheets. Bake in a 350° oven 20 to 25 minutes or until set and golden brown. Immediately remove to racks to cool. Makes about 3 dozen.

## APRICOT MERINGUE COOKIES

4 egg whites
⅛ t. salt
1 t. vanilla
1⅓ c. sugar
1 c. dried apricots, diced
½ c. blanched slivered toasted almonds

Beat the egg whites with salt and vanilla in large mixing bowl until soft peaks form. Gradually add the sugar, over a five minute period, beating until a stiff meringue is formed. Fold in the apricots and almonds. Drop by heaping teaspoons onto brown paper-lined or lightly greased baking sheets. Bake in 350° oven for about 20 minutes. Cookies will have a light brown color. Makes about 5 dozen.

## COCONUT KISSES

3 egg whites
Dash of salt
1 c. sugar
½ t. vanilla
2 c. cornflakes
1⅓ c. flaked coconut
½ c. chopped pecans
2 1-oz. squares semisweet chocolate
2 t. shortening

Beat egg whites with a dash of salt until foamy; gradually add the sugar, beating to stiff peaks. Stir in vanilla, cornflakes, coconut and pecans. Drop from a teaspoon onto well-greased cookie sheet. Bake at 350° for 18 to 20 minutes. Remove immediately to cooling rack. Melt chocolate with the shortening. Swirl chocolate spiral fashion atop kisses. Makes 3 to 4 dozen kisses. Do not freeze.

Meringue cookies absorb moisture readily. Wrap and store cookies in airtight containers.

## PINK KISSES

½ c. superfine granulated sugar
⅛ t. cream of tartar
2 egg whites
Red food coloring
½ c. butter
½ c. confectioners' sugar
1 t. vanilla
1 to 2 T. water

Sift granulated sugar with cream of tartar. Beat egg whites until foamy. Gradually add sugar and continue beating until stiff peaks form. Add food coloring to tint pink. Cover a baking sheet with foil. Using a pastry bag, with star tube, make small swirls of meringue on foil about ½ inch apart. Bake in a 200° oven for 1 hour or until dry. Cool and remove from baking sheet; store in a tightly covered container. About 1 hour before serving, cream butter, confectioners' sugar and vanilla, adding enough water to reach spreading consistency. Spread bottom of each meringue kiss with frosting and put together in pairs. Refrigerate until serving time. Makes about 4 dozen.

*Pictured opposite*
*Apricot Unbeatables, page 25*

## FLAVORFUL FRUIT COOKIES

### RAISIN LEMON TOFFEE COOKIES

½ c. butter, softened
1½ c. sugar
1 egg
1 egg yolk
1½ t. lemon juice
1 T. grated lemon peel
2¼ c. flour
1½ t. baking powder
½ t. salt
½ c. milk
¾ c. raisins
Toffee Topping

Cream butter and sugar until fluffy. Stir in egg, egg yolk, lemon juice and lemon peel. Beat until well blended. Sift together flour, baking powder and salt. Add flour mixture to creamed mixture alternately with milk. Stir in raisins. Drop from teaspoon onto lightly greased cookie sheet, allowing room for spreading. Bake in 350° oven 10 to 15 minutes, or until cookies are lightly golden. Frost each cookie with thin layer of Toffee Topping. Place under broiler and broil until bubbly. Allow to cool. Makes about 3½ dozen cookies.

#### TOFFEE TOPPING

½ c. slivered almonds
6 T. butter
⅔ c. brown sugar
2 T. flour
2 T. milk

Spread almonds evenly on a cookie sheet; bake at 350° for 5 minutes or until toasted. Combine almonds with remaining ingredients in a saucepan and stir over medium-low heat until bubbly.

### BEST RAISIN OATMEAL COOKIES

⅔ c. shortening, melted
1 c. brown sugar
1 egg
1 t. vanilla
1 c. flour
1 t. salt
1 t. baking powder
2 c. uncooked oats
1 c. raisins

Beat together shortening, brown sugar, egg and vanilla. Sift together dry ingredients; add to shortening mixture; beat well. Stir in oats and raisins. Drop by teaspoons onto greased cookie sheets. Bake at 350° 15 to 20 minutes. Remove to racks to cool. Makes about 5 dozen cookies.

Mankind has been preserving fruits by drying since the beginning of recorded history. He certainly discovered grapes drying on the vines thousands of years ago.

The word raisin comes from the Latin "racemus" which means a cluster of grapes or berries; and a raisin is a dried grape.

The dried fruit industry in this nation is indebted to the Mission Fathers who established the chain of California missions. The friars planted the first peaches, apricots, black Mission figs and raisin grapes.

It looked like a tragedy to California grape growers when their grapes dried on the vines during the long, hot summer of 1873. In desperation, one grower shipped his crop to market anyway; and California's first commercial raisins sold like the proverbial hot cakes. Their popularity has never waned.

### SPICY RAISIN BARS

1 c. sifted flour
½ t. baking soda
½ t. salt
1 t. pumpkin pie spice
½ c. shortening
½ c. brown sugar
¼ c. milk
1 t. vanilla
1 c. uncooked oats
1 c. raisins

Sift together flour, soda, salt and spice. Add shortening, sugar, milk and vanilla. Beat until smooth (about 2 minutes). Blend in oats and raisins. Spread batter evenly in greased 11 x 7-inch baking pan. Bake in 350° oven 20 to 25 minutes. Cut into bars. Makes 2 dozen spicy raisin bars.

## RAISIN CRISSCROSS COOKIES

| | |
|---|---|
| ½ c. butter | ¾ t. cream of |
| ¾ c. sugar | tartar |
| 1 egg | ¾ t. baking soda |
| ½ t. lemon extract | ½ t. salt |
| 1¾ c. flour | 1 c. raisins |

Combine butter, sugar, egg, and lemon flavoring. Mix well. Sift together flour, cream of tartar, soda, and salt. Stir into butter mixture. Mix in raisins. Roll in 1-inch balls. Place about 3 inches apart on ungreased baking sheet. Flatten with fork dipped in flour, making a crisscross pattern. Bake 8 to 10 minutes in a 400° oven. Cool on rack. Makes about 3 dozen cookies.

## APRICOT UNBEATABLES

2 c. confectioners' sugar
½ c. flour
½ t. baking powder
½ c. (3 to 4) egg whites
2 c. chopped walnuts
½ c. dried apricots, chopped

Combine sugar, flour, baking powder and egg whites. Add walnuts and apricots; mix well. Drop by teaspoons onto well-greased cookie sheets. Bake at 325° for 15 to 18 minutes. Cool on rack. Makes 3 dozen cookies.

A is for apples, B is for best and C, of course, is for cookie. Apples, either freshly chopped or in a sauce, lend a lovely moist texture to cookies.

Every school child knows the legend of Johnny Appleseed and how he spread apple seeds and graftings of trees across the nation. Apples, one of nature's most perfect health foods, flourished and are now grown commercially in thirty-five states. The first patent on canned apple cider was issued in 1862. Seven years later, in 1869, canned applesauce received a patent. However, it wasn't until 1920 that quantities of apples and applesauce were canned commercially.

## FROSTY APPLESAUCE COOKIES

| | |
|---|---|
| 1 c. butter | ½ t. salt |
| 1 c. brown sugar | ½ t. baking powder |
| 1 egg | ½ t. allspice |
| 1 8½-oz. can | ¼ t. cloves |
| applesauce | 1 c. whole bran |
| 1 T. molasses | cereal |
| 2 c. flour | 1 c. raisins |

Cream butter and brown sugar. Blend in egg, applesauce and molasses. Sift together flour, salt, baking powder and spices and stir into batter. Fold in cereal and raisins. Drop by teaspoons onto ungreased cookie sheet. Bake at 350° for 15 minutes. Cool and frost with Caramel Frosting. Makes 5 dozen cookies.

### CARAMEL FROSTING

½ c. brown sugar
¼ c. butter or margarine, melted
3½ T. milk
1½ c. confectioners' sugar, sifted

Add brown sugar to butter; boil and stir for 1 minute. Cool slightly. Beat in milk. Add confectioners' sugar and beat until smooth.

## SPICED APPLESAUCE COOKIES

½ c. shortening
1 c. sugar
1 egg
2 c. flour
1 t. salt
1 t. baking soda
1 t. baking powder
¼ t. cloves
1 t. cinnamon
1 c. thick, unsweetened applesauce

Cream shortening. Add sugar gradually, creaming until light. Beat in egg. Sift dry ingredients together and add alternately with the applesauce. Blend thoroughly. Drop by teaspoons on greased cookie sheet about 2 inches apart. Bake in 350° oven 10 minutes or until nicely browned. Remove from pan to cool. Makes about 3 dozen cookies.

## APPLE TEA STICKS

¾ c. flour
1 t. baking powder
½ t. cinnamon
¼ t. salt
1 egg
¾ c. light brown sugar
¼ c. milk
1 t. vanilla
½ c. peanut butter
1 c. raw apples, chopped

Sift flour with baking powder, cinnamon and salt. Beat egg until light and gradually beat in sugar. Stir in milk, vanilla and peanut butter. Fold in flour mixture and apples. Spread in greased square pan 8 x 8 x 2 inches. Bake in 350° oven 30 to 35 minutes. Cool in pan for about 5 minutes. Cut into 24 finger-shaped pieces. Roll in sifted confectioners' sugar. Makes 24 sticks.

## MOIST CRANBERRY-APPLE COOKIES

½ c. butter or margarine
1 c. brown sugar
¾ c. sugar
1 egg
¼ c. milk
2 c. flour
1 t. baking powder
1 t. cinnamon
½ t. salt
1 t. grated orange rind
1½ c. pared apples, chopped
1 c. cranberries, chopped

Cream butter and sugars; beat in egg and milk. Sift together flour, baking powder, cinnamon and salt. Stir into butter mixture until well blended. Stir in orange rind, apple and cranberries. Drop by teaspoons onto greased cookie sheets. Bake at 375° for 12 to 15 minutes. Makes about 4 dozen cookies.

When you are using an old-time recipe that calls for brown sugar, you may not need to pack down the sugar. Modern recipes, however, require that brown sugar be packed down in measuring.

## CHERRY CHOCOLATE CHIP COOKIES

1¼ c. flour
½ t. salt
½ t. baking soda
½ c. butter or margarine
½ c. sugar
¼ c. dark brown sugar
1 egg
½ c. red maraschino cherries, drained and chopped
¼ c. chopped walnuts
1 6-oz. pkg. semisweet chocolate chips

Sift together flour, salt and baking soda. Cream butter with sugars; beat in egg. Stir in cherries, walnuts, chocolate pieces and sifted dry ingredients. Drop rounded teaspoons of batter on ungreased baking sheets, about 1 inch apart. Bake in 375° oven 8 to 10 minutes. Let stand ½ minute, then remove from baking sheets. Makes about 4 dozen.

## BANANA TURNOVER COOKIES

1⅓ c. flour
¼ t. salt
¼ t. cinnamon
¼ c. oil
½ c. creamed cottage cheese
1½ T. honey
2 bananas, sliced
¼ c. raisins
2 T. sunflower seeds

Mix together flour, salt and cinnamon. Add oil and stir until mixture resembles coarse meal. Mix together cottage cheese and honey; stir into flour mixture and form into a ball. Roll out ¼ of dough at a time on a board (it is not necessary to sprinkle flour over the board); cut into 4-inch rounds. Place 3 banana slices on half of each dough round. Add 1 teaspoon raisins and ½ teaspoon sunflower seeds to banana slices. Fold far end of dough over filling, to form a turnover. Seal edges. Place on ungreased baking sheet. Bake in 400° oven 10 minutes. Remove and cool. Sprinkle top with confectioners' sugar before serving. Makes 12 turnovers.

## NECTARINE COUNTRY COOKIES

| | |
|---|---|
| 1½ c. nectarines, chopped | ½ c. butter |
| | 1⅓ c. sugar |
| 2 c. flour | 1 egg |
| 1 t. baking soda | ½ c. diced roasted almonds |
| 1 t. salt | |
| ¼ t. cinnamon | ½ c. raisins |
| ⅛ t. cloves | |

Sift flour with soda, salt, cinnamon and cloves. Cream butter with sugar; mix in egg, almonds and raisins. Alternately add flour mixture and chopped nectarines. Drop by tablespoons onto greased baking sheet. Bake at 375° for 13 to 15 minutes. Cool on rack. Store in loosely covered container. Makes 3 to 4 dozen cookies.

---

Follow the recipe carefully in cooling the cookies—in the pan or on a wire rack. Do not stack, pile or overlap warm cookies. Allow them to cool completely before storing.

---

## CHOCOLATE-APRICOT COOKIES

¼ c. butter or margarine
¼ c. shortening
⅓ c. light brown sugar
⅓ c. sugar
1 egg
½ t. vanilla
1 c. flour
½ t. salt
½ t. baking soda
⅔ c. dried apricots, finely chopped
½ c. semisweet chocolate chips or chopped nuts

Cream together butter, shortening and sugars. Beat in egg and vanilla. Sift together flour, salt and soda; stir into creamed mixture until smooth. Stir in apricots and chocolate pieces. Drop by rounded half-teaspoons onto ungreased baking sheets. Bake in 375° oven 8 to 10 minutes or until lightly browned. Cool on wire racks. Makes about 4 dozen 2-inch cookies.

## LEMON LASSIES

2¼ c. flour
1 t. cinnamon
½ t. baking soda
¼ t. salt
½ c. butter or margarine
1 c. sugar
1 egg
¼ c. light molasses

Sift flour with cinnamon, soda and salt. Cream margarine and sugar. Add egg and molasses. Add dry ingredients gradually. Mix well. Divide dough in half. Press half of dough over bottom of an ungreased 13 x 9-inch glass baking dish. Spread with cooled Filling. Chill. Chill remaining half of dough at least 2 hours; then roll out to ⅛-inch thickness between 2 pieces of waxed paper. Place on top of Filling. Bake at 325° for 30 minutes. When slightly cool, cut into bars and remove from dish.

### FILLING

2 eggs, slightly beaten
½ c. sugar
1 T. grated lemon peel
¼ c. lemon juice
1 T. butter or margarine
⅛ t. salt
1 c. grated coconut

In pan, combine eggs, sugar, lemon peel, lemon juice, margarine and salt. Cook over low heat, stirring constantly until thick. Remove from heat. Add coconut. Cool.

---

Sparkling tart red cranberries add an eye-pleasing note to homemade cookies.

Long before the signing of the Declaration of Independence, cranberries grew wild in the United States. The Indians used the berry as a fruit, a dye and as a first-aid remedy.

Though cranberries have always been a part of Thanksgiving, you need not only prepare them in traditional ways. They combine well with other fruits and make a perfect moist cookie.

---

## FRESH ORANGE-CRANBERRY COOKIES

2¼ c. flour
½ t. baking soda
½ t. salt
½ c. butter, softened
½ c. sugar
½ c. brown sugar
1 egg
½ t. vanilla
½ c. orange, unpeeled but finely chopped
¾ c. whole cranberry sauce, drained
1 c. coarsely chopped walnuts

Sift together flour, soda and salt. Cream the butter and sugars until fluffy. Add egg and vanilla. Blend well. To butter mixture alternately add dry ingredients and chopped orange and cranberry sauce. Blend thoroughly. Stir in nutmeats. Drop by teaspoons onto lightly greased cookie sheets. Bake at 375° for 10 to 12 minutes. Cookies will be crisp when cool. Makes 4 dozen cookies.

## MIXED-UP FRUITCAKE COOKIES

½ c. butter or margarine
1 c. sugar
1 egg
¼ c. water
¼ t. brandy extract
1½ c. flour
1¼ t. baking powder
¼ t. salt
1 t. cinnamon
¼ t. nutmeg
¼ t. allspice
½ c. dried apricots, chopped
½ c. raisins
¼ c. mixed candied fruits
½ c. chopped walnuts

Cream butter and sugar until light. Beat in egg, water and brandy extract. Sift together flour, baking powder, salt and spices; gradually stir into butter mixture. Add fruits and nuts. Mix thoroughly. Drop from teaspoons onto ungreased baking sheet. Bake in 400° oven 8 minutes or until lightly browned. Cool on rack. Makes 3 dozen cookies.

## LEMON BLENDER COOKIES

1 lemon
6 T. water
½ c. shortening
1 egg
1 pkg. yellow cake mix

Trim a thin slice from both ends of unpeeled lemon; cut in half lengthwise. Make a shallow V-shape cut; remove white center core. Cut halves in small chunks. In electric blender, puree lemon chunks, adding water. Add shortening and egg; blend until smooth. In large bowl, combine cake mix and lemon mixture; mix well. Drop batter from teaspoons on lightly greased cookie sheets. Bake at 350° for 13 to 15 minutes. Cool on wire racks. Makes about 5 dozen cookies.

## CHERRY OATMEAL COOKIES

½ c. shortening
½ c. butter
1 c. dark brown sugar
1 c. sugar
2 eggs
1 t. vanilla
1½ c. flour
1 t. baking powder
½ t. baking soda
½ t. salt
1 c. red maraschino cherries, drained and chopped
½ c. flaked coconut
2 c. uncooked oats
Red maraschino cherries, drained and cut in pieces for decoration

Cream together shortening, butter, and sugars until light and fluffy. Beat in eggs and vanilla. Sift together flour, baking powder, soda and salt. Gradually add 1 cup chopped cherries, coconut, oats and sifted dry ingredients to creamed mixture. Chill 1 hour. Drop rounded tablespoons of batter on ungreased baking sheets. Place a piece of maraschino cherry (well-drained) atop each cookie. Bake in 375° oven 10 to 12 minutes or until golden brown. After 1 minute, remove cookies to racks and cool. Makes about 6 dozen cookies.

*Peanut Brittle Cookies*

Uncle Curry & Aunt Diane ✓
Charlie & Kathy ✓
Aunt Carol ✓
Owens Family ✓
Darlene K.
Pastor Pingry
Grandma & Grandpa Haslam

Dr. Callahan


Get more tins !!

# NUT FLAVORED COOKIES

Generally the cookie jar is either half full or half empty. It all depends on who you ask, the cookie baker or the cookie eater. However, both will agree that sweet, moist coconut is a succulent addition to a favorite cookie.

Coconut was known as the Indian nut during Biblical times. During the sixteenth century some called it Nargil. This name was dropped by the eighteenth century and cocoanut became the new name. Forty years later, we Americanized the name to coconut.

Coconut, mainly known for its snowy whiteness, is available to cookie bakers in flaked, shredded or grated form. Each form provides a unique texture to enhance your favorite cookie.

## COCO-CHOCO-NUT COOKIES

2¼ c. flour
1 t. baking soda
1 t. salt
1 c. margarine or butter
¾ c. sugar
¾ c. brown sugar
1 t. vanilla
½ t. water
2 eggs
1 c. flaked or shredded coconut
1 c. coarsely chopped nuts
1 6-oz. pkg. semisweet chocolate chips

Sift flour, soda and salt together. Blend butter, sugars, vanilla and water until smooth. Beat in eggs. Add flour mixture gradually, stirring well. Fold in coconut, nuts and chocolate chips. Drop by teaspoons onto greased cookie sheet. Bake at 350° for 10 minutes or until lightly browned. Makes about 9 dozen cookies.

## COCONUT CHERRY BARS

1 c. margarine or butter
1¼ c. sugar
1 egg
1 t. vanilla
2½ c. flour
1½ t. baking powder
½ t. salt
½ c. chopped nuts
½ c. maraschino cherries, chopped
⅔ c. flaked coconut
1 6-oz. pkg. chocolate chips

Cream margarine or butter; add sugar gradually. Blend in egg and vanilla. Sift together flour, baking powder and salt. Stir into creamed mixture. Add nuts, cherries, coconut and chocolate chips. Spread dough in a greased 13 x 9-inch pan. Bake at 375° for about 25 minutes or until bars are firm in the center. Cool slightly; cut into 40 bars.

*Note:* These delightful bars, popular all year around, are an attractive addition to your Christmas cookie tray. Bake a second batch using green maraschino cherries instead of red cherries. Or use ¼ cup each red or green maraschino cherries for a festive holiday touch.

## COCONUT PEANUT BUTTER CRISPS

2 c. flour
1½ t. baking powder
¼ t. salt
½ c. butter
½ c. peanut butter
1 c. brown sugar
1 egg
2 T. honey
1 c. flaked coconut

Sift flour with baking powder and salt. Cream butter, peanut butter and sugar together until light and fluffy. Beat in egg and honey. Fold in flour mixture until blended. Stir in coconut. Shape into rolls about 2 inches in diameter. Wrap in waxed paper and chill in refrigerator overnight or until firm. Slice ⅛ inch thick. Bake on an ungreased baking sheet in a 375° oven for about 12 minutes. Makes about 6 dozen cookies.

*Pictured opposite*
*Peanut Brittle Cookies, page 32*

## PEANUT BRITTLE COOKIES

| | |
|---|---|
| 1 c. flour | 1 egg |
| ¼ t. baking soda | 1 t. vanilla |
| ½ t. cinnamon | 1 c. finely chopped |
| ½ c. butter | salted peanuts |
| ½ c. brown sugar | |

Sift together flour, soda and cinnamon. Gradually add brown sugar to butter. Cream well. Blend in two tablespoons beaten egg (reserve remaining egg) and 1 teaspoon vanilla. Add dry ingredients and ½ cup peanuts. Mix thoroughly. Spread or pat dough on 15 x 10 x 2-inch greased baking sheet. Brush with remaining egg. Sprinkle with remaining peanuts. Bake in a 325° oven 20 to 25 minutes. Do not overbake. Cut or break into pieces while warm.

Crispy, crunchy, delicious cookies filled with peanuts are especially good.

Peanuts were grown thousands of years ago in South America. Peanut-shaped pottery and peanut designs have been found in Inca tombs. Spanish explorers discovered peanuts in Peru. They took them to Spain and traded them to Africans. In time, African slaves brought them to America.

The peanut fame in the United States is credited to the Civil War, the Circus and baseball.

## SALTED PEANUT COOKIES

1 c. butter or margarine
1 c. granulated sugar
1 c. dark brown sugar
2 eggs
1 t. vanilla
1½ c. flour
1 t. baking soda
3 c. uncooked oats
1½ c. salted peanuts

Cream butter and sugars. Add unbeaten eggs and vanilla, beating until fluffy. Sift flour with soda; add oats. Stir in dry ingredients. Add peanuts, mixing well. Drop by rounded teaspoons onto ungreased cookie sheet. Bake at 375° for 12 minutes. Makes 6 dozen.

## PEANUT CHOCOLATE CHIP COOKIES

¼ c. butter or margarine
¼ c. shortening
2 T. peanut butter
½ c. sugar
½ c. light brown sugar
1 egg
1 t. vanilla
1¾ c. flour
½ t. baking soda
½ t. salt
1 c. salted Spanish peanuts
1 6-oz. pkg. semisweet chocolate chips

Cream butter, shortening and peanut butter until soft and fluffy. Stir in sugars, egg and vanilla. Add dry ingredients. Fold in peanuts and chocolate chips. Drop by teaspoons on ungreased cookie sheets about 2 inches apart. Bake in 375° oven 8 to 10 minutes, or until edges of cookies are lightly browned. Cool cookies 5 minutes on cookie sheet. Remove and cool on a rack. Makes 4 dozen.

## CRUNCHY PEANUT COOKIES

| | |
|---|---|
| ½ c. butter | 3 t. baking powder |
| ½ c. peanut butter | ½ t. salt |
| ¾ c. sugar | 1 c. raisins |
| 2 eggs | 1 c. salted peanuts |
| ½ c. milk | 3 c. cornflakes |
| 2 c. flour | |

Cream butter and peanut butter. Stir in sugar, eggs and milk. Sift together flour, baking powder and salt. Add to creamed mixture, beating until smooth. Fold in raisins, peanuts and cornflakes. Drop by heaping teaspoons on greased cookie sheets. Bake in a 350° oven for 15 minutes or until lightly browned. Cool cookies on a rack. Store in tightly covered container in a cool dry place. Makes about 60 2-inch cookies.

Always cover any butter cookie dough while in the refrigerator. This will prevent the delicate dough from absorbing other food flavors and drying out.

## WALNUT SCOTCHIES

1 6-oz. pkg. butterscotch chips
¾ c. butter
2 T. boiling water
1 t. baking soda
1½ c. uncooked oats
1 c. flour
1 c. chopped walnuts
¾ c. sugar
¼ t. salt

Melt butterscotch chips and butter. Remove from heat. Add the boiling water with baking soda and mix well. Gradually blend in remaining ingredients. Drop by slightly rounded teaspoons, 2 inches apart on ungreased baking sheets. Bake at 350° for 10 minutes. Makes 5 dozen.

## GERMAN WALNUT CAKES

1¼ c. flour
⅓ c. sugar
½ c. butter
2 T. milk
½ t. vanilla
½ c. chopped walnuts
1 to 1½ c. walnuts, halves and
    large pieces
    Glaze
4 oz. semisweet or milk chocolate

Combine flour and sugar. Cut in butter until particles are very fine. Sprinkle milk and vanilla over mixture and mix to a stiff dough. Mix in chopped walnuts. Roll dough ¼-inch thick on lightly floured board and cut into rounds. Place on ungreased baking sheet. Cover each cookie with walnut half or piece, pressing them lightly into dough. Bake at 350° for 15 minutes, until edges are very lightly browned. Remove to wire rack and set on baking sheet. Drizzle tops with hot Glaze. Cool. Melt chocolate over warm (not hot) water. Spread bottom of each cookie with chocolate and place on waxed paper until chocolate is set. Makes 2 dozen 2-inch cookies.

### GLAZE

⅓ c. dark brown sugar
⅓ c. light corn syrup

Combine sugar and syrup in small saucepan; stir over moderate heat until sugar is dissolved. Boil one minute.

Butter can be taken directly from the refrigerator and creamed if you cut each stick into about eight pieces. Keep the mixer speed low when starting the creaming. This method is better than allowing the butter to soften before using. If butter becomes too soft, it means adding extra flour to the dough and that cuts down on the shortness or tenderness of the cookies.

## DOUBLE SWIRL WALNUT COOKIES

¾ c. shortening (half butter)
1¼ c. sugar
2 eggs
1 t. vanilla
2½ c. flour
1 t. baking powder
1 t. salt
2 squares unsweetened chocolate
2 T. milk
⅔ c. finely chopped walnuts

Beat together shortening, sugar, eggs and vanilla until fluffy. Sift flour with baking powder and salt. Blend into creamed mixture. Divide dough in half. Blend melted chocolate, milk and half the walnuts into one portion; blend remaining walnuts into light dough. Wrap each portion in waxed paper; chill thoroughly. Roll light dough on lightly floured board to a 8 x 12-inch rectangle. Cover with a sheet of waxed paper and top with a baking sheet. Invert all, remove board and refrigerate dough while rolling chocolate portion to same size. Place light dough over chocolate dough, with shorter sides matching and one longer side about ¼ inch in from edge of chocolate portion. Cut crosswise through center, making two 6-inch sections for easier rolling. Starting from side showing chocolate dough, roll the two together to center. Turn over and roll from the other side to meet the first roll. Wrap in waxed paper and chill until very firm. Cut rolls into ¼-inch slices and place on lightly greased baking sheets. Bake at 400° for about 8 minutes. Let stand a minute, then remove carefully with broad spatula and cool on wire racks. Makes about 40 cookies.

Anytime is a grand time for sampling oven-fresh cookies. A fine addition to any cookie recipe is crisp, crunchy walnuts. The mellow flavor combines well with lively spices. Walnuts are the number one cookie nut.

Walnuts are international travelers. In Biblical times they were grown and eaten in ancient Persia. Traded and transplanted, walnuts eventually reached Italy, Spain and France. English ships carried walnuts all over the world. In time, they became incorrectly known as "English" walnuts. However, they were never commercially grown in England.

In the 1700s Spanish missionaries brought walnuts to California. The trees thrived in the warm climate and rich soil. California now claims to be the walnut capital of the world.

## WALNUT PINWHEELS

⅔ c. butter
1 c. sugar
1 egg
1 t. vanilla
1 t. grated lemon peel
2 T. milk
2½ c. flour
½ t. salt
½ t. baking powder
¾ c. finely chopped walnuts
⅓ c. brown sugar
¼ c. honey
12 candied cherries, halved

Cream butter and sugar. Add egg, vanilla, lemon peel and milk. Sift flour with salt and baking powder; blend into creamed mixture to make stiff dough. Chill about 1 hour. Combine walnuts, brown sugar and honey and mix well for filling. Roll half of chilled dough on lightly floured board to 9 x 12-inch rectangle and cut into 3-inch squares. Place teaspoonful of filling in center of each. Cut diagonally from corners of squares toward center, making 8 points. Fold every other point to center over filling. Press cherry half in center of each. Lift with a broad spatula onto lightly greased baking sheet. Bake at 350° about 12 to 14 minutes. Makes 2 dozen cookies.

## WALNUT JAM CRESCENTS

1⅓ c. flour
¼ t. salt
⅔ c. butter or margarine
½ c. sour cream
⅔ c. walnuts
⅔ c. raspberry jam or orange marmalade

Combine flour with salt. Cut in butter until in fine particles. Add sour cream and mix to a stiff dough. Divide into two even-size portions. Shape each into a round. Wrap in waxed paper and chill well. Meanwhile, chop walnuts very fine. Roll one portion of chilled pastry at a time to an 11-inch round on lightly floured board. Spread with ⅓ cup jam and sprinkle with ⅓ cup walnuts. Cut into quarters, then cut each quarter into 3 wedges. Roll up, one at a time, starting from outer edge, and place on lightly greased cookie sheet. Repeat with second pastry round. Bake in upper half of oven at 375° for 25 to 30 minutes, until lightly browned. Remove to wire racks to cool. Makes 2 dozen crescents.

## WALNUT DIAGONALS

¾ c. butter
½ c. sugar
¼ t. salt
2 egg yolks
1 t. vanilla
2 c. flour

1 c. walnuts, chopped
½ c. brown sugar
¼ c. sour cream
Dash nutmeg

Cream together butter, sugar and salt. Beat in egg yolks and vanilla. Blend in flour. Chill dough about ½ hour. Roll half the cookie dough to a rectangle about 6 x 15-inches. Cut lengthwise into three 2 x 15-inch strips and transfer carefully to cookie sheet, using wide spatula. Put remaining dough through a cookie press fitted with star plate. Force dough along sides and ends of dough strips. (If cookie press is not available, shape dough into ropes about the diameter of a pencil and place along sides and ends of dough strips.) Mix walnuts with brown sugar, sour cream and nutmeg. Spoon this walnut mixture in center and along length of dough. Bake at 350° for 20 to 25 minutes or until lightly browned. Cool, then cut into diagonal slices. Makes about 3 dozen cookies.

*Pictured opposite*
*Double Swirl Walnut Cookies, page 33*

## ALMOND SNOWBALL COOKIES

- 2 c. cornflakes
- 1 c. butter or margarine
- ½ c. sugar
- 1 egg
- 2 t. vanilla
- 1¾ c. flour
- ½ t. salt
- 2 c. finely chopped almonds
- 1½ c. confectioners' sugar

Crush cornflakes into fine crumbs. Set aside. Cream butter and sugar until light and fluffy. Add egg and vanilla and beat well. Sift together flour and salt. With pastry blender, cut flour mixture into butter mixture. Stir in crumbs and almonds. Shape level tablespoons of dough into balls and place on ungreased baking sheets. Bake in 350° oven about 20 minutes or until lightly browned. Cool slightly on baking sheets. Roll in confectioners' sugar. Cool completely before serving. Makes about 5 dozen 1-inch balls.

## COCONUT ALMOND COOKIES

- 1 c. butter
- ¼ t. salt
- 1 c. confectioners' sugar
- 1 t. almond extract
- 1 c. finely grated coconut
- 2¼ c. cake flour
- ¾ c. ground blanched almonds
- Confectioners' sugar

Cream butter with salt. Gradually add sugar, creaming until light and fluffy. Blend in almond extract and coconut. Add flour a little at a time. Stir in almonds. Chill dough. Form into crescents; place on ungreased baking sheets. Bake in 325° oven 18 to 20 minutes. Cool on sheets. Sprinkle with confectioners' sugar. Makes about 4½ dozen cookies.

## BROWN SUGAR ALMOND COOKIES

- ¾ c. butter
- 2 c. brown sugar
- 2 eggs
- 1 t. vanilla
- 3 c. flour
- 2 t. baking powder
- ¾ t. salt
- 1 c. finely chopped almonds
  Whole almonds
  Red or green candied cherries
  Clear Glaze

Thoroughly mix butter, sugar, eggs and vanilla. Blend in flour, baking powder and salt. Stir in almonds. On lightly floured surface roll dough ⅛ inch thick. Cut into circles. Place on ungreased baking sheet. Decorate with whole almonds and cherries. Bake in 375° oven 5 to 7 minutes or until very lightly browned. Brush cooled cookies with Clear Glaze. Makes about 5 dozen 3-inch cookies.

### CLEAR GLAZE

Heat ¼ cup light corn syrup and 2 tablespoons water just to a rolling boil. Cool to lukewarm.

## COCOA PECAN PUFFS

1 c. butter
1½ c. brown sugar
1 egg
1 18¼-oz. can crushed pineapple
3½ c. flour
3 T. cocoa
1 t. baking powder
1 t. cinnamon
½ t. salt
½ c. chopped pecans

Cream butter and sugar until fluffy. Beat in egg until well blended. Fold in pineapple with the syrup. Combine flour, cocoa, baking powder, cinnamon and salt. Stir into pineapple mixture. Fold in pecans. Drop by teaspoons onto lightly greased baking sheets. Bake in 375° oven 12 to 15 minutes or until lightly browned around edges. Remove to racks to cool before storing. Makes 4 to 4½ dozen cookies.

## MILK CHOCOLATE PECAN BARS

1 c. flour
½ c. brown sugar
½ t. baking soda
¼ t. salt
¼ c. butter
Topping
½ c. pecans

In large bowl, combine flour, brown sugar, baking soda and salt; mix well. Cut in butter with pastry blender until mixture resembles fine crumbs. Press evenly into a greased 13 x 9 x 2-inch baking pan. Bake at 350° for 10 minutes. Pour Topping over cookie base; sprinkle with pecans. Return to oven and bake at 350° for 20 minutes. Cool; cut into 4 dozen 2 x 1-inch bars.

### TOPPING

2 c. milk chocolate chips
2 eggs
¼ c. brown sugar
1 t. vanilla
1 t. salt
½ c. chopped pecans

Melt milk chocolate morsels over hot (not boiling) water; remove from heat. In small bowl, combine eggs, brown sugar, vanilla and salt. Beat 2 minutes at high speed on electric mixer. Add melted chocolate; mix well. Stir in pecans.

## LEMON FROSTED PECAN COOKIES

1 c. butter or margarine
¾ c. confectioners' sugar
2 T. milk
1½ c. flour
¾ c. cornstarch
¾ c. chopped pecans
2½ c. confectioners' sugar
1 T. butter
3 T. lemon juice
Yellow food coloring

Stir butter to soften. Add confectioners' sugar, milk, flour and cornstarch. Cream until well blended; chill. Place small spoonfuls of chopped pecans 2 inches apart on an ungreased baking sheet. Shape dough into small balls (about 1 teaspoon) and flatten each over a few pecans. Bake in 350° oven for 12 to 15 minutes. Cool. Combine remaining ingredients. Spread over cookies. Makes 4 dozen.

## GIFTS OF LOVE

It's time to make another batch
Of cookies good and sweet
To keep the jar brimming full
Of fresh-baked cookie treats.

There's nothing quite as pleasing
When a friend drops in for tea,
As delicious homemade cookies
That demand the recipe!

And when the children return from school,
As hungry as can be,
Fill them up with milk and cookies
And special memories.

So keep the jar upon the shelf
Brimming full indeed
Of confections you have made,
Gifts of love are these!

*Betty Dollar Wallace*

# OLD-FASHIONED CEREAL AND GRAIN COOKIES

## CANDIED OATMEAL DROPS

1 c. candied citron or glazed cherries, halves
¼ c. brandy
1½ c. flour
1 t. salt
1 t. cinnamon
½ t. baking soda
½ t. cloves
1 c. brown sugar
¾ c. butter or shortening
2 eggs, beaten
3 c. uncooked oats
1 c. chopped nuts

Soak candied fruit in brandy while preparing dough, or soak overnight. Stir together flour, salt, cinnamon, soda and cloves. Beat together sugar, butter and eggs. Stir in flour mixture, then fold in soaked fruit, oats and nuts. Drop by level tablespoons onto lightly greased baking sheets. Bake in 375° oven 10 to 12 minutes or until lightly brown. Cool. Makes 5½ dozen.

There are cookies and there are cookies, but oatmeal cookies are always special. These welcome and nourishing cookies have kept cookie jars filled for generations.

Perhaps the forerunner of our classic oatmeal cookie is the Scottish oatcake or bannock. The oatcakes are made in circles, then cut in wedges called farls.

Oats arrived in the Colonies in the early 1600s. Creative early American cooks gradually incorporated oats into a vast array of recipes. Most of us will agree the oatmeal cookie was the best invention of all.

## CHEWY OATMEAL COOKIES

1 c. flour
1 t. cinnamon
¾ t. baking soda
½ t. salt
¼ t. nutmeg
¾ c. shortening
1⅓ c. brown sugar
2 eggs
1 t. vanilla
2 c. uncooked oats
1 c. raisins

Sift together flour, cinnamon, soda, salt and nutmeg. Cream shortening and sugar. Add eggs and vanilla; beat until smooth. Add flour mixture. Stir in oatmeal and raisins. Drop rounded teaspoons of dough onto greased cookie sheets. Bake in 350° oven 12 to 15 minutes. Makes about 3½ dozen cookies.

## CEREAL 'N CHOCOLATE CHIP COOKIES

1¾ c. flour
1 t. baking soda
½ t. salt
1 c. butter or margarine
¾ c. granulated sugar
¾ c. brown sugar
2 eggs
1 t. vanilla
2 c. oven-toasted rice cereal
1 6-oz. pkg. semisweet chocolate chips

Stir together flour, soda and salt. Set aside. Cream together butter and sugars. Add egg and vanilla and beat well. Stir in dry ingredients. Add rice cereal and chocolate chips. Drop by level tablespoons onto greased baking sheets. Bake in 350° oven about 10 minutes or until lightly browned. Cool about 1 minute before removing from baking sheets. Place on wire racks. Makes about 6 dozen 2½-inch cookies.

### PEANUT BUTTER COOKIES

Mix ¾ cup peanut butter into butter-sugar mixture.

### CHOCOLATE CHIP RAISIN COOKIES

Add 1 cup seedless raisins with the chocolate chips.

### HOLIDAY FRUIT COOKIES

In place of chocolate chips, use 1 cup finely cut, mixed candied fruit.

*Pictured opposite
Cereal 'N Chocolate Chip Cookies*

Here's what's cookin' *Cereal 'n Chocolate Chip Cookies*
Recipe from the kitchen of MRS. B.

| | |
|---|---|
| 1 3/4 C FLOUR | 1/2 t SALT |
| 1 t BAKING SODA | 1 C BUTTER |
| 3/4 C SUGAR | 1 t VANILLA |
| 3/4 C BROWN SUGAR | 2 EGGS |
| 2 C TOASTED RICE CEREAL | |
| 1 6 OZ 7KG CHOCOLATE CHIPS | |

STIR TOGETHER FLOUR, SODA,
SET ASIDE. MEASURE

## JELLY BEAN JOLLIES

½ c. butter
⅓ c. sugar
⅓ c. light brown sugar
1 egg
½ t. baking soda
½ t. baking powder
½ t. salt
½ t. vanilla
1¼ c. flour
½ c. uncooked oats
1 c. jelly beans or gumdrops, cut up

Cream together butter and sugars. Beat in egg, baking soda, baking powder, salt and vanilla. Stir in flour and oats until blended. Add jelly beans. Drop rounded spoonfuls of batter about 2 inches apart on lightly greased cookie sheet. Bake in 375° oven 10 to 12 minutes or until lightly browned. Makes 3 to 3½ dozen cookies.

The word "cereal" is kin to Ceres, the Roman goddess of vegetation.

It's best to cool large cookies for one to two minutes before removing from the cookie sheet, unless the recipe directions tell you otherwise. That's because just-baked cookies are very tender and need the time to firm a bit before they're removed with a wide metal spatula.

## CHOCOLATE BRAN CRISPS

2 c. flour
½ t. baking soda
½ t. salt
1 c. butter or margarine
1½ c. sugar
2 eggs
1 t. vanilla
1 c. whole bran cereal
1 6-oz. pkg. semisweet chocolate chips

Sift together flour, soda and salt. Set aside. Beat butter and sugar until light and fluffy. Add eggs and vanilla, beating well. Stir in bran cereal and chocolate chips. Add sifted dry ingredients. Mix well. Drop by level tablespoons onto ungreased baking sheets. Bake in 375° oven about 12 minutes or until lightly browned. Makes about 5½ dozen crisp cookies.

## RANGER COOKIES

½ c. shortening
½ c. granulated sugar
½ c. brown sugar
1 egg
½ t. vanilla
1 c. flour
½ t. baking soda
¼ t. baking powder
¼ t. salt
1 c. uncooked oats
1 c. whole wheat flakes
½ c. shredded coconut

Thoroughly mix shortening, sugars, egg and vanilla. Stir in remaining ingredients. Drop dough by rounded teaspoons 2 inches apart onto ungreased baking sheet. Bake in 375° oven 10 minutes. Immediately remove from baking sheet. Makes 3 dozen cookies, chewy on the inside, and crisp on the outside.

## HONEY OAT DROPS

¾ c. flour
¼ t. salt
¼ t. baking soda
¼ c. butter or margarine
⅓ c. honey
¼ c. sour cream
½ t. vanilla
½ c. uncooked oats
½ c. coarsely chopped walnuts
¼ c. pitted dates, chopped

Sift flour with salt and baking soda. Cream together butter and honey. Stir in sour cream and vanilla. Blend in flour mixture and oats. Stir in walnuts and dates. Drop by rounded tablespoons onto greased and floured cookie sheets. Bake just above oven center at 325° about 15 minutes, until lightly browned. Let stand a minute, then remove to wire racks to cool. Makes 1½ dozen.

## HONEY CEREAL COOKIES

2 c. flour
1 t. baking soda
½ t. baking powder
½ t. salt
1 c. butter
½ c. brown sugar
¾ c. granulated sugar
½ c. honey
1 egg
2 c. crisp whole wheat flakes
2 c. crisp sweetened rice cereal
1 c. flaked coconut

Sift flour with soda, baking powder and salt. Cream butter and sugars; add honey, egg and the flour mixture. Add cereals and coconut; mix thoroughly. Drop from teaspoon onto ungreased baking sheets. Bake at 375° for 8 to 10 minutes, or until golden brown. Let stand a few seconds before removing from baking sheet. (Cookies will become crisp when cool.) Makes about 8 dozen.

## BANANA GRANOLA COOKIES

⅓ c. shortening
½ c. sugar
¼ c. molasses
1 egg
1⅓ c. ripe bananas, mashed (4 medium)
¼ c. nonfat dry milk powder
1¼ c. flour
1 t. baking powder
½ t. salt
¼ t. baking soda
⅛ t. ginger
½ t. grated lemon rind
½ c. flaked coconut
2 T. sesame seeds
¾ c. raisins
1 c. uncooked oats

In large mixing bowl, cream shortening and sugar. Beat in molasses and egg. Stir in bananas and dry milk powder. Sift together flour, baking powder, salt, baking soda and ginger; blend into batter. Stir in lemon rind, coconut, sesame seeds, raisins and oats. Drop by teaspoons onto greased baking sheets. Bake in 400° oven 10 minutes. Remove to rack and cool. Makes 4 dozen.

## CHOCOLATE SNOW DROPS

1 c. flour
1 t. baking powder
¼ t. baking soda
¼ t. salt
½ c. coarsely chopped nuts
⅓ c. butter or margarine
1 c. brown sugar
1 egg
2 1-oz. squares unsweetened chocolate, melted
½ c. whole bran cereal
½ c. buttermilk or sour milk
½ t. vanilla flavoring

Sift together flour, baking powder, soda and salt; stir in nuts. Set aside. Cream together butter and sugar. Add egg and melted chocolate; mix thoroughly. Stir in bran cereal, buttermilk and vanilla. Add sifted dry ingredients; mix until combined. Drop by level tablespoons onto lightly greased baking sheets. (A walnut half can be gently pressed into top of each cookie.) Bake in 375° oven about 12 minutes or until cookie springs back when lightly touched. Remove immediately from baking sheets; cool on wire racks. Top cookies with confectioners' sugar frosting if desired. Makes about 3½ dozen 2¼-inch cookies.

## CHOCOLATE WHEAT GERM BUTTERBALLS

¾ c. toasted wheat germ
¾ c. sugar
2 1-oz. squares semisweet chocolate
2 T. milk
1 c. butter
1½ t. vanilla
2½ c. flour
¼ t. salt
⅓ c. diced roasted almonds

Combine 1 tablespoon EACH of the wheat germ and sugar; reserve for coating. Melt chocolate and milk over low heat. Beat together butter and sugar. Stir in vanilla and melted chocolate. Gradually add flour mixed with salt and wheat germ. Mix in almonds. Shape dough into 48 balls. Dip into sugar and wheat germ. Place on ungreased baking sheet. Bake in 375° oven 11 to 12 minutes. Cool on rack. Makes 4 dozen.

## GLAZED WHEAT GERM FLORENTINES

¼ c. shortening
⅔ c. toasted wheat germ
½ c. sugar
¼ c. flour
¼ t. salt
3 T. whipping cream
1 t. vanilla
¼ c. finely chopped almonds
3 1-oz. squares semisweet chocolate, melted

Melt shortening. Mix in all ingredients except chocolate. Drop teaspoon measures of mixture onto lightly greased baking sheet. Flatten with back of spoon. Bake in 350° oven 7 to 8 minutes or until lightly browned. Cool on baking sheet 2 minutes. Carefully remove and cool on racks. Spread bottoms of cooled cookies with melted chocolate. Store between layers of waxed paper. Makes about 3 dozen cookies.

## TOASTED WHEAT GERM VIENNA BARS

2 eggs, separated
½ c. sugar
6 T. butter
2 t. grated lemon peel
1 t. vanilla
1¼ c. flour
¼ t. salt
¾ c. toasted wheat germ
¼ c. finely chopped walnuts
½ c. apricot jam
Confectioners' sugar

Beat egg yolks with ¼ cup sugar. Beat in butter, lemon peel, vanilla, flour, salt and ½ cup wheat germ. Spread dough on greased baking sheet into 10 x 5-inch rectangle. Build up edges about ½ inch. Bake in 350° oven 12 to 15 minutes. Meanwhile, beat egg whites until foamy. Add remaining ¼ cup sugar gradually and beat until stiff. Fold in walnuts and remaining ¼ cup wheat germ. Spread jam over hot crust. Spread egg mixture on top. Return to oven and continue baking 15 to 18 minutes longer or until golden brown on top. Cool. Dust with confectioners' sugar. Cut into small bars. Makes about 3 dozen bars.

## SOUR CREAM OATMEAL COOKIES

| | |
|---|---|
| ¾ c. butter | 1 t. baking soda |
| 2 c. brown sugar | 2 c. uncooked oats |
| 2 eggs, beaten | ½ t. salt |
| ¾ c. sour cream | ½ t. cinnamon |
| 1 t. vanilla | 1 c. raisins |
| 2 c. flour | ½ c. chopped nuts |

Cream butter and sugar until fluffy. Add eggs, sour cream and vanilla. Beat well. Sift together flour, soda, salt and cinnamon and add alternately with oats, nuts, and raisins. Beat until smooth. Drop by teaspoons on a greased cookie sheet. Bake at 350° about 15 minutes or until cookies are lightly browned and firm to touch. Cool on rack. Makes about 4½ dozen.

## LUSCIOUS APRICOT BARS

⅔ c. dried apricots, finely chopped, or
¾ c. finely chopped prunes
½ c. butter or margarine
¼ c. granulated sugar
1 c. flour
½ c. whole bran cereal
½ t. baking powder
¼ t. salt
1 c. brown sugar
2 eggs
½ t. vanilla
½ c. finely chopped nuts
  Confectioners' sugar

Rinse apricots; place in small mixing bowl. Cover with very hot water and let stand 10 minutes or until fruit is tender. Drain well. Set aside. For crust, measure butter, granulated sugar and ½ cup flour into small mixing bowl; beat until smooth and creamy. Mix in bran cereal. Spread mixture evenly in bottom of ungreased 8 x 8 x 2-inch baking pan. Bake in 350° oven about 25 minutes or until lightly browned. Remove from oven; cool slightly. While crust is baking, sift together the remaining ½ cup flour, baking powder and salt. Set aside. Place brown sugar and eggs in large mixing bowl; beat well. Add sifted dry ingredients, vanilla, nuts and apricots; mix well. Spread mixture over baked crust. Return to 350° oven; bake 50 minutes or until lightly browned. Cool. Cut into bars. Roll in confectioners' sugar. Makes 32 bars.

## PRIZE BROWNIES

Brownie lovers come in all sizes and ages. Some prefer a rich, moist, fudgy brownie. Others favor a nutty, frosting-covered cake-like bar.

In fact, some claim that the original brownie resulted from a disaster when an inventive baker rescued a fallen chocolate cake.

## CHARLIE'S BROWNIES

1¼ c. flour
1 c. sugar
1 c. brown sugar
1 t. baking powder
1 t. salt
1 t. vanilla
½ c. butter, softened
¼ c. shortening
4 eggs
3 1-oz. envelopes pre-melted unsweetened chocolate
½ c. chopped nuts (optional)

Combine all ingredients in large mixing bowl. Beat at medium speed for 1 minute. Spread in greased 15 x 10-inch pan. Bake in preheated 350° oven for 25 to 30 minutes. Cool and frost. For thicker brownies, bake in a greased 13 x 9-inch pan for 30 to 35 minutes.

### CHOCOLATE ICING

3 T. butter
3 T. milk
1 1-oz. envelope pre-melted unsweetened chocolate
2½ c. confectioners' sugar

Melt butter, milk and chocolate. Stir in sugar; beat until smooth. Spread on cooled brownies.

## GROWN-UP BROWNIES

### COOKIE BASE

½ c. brown sugar
¼ c. butter or margarine
¾ c. flour
¼ t. baking powder

Cream brown sugar and butter. Sift flour and baking powder and blend into sugar and butter mixture. Press into a greased 8- or 9-inch square pan. Bake at 350° for 10 minutes.

### TOPPING

1¼ c. sugar
2 eggs
⅓ c. butter or margarine, melted
2 1-oz. envelopes pre-melted or
2 1-oz. squares unsweetened chocolate, melted
⅔ c. flour
½ t. baking powder
¼ t. salt
½ c. chopped nuts

Combine sugar and eggs; beat well. Stir in melted butter and chocolate. Sift together and blend in flour, baking powder and salt. Stir in chopped nuts. Spread Topping over partially baked cookie base. Bake at 350° for 25 minutes if using 9-inch pan; 35 minutes for 8-inch pan. Cool before cutting into squares. Makes 3 dozen 1½-inch squares.

## GRAHAM CRACKER BROWNIES

½ c. brown sugar
½ c. granulated sugar
½ t. salt
1 t. vanilla
1 c. graham cracker crumbs
¾ c. raisins
⅓ c. chopped walnuts
2 eggs, beaten

Combine sugars, salt, vanilla, graham cracker crumbs, raisins and nuts. Add to beaten eggs and mix well. Spread evenly in greased and floured 8-inch square pan. Bake in a 350° oven for 25 minutes. Cool slightly; then turn out and cut into squares. Dust with confectioners' sugar, if desired. Makes 16 squares.

## CHOCOLATE PEPPERMINT BROWNIES

4 1-oz. squares unsweetened chocolate
½ c. butter
2 c. sugar
4 eggs, beaten
1 c. flour
1 t. vanilla
1 c. coarsely chopped walnuts
15 to 20 chocolate peppermint patties

Melt chocolate and butter together over hot water. Cool slightly. Gradually add sugar and eggs, beating thoroughly after each addition. Blend in chocolate mixture. Stir in flour. Then add vanilla and nuts. Spread in greased 9-inch square pan. Bake in 325° oven about 40 minutes. Arrange chocolate peppermint patties over top of hot brownies; return to oven about 3 minutes to soften patties. Then spread to cover entire top of the brownies. Cool and cut into bars. Makes about 2 dozen brownies.

> It's best to shell walnuts and keep the kernels refrigerated in airtight containers. Kept fresh, kernels break with a snap, taste crisp and clean.

## WALNUT BROWNIES

⅓ c. shortening
1 6-oz. pkg. semisweet chocolate chips
¾ c. cake flour
½ c. sugar
½ t. baking powder
¼ t. salt
2 eggs
1 t. vanilla
1 c. coarsely chopped walnuts

Combine shortening and chocolate chips and melt over hot water. Cool slightly. Meanwhile, sift flour with sugar, baking powder and salt. Combine chocolate mixture, eggs and vanilla. Add dry ingredients and mix until smooth. Stir in walnuts. Spread into greased 8-inch square pan. Bake at 350° for about 30 minutes, just until top feels firm to touch. Cool in pan. Cut into squares or bars. Makes 15 brownies.

## BUTTERSCOTCH BROWNIES

¼ c. butter
½ c. evaporated milk
2 c. light brown sugar
2 eggs, slightly beaten
½ t. salt
1½ c. flour
2 t. baking powder
1 t. vanilla
1 c. chopped pecans

In saucepan melt butter; remove from heat. Add evaporated milk, sugar, eggs and salt. Stir until well blended. Sift together flour and baking powder. Stir into egg mixture. Add vanilla and pecans. Spread evenly in greased 13 x 9-inch pan. Bake at 350° for 30 to 35 minutes. Cool in pan on wire rack. Cut into rectangles. Makes 3 dozen brownies.

## PEANUT SWIRL BROWNIES

1 6-oz. pkg. semisweet chocolate chips
6 T. butter or margarine
⅓ c. honey
2 eggs, beaten
1 t. vanilla extract
½ c. flour
½ t. baking powder
1 c. peanut butter
½ c. sugar
½ c. milk
1 egg
Dash of salt
½ c. chopped peanuts

Lightly grease a 9 x 9 x 2-inch baking pan. In a saucepan, over low heat, melt chocolate chips and butter, stirring constantly; cool. Gradually add honey to 2 beaten eggs. Blend in cooled chocolate mixture and vanilla. Stir together flour and baking powder. Add to chocolate mixture and stir just until dry ingredients are moistened. Pour half (1 cup) of brownie mixture into a lightly greased baking pan. Bake in a preheated 350° oven for 10 minutes. Blend peanut butter with sugar and beat in milk, egg and salt. Stir in nuts. Pour peanut mixture over partially baked brownie layer. Carefully spoon remaining brownie batter over peanut layer. Swirl slightly. Bake in a 350° oven about 30 to 35 minutes or until done. Makes about 24 bars.

# RICH CHOCOLATE COOKIES

## CHOCOLATE THUMBPRINTS

1 1-oz. square unsweetened chocolate
½ c. butter or margarine
½ c. sugar
1 egg, separated
¼ t. vanilla
1 c. flour
¼ t. salt
¾ c. finely chopped nuts
1 6-oz. pkg. semisweet chocolate chips

Melt chocolate over hot, not boiling, water. Cool slightly. Cream butter; add melted chocolate. Add sugar, egg yolk and vanilla and mix thoroughly. Sift together flour and salt. Add to chocolate mixture. Slightly beat egg white with fork. Roll dough into balls (about 1 teaspoon per ball); and dip balls in egg white to coat. Roll in nuts. Place about 1 inch apart on ungreased cookie sheet; press thumb gently in center of each. Bake in preheated 350° oven 10 to 12 minutes or until set. Transfer to cake rack. Immediately place 3 or 4 chocolates chips in the "thumbprint." When the chips have melted, spread evenly over the thumbprint. Makes about 3 dozen cookies.

The story of the cocoa bean is a romantic one. It could be labeled "the little brown bean that made good." Spaniards recognized the possibilities of chocolate, but kept it a secret for nearly one hundred years.

As late as the Eighteenth century, some Latin American growers ate only the slightly sweet flesh of the cocoa pod. They considered the bean a waste or, following the example of the Aztecs and Mayans, used it as currency.

## CHOCOLATE COFFEE DROPS

2¼ c. flour
1 T. baking powder
1 t. salt
2 t. nutmeg
2 t. cinnamon
2 T. boiling water
2 T. instant coffee
⅔ c. shortening
1 c. dark brown sugar
1 egg
1 t. vanilla
1 12-oz. pkg. mini-chocolate chips
½ c. chopped nuts

Stir together flour, baking powder, salt, nutmeg and cinnamon and set aside. In small bowl, pour boiling water over coffee. Let cool. Cream shortening and sugar until light and fluffy. Beat in egg and vanilla. Add flour alternately with coffee. Stir in chocolate chips and nuts. Drop by level tablespoons on greased cookie sheet. Bake in preheated 375° oven 6 to 8 minutes. Makes about 4½ dozen.

## CHOCOLATE BANANA COOKIES

3 c. flour
4½ t. baking powder
1½ t. salt
1 t. baking soda
1 c. butter
¾ c. sugar
½ c. light brown sugar
1 t. vanilla extract
1 egg
1 c. mashed banana
2 1-oz. squares semisweet or
　 unsweetened chocolate, melted
1 c. chopped nuts
　 Confectioners' sugar

Sift together flour, baking powder, salt and soda. Cream together butter and sugars. Beat in vanilla and egg. Blend in banana, cooled chocolate and nuts. Stir in flour mixture. Drop by level tablespoons onto greased baking sheets. Bake in preheated 350° oven 12 to 14 minutes. Cool on wire racks. Sprinkle with confectioners' sugar. Makes about 6½ dozen.

# SUGAR AND SPICE COOKIES

## CRACKLE-TOP MOLASSES COOKIES

| | |
|---|---|
| 1 c. shortening | 2 t. baking soda |
| 2 c. brown sugar | 2 t. dry mustard |
| 1 egg, well beaten | 1 t. vanilla |
| 1 c. molasses | 1 t. lemon extract |
| 4 c. flour | Sugar |
| ½ t. salt | |

Cream shortening; add brown sugar. Blend in egg and molasses. Beat until light and fluffy. Sift dry ingredients; gradually blend into creamed mixture. (Dough should be soft but not sticky.) Add vanilla and lemon extract. Shape into 1-inch balls and place on a greased baking sheet. (Do not flatten.) Bake at 350° for 12 to 15 minutes, or until brown. Sprinkle with sugar; remove from baking sheet. Makes about 5 dozen.

## PEANUT BUTTER HONEY SLICES

4 c. flour
1 t. baking soda
½ t. salt
1 t. cinnamon
1 c. smooth peanut butter
½ c. butter
½ c. sugar
1 c. honey
2 t. vanilla
2 eggs, well beaten

Sift together flour, soda, salt and cinnamon. Set aside. Cream peanut butter and butter. Add sugar, honey and vanilla and beat until fluffy. Add eggs. Stir in flour mixture. Shape into four 8-inch rolls. Wrap in waxed paper. Chill. Cut into ⅛-inch slices. Bake in 400° oven 5 to 8 minutes. Makes 6 dozen.

## ORANGE SUGAR COOKIES

½ c. butter
½ c. sugar
2 eggs
1 T. orange juice concentrate, thawed
1 T. grated orange rind
2 c. flour
2 t. baking powder
½ c. sugar mixed with 2 T. grated orange rind

Cream butter and sugar. Beat in eggs, one at a time. Blend in undiluted orange concentrate and 1 tablespoon orange rind. Sift together flour and baking powder and blend into creamed mixture. Wrap in waxed paper and refrigerate 3 hours. Roll out on lightly floured surface to ¼-inch thickness. Cut with a 2-inch cookie cutter. Place on greased baking sheet and sprinkle with sugar mixed with orange rind. Bake in 375° oven for 8 to 10 minutes. Makes 5 dozen cookies.

> Cool cookie sheets before placing rolled cookie dough on to bake. If cookie sheet is warm when cookies are placed on, they will have a bubbly appearance when baked.

## GINGER HONEY BARS

2 c. cake flour
1¼ c. sugar
1 t. nutmeg
¼ t. baking soda
¼ t. salt
½ c. butter, melted
½ c. honey
4 egg whites
2 T. milk
½ c. crystallized ginger, diced

Sift flour with sugar, nutmeg, soda and salt. Add butter, honey, egg whites and milk, stirring until blended. Fold in crystallized ginger. Turn batter into two well greased and waxed paper lined 8 x 8 x 2-inch pans. Bake in 350° oven 35 minutes or until top is firm when pressed lightly. Turn out onto wire racks. Remove paper at once. Cool. Cut each cake into 24 squares. Store in a tightly covered container at least 2 to 3 days before serving. Flavor and texture improves with age. Makes 48 squares.

## TULIP COOKIES

¾ c. sugar
½ c. butter
1 egg
1 egg yolk
1 t. grated orange rind
2 T. orange juice
2¼ c. flour
1 T. baking powder
1 t. salt
  Glaze

Cream sugar and butter until light and fluffy. Blend in egg and egg yolk (reserving white for Glaze), orange rind and juice. Sift together dry ingredients. Gradually add to creamed mixture, blending thoroughly. Divide dough into 2 portions and chill 1 hour in refrigerator or 15 minutes in freezer. Roll out on lightly floured surface to ¹⁄₁₆-inch thickness. Cut circles with 4-inch round cookie cutter. Cut 3 petals from each circle, using about ⅓ of edge of cookie cutter. Arrange 3 petals in tulip shape for each cookie on lightly greased baking sheet. Bake in preheated 375° oven 5 to 6 minutes or until just golden at edges. Cool on racks. Spread with Glaze. Makes 3 dozen cookies.

### GLAZE

1 egg white
1½ c. confectioners' sugar
1½ T. orange juice
  Yellow food coloring
  Red food coloring

Beat egg white until foamy. Blend in sugar and orange juice. If necessary, add more orange juice to make a thin glaze. Tint half of glaze pink and half yellow.

---

In Colonial times when sugar was scarce, or not available at all, molasses was used as the sweetener. Shipped in huge barrels from the West Indies, it was often called "long sweetening" whereas sugar was referred to as "short sweetening."

Today, molasses is still a popular ingredient, but most molasses cookie recipes call for a combination of molasses and sugar.

---

## BROWN-EYED SUSANS

1 c. butter
1 c. confectioners' sugar
1 egg
1½ t. orange extract
2½ c. flour
1 t. salt
  Glaze

Cream butter; add sugar gradually. Beat in egg and extract. Blend in dry ingredients. Chill. Roll dough ¼ inch thick on floured surface. Cut with large and small daisy cutters. Place on ungreased cookie sheets. Bake at 375° about 10 minutes, depending on size. Make Glaze.

### GLAZE

1 c. confectioners' sugar
2 T. milk
½ t. orange extract
  Yellow food coloring
  Cocoa

Combine sugar, milk and orange extract. Use several drops of food coloring to tint mixture a pale yellow. Brush warm cookies with the glaze. Add a small amount of cocoa and additional confectioners' sugar to remaining glaze to make dark chocolate frosting. Place ¼ teaspoonful frosting on center of large daisy cookie. Top with small daisy cookie. Decorate with bit of frosting. Makes 2½ dozen cookies.

## CINNAMON CRISPS

1 c. butter or margarine
1 c. extra fine granulated sugar
1 egg, beaten
2½ c. flour
½ t. salt
2¼ t. cinnamon
1 c. coarsely chopped blanched almonds

Cream butter and sugar until light and fluffy. Add egg and mix well. Sift together dry ingredients and add to creamed mixture. Stir in chopped almonds. Mix well. Form into rolls 1½ inches in diameter. Wrap in waxed paper and place in refrigerator overnight. Slice ¼ inch thick. Bake on greased cookie sheets in a 350° oven 12 to 15 minutes. Makes 3½ dozen.

## FAMILY FAVORITES

### PINEAPPLE-FILLED COOKIES

1 c. butter
½ c. sugar
½ c. confectioners' sugar
1 egg
1½ t. vanilla
2¾ c. flour
¼ t. salt
½ t. baking soda
½ t. cream of tartar

Cream butter; add sugars gradually. Beat in egg and vanilla. Blend in dry ingredients. Chill. Make Pineapple Filling.

#### PINEAPPLE FILLING

1 T. water
1 T. cornstarch
½ c. pineapple jam

Combine all ingredients in saucepan. Cook at low heat until thick and clear. Cool.

Roll dough ⅛ inch thick on floured surface; cut with 2-inch scalloped cutter. Place half of the cookies on lightly greased cookie sheets. Place ½ teaspoons of filling in center of each cookie. Cut small holes in centers of remaining cookies; place on top of filling, sandwich fashion. Press each scallop together lightly with tip of finger. Bake at 350° about 12 minutes. Makes about 5 dozen cookies.

> Remove cookies from baking sheet with a spatula as soon as they come out of the oven.

### MINCEMEAT COOKIES

1½ c. flour
1½ t. baking soda
¼ c. water
2 eggs
⅓ c. shortening
¾ c. brown sugar
¾ t. cinnamon
¼ t. nutmeg
½ t. salt
½ c. chopped nuts
½ c. dry mincemeat

Sift together flour and baking soda. Set aside. Put next 7 ingredients into blender and blend until smooth. Add nuts and mincemeat and blend another second. Pour blended mixture into flour and stir until mixed. Drop by teaspoons onto greased baking sheet. Bake at 375° for 10 minutes. Immediately place on a wire cooling rack. Makes about 4 dozen cookies.

### WHIRLIGIGS

3 c. flour
1 t. salt
¾ t. baking soda
¾ c. butter
1½ c. sugar
1 egg
2 t. vanilla
3 T. water
2 1-oz. squares unsweetened chocolate
Hot milk

Sift together flour, salt and soda. Cream butter and sugar until fluffy. Add egg and vanilla. Blend well. Add sifted dry ingredients and water. Mix well. Divide dough in half. Add melted chocolate to half of the dough. Shape each piece of dough into 2 rolls about 2 inches in diameter. Wrap in waxed paper. Refrigerate overnight. Cut each roll lengthwise into 4 equal quarters. Brush cut sides with hot milk. Place 4 strips of alternating color together to form a round cookie. Press firmly together. (There will be alternating chocolate and yellow quarters in each roll.) Return to refrigerator to firm. Cut into ⅛-inch slices. Bake on greased cookie sheets at 325° for 8 to 10 minutes or until cookies are slightly golden at edges. Cool on racks. Makes 12 dozen 2-inch cookies.

*Pictured opposite*
*Tulip Cookies, page 49*
*Brown-Eyed Susans, page 49*

## ALMOND BRITTLE BARS

1 c. butter or margarine
2 t. instant coffee
1 t. salt
¾ t. almond extract
1 c. sugar
2 c. flour
1 6-oz. pkg. semisweet chocolate chips
½ c. flaked coconut
½ c. finely chopped almonds

Beat together butter, coffee, salt and almond extract. Gradually add sugar, beating until light and fluffy. Stir in flour, chocolate chips and coconut. Press batter into ungreased 15½ x 10½ x 1-inch jelly roll pan. Sprinkle almonds over top. Bake in 375° oven 23 to 25 minutes or until golden brown. Set pan on rack; cut 2½ x 1½-inch bars while warm. When cool, remove from pan. Makes 40 bars.

*Note:* If you want to break the cookies in irregular pieces, cool baked cookie dough in pan on rack, then break it in pieces with your fingers. Cookies are crisp.

## UNIQUE DATE COOKIES

| | |
|---|---|
| 1 c. sugar | 4 c. flour |
| 1 c. brown sugar | 1 t. salt |
| 1 c. butter | 1 t. baking soda |
| 3 eggs | Filling |
| 1 t. vanilla | |

Cream butter and sugars until light. Add eggs and beat until light and fluffy. Mix in vanilla. Add sifted dry ingredients. Mix well. Chill dough. Roll out on lightly floured board and spread with filling. Roll up like jelly roll. Chill again overnight. Slice ⅛-inch thick and place on lightly greased baking sheets. Bake in 375° oven for 10 to 12 minutes or until lightly browned. Makes about 6 dozen cookies.

### FILLING

1 lb. dates, finely chopped
½ c. sugar
½ c. water

Combine ingredients in saucepan. Bring to a boil over medium heat, stirring constantly. Boil 1 minute. Remove from heat and set aside to cool.

## CHERRY COCONUT CHEWS

2 c. flour
½ t. baking powder
½ t. baking soda
½ t. salt
⅔ c. shortening
⅔ c. sugar
1 egg
½ c. milk
1 t. vanilla
1 c. flaked coconut
¼ c. maraschino cherries, chopped and drained

Sift flour, baking powder, soda and salt together. Set aside. In a large bowl, cream shortening with sugar until fluffy. Beat in egg, milk and vanilla. Stir in flour mixture until well blended. Stir in coconut and cherries. Drop by rounded teaspoonsful onto lightly greased cookie sheets. Bake in 375° oven 10 minutes or until firm and lightly golden around edges. Remove from cookie sheets to cool. Makes about 4½ dozen.

## CHOCOLATE DATE JUMBLES

2 1-oz. squares unsweetened chocolate
½ c. shortening
1½ c. sugar
1 t. vanilla
2 eggs
1 c. sour cream
2¾ c. flour
½ t. baking soda
½ t. baking powder
1 t. salt
1 8-oz. pkg. pitted dates, cut up
1 c. chopped walnuts

Melt chocolate over hot water. Cool. Cream shortening and sugar until creamy; add vanilla and eggs and beat until fluffy. Stir in chocolate and sour cream. Sift together next four ingredients. Add with dates and nuts to sugar mixture. Blend well. Drop by teaspoons about 2 inches apart on greased cookie sheet. Bake in a 400° oven 8 to 10 minutes or until done. Remove to rack to cool. Makes 4½ dozen cookies.

# COOKIES WITH A FOREIGN ACCENT

## AMARETTI
### (ITALIAN MACAROONS)

½ lb. ground blanched almonds
1 c. sugar
¼ t. salt
2 egg whites, stiffly beaten
½ t. almond extract
   Confectioners' sugar
   Colored sugar and decorators

Combine almonds, sugar, and salt; fold into beaten egg whites. Add almond extract. Drop by teaspoons (or roll into small balls) on greased and floured cookie sheets. Sprinkle with confectioners' sugar, then with colored sugar or decorators. Let stand 2 hours before baking. Bake at 300° about 20 to 25 minutes or until lightly browned. Makes about 3 dozen.

---

Some of the most enchanting concoctions to emerge from European kitchens are the delectable desserts baked in fanciful shapes. Austrians delight in the "Rebrucken," a chocolate frosted "saddle of venison"; whereas the German specialty is the "Igel," a cake resembling a hedgehog with raisins for eyes and split almonds for quills. In Lithuania, the favorite goodie is "Grybai," crisp, frosted cookies in the shape of plump mushrooms that look as if they had just been picked from a cool forest floor. Grybai in their charming mushroom shapes are traditional Lithuanian Christmas cookies.

Though easy to make, Grybai do take a little time and patience to frost. Bake a batch of Grybai in assorted sizes—some tiny buttons, others fat and sassy. Packaged in pretty flowerpots or straw baskets, they make charming and welcome gifts.

---

## GRYBAI
## (SPICED MUSHROOM COOKIES)

3 T. butter
¼ c. sugar
1 egg
½ c. honey, heated and cooled to lukewarm
2 c. flour
2 T. lemon-flavored instant tea
¾ t. baking soda
½ t. cinnamon
¼ t. cloves
¼ t. ginger
¼ t. nutmeg
   White Icing
   Chocolate Icing

In large bowl, blend butter and sugar; beat in egg and honey. Sift together dry ingredients. Gradually add to butter mixture, blending well. Wrap dough in waxed paper and chill at least 1 hour. Preheat oven to 350°. Shape ⅓ of the dough into mushroom-like stems ¼ inch in diameter and 1½ inches long. Shape remaining dough into an equal number of balls 1 inch in diameter. Indent 1 side of each ball with thumb to form a mushroom-like cap. Place balls rounded side up, laying stems separately on sides, on greased cookie sheets. Bake 10 minutes; cool on wire racks. Makes about 3 dozen cookies.

To assemble, dip end of stem into White Icing and fit into indentation of cap; allow icing to set. Coat stem and underside of cap with White Icing, then top cap with Chocolate Icing.

### WHITE ICING

In small bowl, blend 2½ cups confectioners' sugar with 3 to 4 tablespoons milk.

### CHOCOLATE ICING

In small bowl, blend 2 cups confectioners' sugar, 1 tablespoon cocoa and 2 to 3 tablespoons milk.

---

When cookies are cool and ready for storage, place in a cookie jar or can which has a tightly fitting cover. Store only one kind of cookie in each container.

## GERMAN PFEFFERNUESSE

½ c. butter, melted
1 c. sugar
2 eggs
½ t. grated lemon rind
½ t. anise oil
2 c. flour
1½ t. cinnamon
½ t. cloves
½ t. baking soda
½ c. citron, finely chopped
1½ c. finely chopped blanched almonds
Confectioners' sugar

Combine melted butter, sugar and eggs. Blend well. Add lemon rind and anise oil. Sift together flour, cinnamon, cloves and soda. Add to butter mixture. Add citron and almonds. Blend. Shape into small balls, using 1 teaspoon of dough. Place on greased cookie sheets. Bake at 350° for 12 to 14 minutes. While warm roll in confectioners' sugar. Store in airtight container and allow to mellow 2 to 3 weeks. Makes about 15 dozen cookies.

## NORWEGIAN BUTTER COOKIES

1 c. butter
½ c. sugar
2 hard-boiled egg yolks
2 raw egg yolks
2½ c. flour
1 egg white, slightly beaten
Granulated sugar

Cream butter and sugar until light and fluffy. Force hard-boiled egg yolks through a wire sieve. Add sieved egg yolks and raw egg yolks to creamed mixture, mixing thoroughly. Add flour and mix until smooth. Chill dough for several hours or overnight. Pinch off small balls of dough about ½- to ¾-inch diameter. Roll into strips 4 to 5 inches long and about the size of a lead pencil. Tie each strip into a knot. Place on lightly buttered cookie sheet. Brush with egg white and sprinkle with sugar. Bake in 350° oven 8 to 10 minutes or until lightly browned. Carefully remove from cookie sheet to avoid breaking and place on cooling rack. Makes 4 dozen cookies.

## MEXICAN CINNAMON TEA CAKES

1¼ c. sugar
1 c. butter or margarine, softened
1½ t. cinnamon
¼ t. baking soda
2¾ c. flour

Cream the butter with 1 cup of the sugar, ½ teaspoon of the cinnamon and soda. Add flour. Roll on lightly floured board to ⅛-inch thickness. Shape with 1½-inch cookie cutters. Place on ungreased cookie sheets. Bake in a 400° oven 8 to 10 minutes or until cookies are lightly browned around edges. While still hot, combine remaining sugar and cinnamon and sprinkle over tops of cookies. Store in a tightly closed cookie jar. Makes 4½ dozen.

## ENGLISH TEA LOGS

5⅓ c. flour
1½ c. butter or margarine
2 eggs
2 t. sugar
1 t. salt
1½ c. finely chopped apple
¾ c. raisins
3 T. sugar
1 T. lemon-flavored instant tea
1 t. cinnamon
Confectioners' sugar

Place flour in large bowl, making a well in center. Into the well, put butter, eggs, sugar and salt. Using the fingertips, make a paste of the center ingredients, gradually incorporating flour until a smooth, firm ball is formed. Wrap in waxed paper; refrigerate 2 to 3 hours. In small bowl, combine apples, raisins, sugar, lemon-flavored instant tea and cinnamon. Between lightly floured waxed paper, roll half the dough into an oblong, ⅛ inch thick. Cut dough into 2-inch squares. Place a teaspoon of filling in the center of each square. Roll square like a log and seal ends. Place on ungreased cookie sheet, seam side down. Repeat above procedure for other half of dough. Bake in 375° oven 20 minutes. Sift confectioners' sugar over logs while still hot. Makes about 5 dozen tea logs.

*Kriskletts*

## KRISKLETTS
## (MOROCCAN ANISE TIDBITS)

| | |
|---|---|
| 3 c. flour | 1 T. anise seed, |
| 1 c. sugar | crushed |
| 3 t. baking powder | ¾ c. water |
| ½ t. salt | 3 T. salad oil |

Sift flour with sugar, baking powder and salt. Stir in anise seed. Add approximately ¾ cup water, a little at a time, mixing until dry ingredients are moistened (dough should be slightly rubbery.) Work oil into dough. Shape dough into pencil-thin rolls by rolling dough with the palms of your hands on a lightly floured board. Cut each roll into ½-inch pieces. Place on greased cookie sheets and bake in a 350° oven 15 to 20 minutes. Cool and store in a dry place. Serve with minted tea if desired. Makes about 1½ pounds.

# COOKIE SPECTACULARS

## TRI-CORNERED HATS

½ c. lemon-flavored instant tea
¾ c. butter or margarine, softened
1 egg
1 t. vanilla
2¾ c. flour
¼ c. milk
2¼ c. ready-to-use mincemeat
2 T. rum or ⅛ t. rum extract
Confectioners' sugar

Blend tea and butter until light and fluffy. Add egg and vanilla. Alternately stir in flour and milk, blending well. Chill 1 hour. On lightly floured board, roll ¼ of the dough at a time ⅛ inch thick. Cut with 3-inch round cookie cutters. Combine mincemeat and rum. Place ½ tablespoon mincemeat in center of each circle. Form hat by lifting edges up and pinching together tightly at 3 points equally distant from each other, leaving filling exposed. Bake on ungreased cookie sheets in 350° oven 10 to 12 minutes. Cool. If desired, pipe edges with softened cream cheese or sprinkle with confectioners' sugar. Makes about 4 dozen.

Austrian peach cookies are the inspiration of a clever Austrian baker.

The peach, held in high esteem since the Middle Ages, is often called the "gold that grows on trees." Some believe the peach originated in China 3,000 years ago. The peach reached the New World in the fifteenth century.

This richly decorated little peach confection is a delightful gift to bake for a friend or serve for a special luncheon.

## AUSTRIAN PEACH COOKIES

1 c. sugar
¾ c. vegetable oil
½ c. milk
2 eggs
¾ t. baking powder
½ t. vanilla
3½ to 4 c. flour
Apricot filling
Red and Yellow-Orange Sugars

In large bowl, combine sugar, oil, milk, eggs, baking powder and vanilla. Blend in enough flour to form a soft dough. Roll into walnut-size balls and bake on ungreased cookie sheets in 325° oven 15 to 20 minutes (cookies will be pale). Cool completely. Scrape out cookies by gently rotating tip of sharp knife against flat side of cookie, leaving shell and reserving crumbs. Fill cookies with apricot filling. Press two cookies together to form a "peach." Brush lightly with additional brandy or water and immediately dip one spot in Red Sugar for blush, then roll entire cookie in Yellow-Orange Sugar for peach color. If desired, insert a piece of cinnamon stick "stem" through green gumdrop "leaf" into the stem of each peach. Makes 2½ dozen.

### APRICOT FILLING

2 c. reserved cookie crumbs
1 c. peach or apricot preserves
½ c. chopped almonds
1 3-oz. pkg. cream cheese, softened
2 T. instant tea
2 to 3 T. peach, apricot or plain brandy
¾ t. ground cinnamon

In medium bowl combine 2 cups reserved crumbs, preserves, almonds, cream cheese, instant tea powder, brandy and cinnamon.

### RED AND YELLOW-ORANGE SUGARS

1 c. sugar
Red food coloring
Yellow food coloring

To make red sugar: blend ⅓ cup sugar with a few drops of red food coloring. To make yellow-orange sugar: blend ⅔ cup sugar with 2 to 3 drops red food coloring and enough yellow food coloring to make a peach color.

## FORTUNE TEA COOKIES

3 egg whites
¾ c. sugar
⅛ t. salt
½ c. butter or margarine, melted
¼ t. vanilla
1 c. flour
1 T. instant tea
2 T. water
    Freezer paper cut in 2 x 2½-inch strips
    with fortunes written on them

In medium bowl, combine egg whites, sugar and salt. Stir in thoroughly, one at a time, butter, vanilla, flour, tea and water. Chill at least 20 minutes. Make only 2 cookies at a time. On greased baking sheet, drop 2 slightly rounded teaspoonsful of dough 4 inches apart. Spread dough very thin with back of spoon to about 3 inches in diameter. Bake in 350° oven 5 minutes or until edges turn lightly brown. Remove immediately to wire rack. Cookies should be paper thin. Working quickly, place one fortune in center of each cookie. Fold cookie in half, enclosing fortune, to form a semicircle. Grasp rounded edges of semicircle between thumb and forefinger of one hand. At center of folded edge, push in with forefinger of other hand. Solid sides of cookie will puff out. Keeping forefinger in place, bring edges of fold downward around forefinger. Place each cookie in small-size muffin tin, open edges up, until cookie sets. Store in airtight container. Makes about 4 dozen cookies.

The ever popular Chinese fortune cookie appears to be inspired by the West. It is unlikely that you will find a recipe for it in an authentic Chinese cookbook.

According to one legend, fortune cookies were created in a moment of inspiration by a Japanese chef in San Francisco. Ironically, these whimsies with fortune slips have become a standard and fascinating end to many Oriental meals.

No newcomer to the snack scene, pretzels may once have been a symbol of the solar cycle and date back to Roman times. No one really knows who baked the first pretzel or twisted it into a circular shape.

Some legends claim, however, that a monk in the monastery bakery twisted bread scraps into a circle, twisting the ends to symbolize arms crossed in prayer. Priests later used pretzels to reward students for learning their prayers. These twisted shapes were called *pretiola*, Latin for small reward.

Pretzels eventually became a holy symbol of prayer and penance. Later, they were known by still another Latin name, *bracellae*, which means little arms. By the fifth century, pretzels were a popular Christian Lenten bread. Since the original pretzel recipes did not call for eggs, shortening, or milk, the flour, water and salt product was acceptable to eat during Lent.

Today pretzels, salted or plain, come in all sizes and shapes: long and short, thick and thin, nuggets, and the familiar ring with crossed ends.

## PRETZEL COOKIES

¾ c. butter
½ c. sugar
1 t. vanilla
1¾ c. flour
2 T. milk
1 egg, slightly beaten
    Colored sugar

Cream butter, sugar and vanilla until light and fluffy. Gradually add flour and milk, mixing until well blended. Chill dough for ease in handling. Divide dough into 4 equal parts. Work with one part of dough at a time, refrigerating remaining dough. Divide each part into 8 pieces. Roll each piece between hands to form an 8-inch strand. Place on cookie sheet, twisting into pretzel shape. Brush dough with egg and sprinkle with sugar. Bake in preheated 400° oven 8 to 10 minutes or until lightly browned. Remove to wire racks to cool. Makes 32 pretzel cookies.

# HOLIDAY COOKIES

## CHOCOLATE SUGAR PUFFS

½ c. salad oil
4 1-oz. squares unsweetened chocolate
2 c. sugar
4 eggs, beaten
2 t. vanilla
2½ c. flour
2 t. baking powder
½ t. salt
½ c. chopped walnuts or pecans (optional)
1 c. confectioners' sugar

Combine oil, melted chocolate and sugar. Stir in eggs and vanilla. Sift together flour, baking powder and salt; add to sugar mixture. Stir in nuts. Chill dough 2 to 4 hours or overnight. Shape dough into small balls, about ¾ inch in diameter. Roll in confectioners' sugar. Place on lightly greased cookie sheets. Bake at 350° for 10 to 12 minutes. Makes about 6 dozen cookies.

## SANTA'S WHISKERS

1 c. butter or margarine
1 c. sugar
1 t. almond extract
2½ c. flour
¾ c. maraschino cherries, finely chopped
½ c. finely chopped pecans
¾ c. flaked coconut

Cream butter and sugar, blend in extract. Stir in flour, cherries and nuts. Form in 2 rolls, each 2 inches in diameter and 8 inches long. Roll in coconut. Wrap and chill several hours or overnight. Slice ¼ inch thick; place on ungreased cookie sheet. Bake at 375° for 12 minutes or until edges are golden. Makes 5 dozen.

## BON BON COOKIES

1 c. dates, finely ground
½ c. finely ground walnuts
½ t. vanilla
2 egg whites
⅛ t. salt
⅔ c. sugar
½ t. vanilla
Red food coloring
Green food coloring

Combine dates, nuts and vanilla. Shape into small balls using ½ teaspoon of mixture. Beat egg whites and salt until stiff but not dry. Add sugar gradually. Beat until mixture holds a firm peak. Add vanilla. Blend. Divide meringue in half. Tint one half green and the other pink. Drop balls into meringue. Cover with meringue. Remove each ball with a teaspoon. Place on greased cookie sheet. Swirl top. Bake at 250° about 30 minutes. Makes about 4 dozen cookies.

## HOLIDAY FRUIT DROPS

1 c. shortening
2 c. brown sugar
2 eggs
½ c. buttermilk
3½ c. flour
1 t. baking soda
1 t. salt
1½ c. pecan pieces
2 c. candied cherries, halved
2 c. dates, cut up

Mix shortening, sugar and eggs. Stir in buttermilk. Sift dry ingredients. Stir into shortening mixture. Fold in pecans, cherries and dates. Chill at least 1 hour. Drop rounded teaspoons of dough about 2 inches apart on lightly greased baking sheet. Place a pecan half on each cookie, if desired. Bake in 400° oven 8 to 10 minutes, until almost no imprint remains when touched lightly. Holiday Fruit Drops improve with storing. Makes about 8 dozen.

---

Avoid working in too much flour in rolled cookies. Chill dough thoroughly before rolling.

---

*Pictured opposite*
*Fortune Tea Cookies, page 57*

# ROLLED SPICED CHRISTMAS COOKIES

4 c. flour
1¾ c. sugar
1 t. allspice
1 t. cinnamon
1½ c. butter or margarine
2 eggs, lightly beaten
3 T. cold water

Sift together first 4 ingredients. Cut in butter until mixture resembles coarse meal. Stir in eggs and water, mixing well. (Dough will be stiff but do not add more water.) Chill until dough can be handled easily, about 1 hour. Roll to ⅛-inch thickness on a lightly floured board. Shape with assorted cookie cutters. Bake on ungreased cookie sheets in a 400° oven 7 to 8 minutes or until lightly browned around the edges. Cool on wire racks. Frost as desired with confectioners' sugar icing. Decorate with colored sugar, cinnamon drops and bits of candied fruits. Makes about 9 dozen cookies of assorted shapes and sizes.

# GINGERBREAD MEN

4 c. flour
1 T. ginger
1 t. baking soda
1 t. salt
1 t. cinnamon
1 c. butter, softened
1 c. light brown sugar
½ c. light molasses

Sift together dry ingredients and set aside. Cream butter and sugar until light and fluffy. Blend in molasses. Gradually add flour mixture. Mix thoroughly. Chill until firm, 1 to 2 hours. Divide dough into quarters. On large ungreased baking sheets roll each quarter out to ⅛-inch thickness. Cut with 5-inch tall gingerbread man cutter. Remove dough between cookie cutouts; re-roll excess dough on another baking sheet. Bake cookies in a 375° oven 7 to 8 minutes, or until lightly browned. Cool slightly before removing from baking sheets. Cool completely; decorate as desired. Makes 4 to 5 dozen.

Giving gifts of Christmas cookies is not a new idea or even entirely American.

According to an old Danish legend, no Christmas visitor is allowed to leave the house without taking a bag of Christmas cookies. Otherwise the host and hostess run the risk of the holiday visitor carrying the Christmas Spirit away in his empty hands.

# MARZIPAN BARS

½ c. butter
½ c. brown sugar
1 egg yolk
1 t. vanilla
½ t. baking soda
2 c. flour
¼ t. salt
¼ c. milk
1 c. red raspberry jelly

Cream butter and sugar. Beat in egg yolk and vanilla. Sift together flour, soda and salt. Add dry ingredients and milk. Spread onto bottom of greased 10 x 15 x 1-inch pan; cover with jelly. Make filling.

## ALMOND PASTE FILLING

1 8-oz. can almond paste, cut in small pieces
1 egg white
½ c. sugar
1 t. vanilla
3 T. butter
3 eggs
Green food coloring

Blend almond paste, egg white, sugar, vanilla and butter until smooth. Add eggs one at a time and beat well. Tint mixture a delicate green; pour over jelly layer. Bake at 350° for 35 to 40 minutes. Cool. Make icing.

## CHOCOLATE ICING

2 1-oz. squares unsweetened chocolate, melted
1 T. butter
1 t. vanilla
2 c. confectioners' sugar
About ¼ c. hot milk

Combine all ingredients; beat until smooth. Spread over almond layer and cut into small bars.

## CHEESECAKE COOKIES

1 c. butter, softened
1 c. sugar
½ t. vanilla or almond extract
2 c. self-rising flour
   Cream Cheese Topping
2 c. sliced almonds (optional)

Cream butter and sugar until light and fluffy. Stir in flavoring. Gradually add flour and mix well. Pat or spread dough evenly over bottom of ungreased 15½ x 10½ x 1-inch jelly roll pan. Bake in 350° oven 20 minutes or until lightly browned. Cool. Spread crust with Cream Cheese Topping. If desired, sprinkle top with almonds. Continue baking in 350° oven 30 to 35 minutes. Cool completely before cutting into bars. Makes 4 dozen.

### Cream Cheese Topping

2 8-oz. pkgs. cream cheese, softened
2 eggs
½ t. vanilla or almond extract
½ c. confectioners' sugar
1 c. sour cream

Beat cream cheese until smooth. Add eggs and flavoring, beating until smooth. Stir in sugar. Fold in sour cream.

## SNOWBALLS

¼ c. butter
4 c. miniature marshmallows
5 c. crisp rice cereal
1⅓ c. flaked coconut

Melt butter in large saucepan. Add marshmallows. Cook over low heat, stirring constantly, until marshmallows are melted and mixture is very syrupy. Remove from heat. Add rice cereal; stir until well coated. With buttered fingers, shape into 24 balls about 2 inches in diameter. Roll in coconut. Let stand until cool. Makes 24 2-inch Snowballs. *Note:* To store Snowballs in freezer, wrap tightly or place in airtight container.

### Peppermint Snowballs

Add ½ cup crushed hard peppermint candy with the rice cereal. For variety use other flavored hard candy.

## PEANUT BUTTER CANES

½ c. margarine      1 egg
½ c. sugar          ½ t. vanilla
½ c. brown sugar    1¼ c. flour
1 c. creamy peanut  ½ t. salt
   butter           ½ t. baking soda

Cream margarine and sugars until fluffy. Beat in peanut butter, egg and vanilla. Add flour, salt and soda, blending well. For each cookie, shape 1 level tablespoon of dough into pencil shape about 6 inches long and ¼ inch thick. Shape in the form of a candy cane. Bake on ungreased baking sheets in 375° oven about 10 minutes or until done. Cool cookies on brown or other absorbent paper. When cool, decorate with red and white Confectioners' Sugar and Water Icing and sprinkle with colored sugar, if desired. Tie bow around stem of cane with red and green ribbon. Makes about 4 dozen.

---

When a cookie recipe calls for chopped candied fruit, dates, prunes, raisins or other dried fruit, it's easier to cut them with a kitchen shears rather than a knife.

---

## POINSETTIA COOKIES

2 c. confectioners' sugar
1 c. butter or margarine
2 eggs
1 t. vanilla
½ t. rum extract
3 c. flour
1 t. salt
1 c. shredded coconut
1 c. butterscotch chips
   Granulated sugar
½ c. candied red cherries, cut in wedges

Beat together confectioners' sugar and butter. Add eggs and extracts. Sift together flour and salt and stir into butter mixture. Add coconut and ¾ cup of the butterscotch morsels. Chill dough until firm. Roll into 1-inch balls. Place on ungreased cookie sheets. Flatten cookie with bottom of glass dipped in granulated sugar. Place a butterscotch morsel in center of each cookie. Place cherry wedges in a circle to resemble a poinsettia. Bake at 375° about 12 minutes. Makes about 5 dozen.

# Book III Index